Cold War Bombers

'The Cold War'. Three words that still have the power to chill the blood. After the devastation of World War 2, the world entered a terrifying age of political and military tension between East and West. Each side had a nuclear deterrent that prevented an attack by the other, on the basis that such an act would lead to total annihilation: the doctrine of mutually assured destruction (MAD). But there was no point in having a deterrent if you did not have the means to deliver it. Enter the age of the nuclear bomber, the age when B-52s, Hustlers, Vulcans, Victors, 'Bears' and 'Badgers' ruled the skies.

'Keepers of the peace' or 'destroyers of the world'? No matter how you view these mighty beasts, there was no denying that they were technological masterpieces, the ultimate war machines of their time. As the superpowers 'fought' for supremacy, it was the bombers that were at the sharp end of the technological battle, flying ever faster, further and higher. Thankfully these 'Gods of War' were never called upon to unleash their destructive abilities to the full, but their awesome power and futuristic design resulted in some of the most iconic flying machines the world has ever seen.

The reign of the nuclear bomber was not to last, its mission superseded by the development of less vulnerable ballistic missiles, but its legacy lives on today...

AVIATION ARCHIVE SERIES

'Cold War Bombers' is No 28 in the Aviation Archive series. Subject aircraft are listed chronologically from the dates of their maiden flights and are filed under nation of manufacture. The extensive photographic coverage includes many exclusive and rare shots that have never been published before. As ever, the words and photographs are complemented by 'period' cutaways from the talented pens of the 'Flight' and 'Aeroplane' artists of the era, together with specially-commissioned aircraft profiles.

Aviation Archive Series

Cold War Bombers: The world's deadliest aircraft

• **Author:** Denis J. Calvert • **Editor:** Allan Burney • **Design:** Key Studio

• **Publisher and Managing Director:** Adrian Cox • **Executive Chairman:** Richard Cox • **Commercial Director:** Ann Saundry • **Group Editor:** Nigel Price

• **Distribution:** Seymour Distribution Ltd +44 (0)20 7429 4000 • **Printing:** Warners (Midlands) PLC, The Maltings, Manor Lane, Bourne, Lincs PE10 9PH.

Cold War Bombers
The world's deadliest aircraft

◎ Dassault Mirage IV

Dassault Mirage IVA

Crew:	2
Length:	76ft 6in (23.32m)
Wingspan:	38ft 10in (11.84m)
Height:	17ft 9in (5.42m)
Weight empty:	31,990lb (14,510kg)
Max. T/O weight:	70,550lb (32,000kg)
Max Speed:	Mach 2.2 (1,450mph) at altitude
Range:	2,500 miles (4,000km)
Powerplant:	2 x SNECMA ATAR 9K turbojets rated at 10,380lb (4,710kg) dry and 14,770lb (6,700kg) in afterburner
Armament:	AN-11, AN-22 free-fall nuclear weapons

In the aftermath of World War 2, France had an ambivalent attitude towards its membership of NATO. While it undoubtedly needed the degree of mutual support and protection that NATO offered, there was a deep-seated distrust of relying upon a foreign power to provide its ultimate, nuclear security. The country's defence plan for 1955-59 provided for the development of a French nuclear weapon, its packaging into a small air-droppable form and the construction of a bomber to provide the delivery method.

Dassault Aviation, already having considerable success with its single-engined Mirage III series of fighters, proposed a twin-engined (SNECMA Atar) variant scaled up by 50% in each dimension, this resulting in an aircraft with more than twice the all-up weight. Thus was born the Mirage IV, which would become the spearhead of France's 'Force de Frappe' (strike force) and a source of great national pride (a true Gallic symbol) over several decades. As with pretty much everything else in the Mirage IV programme, the nuclear weapon carried – either the early AN-11 or the later AN-22 – was wholly French-designed and produced. Unlike the independent nuclear deterrent of several countries, the French strike force was exactly that – independent.

The first prototype Mirage IV got airborne from Melun Villaroche on 17 June 1959, piloted by Roland Glavany. The following day, on its second flight, the aircraft made a single pass at the le Bourget Salon, flying at 300ft and 350kts for maximum effect.

There were three pre-series Mirage IVA, to be followed by a production batch of 50, the first of which flew on 7 December 1963. The Mirage IVA was not a large aircraft and the fact that its combat radius did not exceed 1,000 miles limited the targets (in the Soviet Union) that could be reached. It did not have a bomb bay as such; rather, the single weapon was carried, semi-recessed into the centre fuselage. The pilots of France's FAS (Forces Aériennes Stratégiques) came to accept that, in delivering the single free-fall AN-22 nuclear

Left: **The Mirage IV might not have been large by bomber standards, but take-offs were always a spectacular and noisy affair, especially when it was fitted with 12 JATO (jet-assisted take-off) bottles to help it operate out of relatively short strips. The 'P' variant pictured here could carry a pair of ASMP (Air-Sol Moyenne Portée) missiles.**

Right: **The sharp end (literally) of the first Mirage IV, very much a product of the Dassault bureau. The 'makeshift' bomber was effectively a twin-engined scaled-up version of the Mirage III.**

weapon into Eastern Europe, their mission was probably one-way. The agreement by the US government to authorise the sale of 12 KC-135 (C-135F – 'F' for 'France') flight refuelling tankers greatly improved the force's effectiveness and its targeting options. The first of these flew in February 1964, and 11 of the original 12 remain in service today.

As designed, the Mirage IVA was intended for a high-high flight profile at Mach 1.8 to deliver its single nuclear store, but the increasing threat posed by Soviet surface-to-air missiles in the 1960s forced a rethink. Twelve further Mirage IVA were ordered in 1964, these incorporating structural and flight control changes to suit them for the low-level role that would become increasingly important. In time, these same changes were incorporated in all remaining aircraft of the first batch. At its peak, the FAS had nine escadrons (squadrons) of Mirage IV, each with

four aircraft, along with its 12 C-135F tankers. The need to disperse the force to guard against a possible pre-emptive strike saw each squadron based at a different airfield.

A nuclear ground alert was held from 5 October 1964. Mont-de-Marsan was selected as the first base, but the alert was gradually extended to the Mirage IV squadrons on other bases. Alert states varied from a relatively relaxed 15 minutes (ie 15 minutes from launch signal to take-off) to 5 minutes and, in extremis, to an alert state with the crews ready in cockpit. Unlike SAC, FAS did not have the resources to mount an airborne alert, although there is a persistent story doing the rounds that a Mirage IVA complete with AN-11 nuclear weapon on ground alert was launched in error in 1965 as the result of problems of communication and authorisation.

The Mirage IV force was alone in holding the French nuclear alert until the early 1970s, when two further 'legs' of what would become France's nuclear triad became operational.

Eighteen silo-launched ballistic missiles were declared operational on the Plateau d'Albion in the south of the country in August 1971, while the country's first ballistic missile-armed submarine 'le Redoutable' was commissioned on 1 December of the same year. Both these offered a more capable and less vulnerable delivery system than the Mirage IV with a free-fall bomb, and the front-line strength of Mirage IVs was progressively reduced.

To keep the Mirage IV fleet viable in the context of a possible central European war, the decision was taken in October 1979 to rebuild 18 Mirage IVA to a new IVP ('P' for 'penetration' – the same in English as in French) standard. The main change was the ability to carry a pair of ASMP (Air-Sol Moyenne Portée) missiles to provide a decent stand-off range. The first IVP flew on 12 October 1982 and gave the Mirage IV a new lease of life, the type only finally being retired in 2005, although its final years were in the reconnaissance role fitted with the CT52 recce pod.

Below: **For many years the Mirage IV was a vital part of the nuclear triad of the 'Force de Frappe', France's nuclear deterrent striking force. It did not have a bomb bay as such; rather, the single weapon was carried, semi-recessed into the centre fuselage. The Mirage IV was retired from the nuclear strike role in 1996, and the type was entirely retired from operational service in 2005.**

⭐ Tupolev Tu-4 'Bull'

When three USAAF B-29s landed by chance in the east of the Soviet Union in 1944, they were given to Soviet engineers who examined them in great detail. The result was a reverse-engineered B-29, in almost every respect a copy of the Boeing-built original, but with little or no parts commonality.

Given the designation Tu-4 to reflect Tupolev's management of the project, the new 'Russian' aircraft was put into priority production, the first example flying on 19 May 1947. From both a design and production point of view, the Soviet aircraft industry learnt a lot from this exercise.

The Tu-4 gave the Soviets a state-of-the-art strategic bomber much sooner than would otherwise have been possible. Some 850 examples were produced and the type remained in the bomber role into the early 1960s. A Tu-4 dropped the first Soviet nuclear weapon, the RDS-1, in 1949 and for a number of years provided the Soviet Air Force's only strategic nuclear delivery system.

*Above: **Tupolev Tu-4 'Bull', bort 24 black, c/n 220504, built in Kazan plant No 22, and based at Bagerovo AB near Kerch, Ukraine, late 1950s.***
Artwork © Zaur Eylanbekov

*Below: **The B-29 ancestry of the Tu-4 'Bull' is all too apparent. The aircraft were in fact reverse-engineered with differences being limited to the engines, the defensive weapons, the radio and the identification friend or foe (IFF) system. The Soviet engine, the Shvetsov ASh-73 was a development of the Wright R-1820 but was not otherwise related to the B-29's Wright R-3350.***
Foxbat Files Image Library

⭐ Ilyushin Il-28 'Beagle'

Occupying very much the same place in the Soviet Air Force as did the Canberra in the RAF and the B-45 in the USAF, the Il-28 was a twin-jet light attack bomber with a tactical nuclear capability. Built to a total of 6,316 examples, this was the Cold War's most numerous bomber type.

The Il-28's origins date to late 1947, when Sergey Ilyushin proposed a relatively conservative design, straight-winged (but with a swept tailplane and fin) and powered by two Rolls-Royce Nene centrifugal turbojets. Soviet access to the latest jet engine technology was the result of an ill-judged decision by the post-war British government to present 25 Rolls-Royce Nene turbojets to the country 'for research purposes'. Breaking both the letter and the spirit of these undertakings, the Soviets reverse engineered the Nene to produce their own RD-45. The prototype Il-28, which flew on 8 July 1948 from the test centre at Zhukovsky, had two original Nenes; later examples would be fitted with unlicensed-copy RD-45s. In the best Soviet traditions, the Il-28 was a rugged aircraft, capable of operation from rough strips and with the ability to fit two JATO bottles further to improve take-off performance. Handling was assessed as good; the pilot could easily trim out the aircraft in the case of an engine failure and the prototype reached a top speed of 460kts. Production aircraft fitted with the Klimov VK-1, a development of the RD-45, were able to achieve almost 500kts.

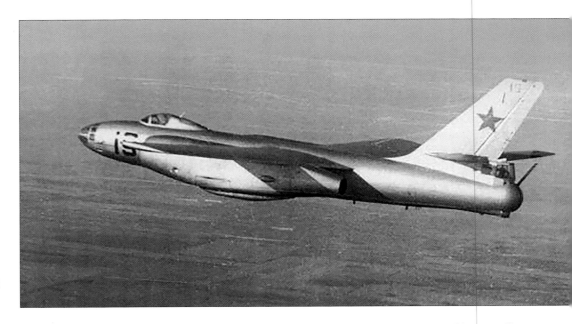

Above: **The Il-28 design was conventional in layout, with high, unswept wings and a swept horizontal tail and fin. The engines were carried in bulky engine nacelles slung directly under the wings.**

The Il-28 made its first public appearance at the May Day parade in Moscow in 1950. It was promptly allocated the NATO reporting name of Beagle. By this time, the type was in production at three separate factories and large numbers were soon coming off the production lines. As Soviet units started re-equipment with the Il-28, priority was given to those in the west which were closest to the NATO borders. The aircraft was radar-equipped and had a decent avionics fit. Once crews had worked up to combat ready status and had been issued with the RDS-4 nuclear weapon, the increasing number regiments of Il-28s constituted a viable, near all-weather tactical nuclear force. As such, it caused NATO serious worries in the European theatre.

The Il-28 was produced in numerous variants in the Soviet Union, Czechoslovakia and China and went on to serve with some 20 friendly (to the Soviet Union, that is) countries. Il-28s took part in the Korean War, while a batch of nuclear-capable Il-28N was deployed to Cuba in September 1962, arriving by sea alongside the Soviet ballistic missiles. In central Europe, however, the type was obsolescent by 1960 and mass withdrawals followed. Many Il-28s remained in service in second-line roles and the Romanian Air Force operated its last example (a Chinese-built H-5) until written off in a crash in 2001.

Above: **An unarmed training version of the Il-28 was fitted with a new nose housing a cockpit for the instructor, while the trainee sat in the normal cockpit. Designated Il-28U, the variant was given the NATO reporting name 'Mascot', one of its operators being Egypt, as illustrated. Egypt received 70 Czechoslovakian-built Il-28s in 1956, shortly before the Suez Crisis. The Israelis rated the Il-28 as a high priority target during the Six-Day War.**

⭐ Tupolev Tu-16 'Badger'

Tupolev's Tu-16 was a twin-jet bomber from the early 1950s, born of the need to produce an aircraft capable of delivering Soviet weapons of the time over a long distance at speeds much greater than those of the Tu-4. The weapon around which the design was based was the high-explosive FAB-9000, which was a 9000kg/20,000lb weapon, this dictating the size of the bomb bay.

Tupolev's design featured a highly swept wing (with a 41-degree sweep on the inboard leading edge), two Mikulin AM-3 axial flow turbojets in the wing root and a novel undercarriage arrangement that would become a trademark of the Tupolev design bureau. This featured a tricycle arrangement in which the main gear retracted rearwards into streamlined pods that projected beyond the trailing edge of the wing. To place the aircraft in context, the Tu-16 was to the Soviet Air Forces what the Valiant was to the RAF or the B-47 to SAC – a first-generation medium bomber that would prove adaptable to many other roles.

The first prototype was designated Tu-88 and flew on 27 April 1952. Performance, though, was disappointing as weight growth had eroded range and weapons load. A disciplined effort to produce a lighter aircraft gave rise to the Tu-16A, the production version that was the basis of the many variants that would be produced, either as new-build or by conversion. This was dubbed 'Badger-A' by NATO. Full-scale production was authorised in 1953 and nine aircraft overflew Red Square in Moscow on 1 May 1954.

Over 1,500 Tu-16s of all variants would be built before construction ended in the early 1960s. 'Badger-A' was primarily employed to deliver the Soviet nuclear arsenal, a task it carried out admirably until the widespread deployment of SAMs made penetrating western air defences more dangerous and ICBMs seemed to offer better deterrence at less cost. As a result, Tu-16s were increasingly converted to take on other roles. Variants included aircraft for air-to-air refuelling using the probe and drogue or the 'wingtip to wingtip' method, specialised anti-shipping with ASMs including the AS-1 Kennel, maritime reconnaissance, ELINT and electronic jamming. These were designated 'Badger-A' through 'Badger-L'. The Tupolev Tu-104, the first Soviet jet airliner, was based on the Tu-16 and a

*Above: **A rare air-to-air colour image of a Soviet Tu-16 'Badger' pictured against a setting sun.***
Foxbat Files Image Library

*Right: **Underside view of a Soviet 'Badger-C' equipped with a Raduga KSR-5 missile under the wing. Given the NATO reporting name AS-6 'Kingfish', this long-range, air-launched cruise missile and anti ship missile was essentially a scaled down version of the Raduga Kh-22 'Kitchen', built specifically for the Tu-16.***
Photo courtesy of Joint Services Recognition Journal via FoxbatFiles.com

number of de-militarised Tu-16G/'Badger-A' were issued to Aeroflot for crew training and mail services prior to the Tu-104 entering airline service in 1956.

China set up a production line, this time with permission, under a Sino-Soviet accord signed in 1957. Chinese aircraft were based on the 'Badger-A' and were known as the Xian H-6. Most served in the bomber or anti-shipping roles, with more than 100 believed still to be in service.

Tupolev Tu-16 'Badger-A'

Crew:	6
Length:	114ft 2in (34.8m)
Wingspan:	108ft 3in (33.0m)
Height:	34ft (10.4m)
Weight empty:	83,500lb (37,900kg)
Max. T/O weight:	160,000lb (72,600kg)
Max Speed:	650mph (1,050km/h)
Range:	4,500 miles (7,250km)
Powerplant:	2 x Mikulin AM-3 turbojets rated at 19,300lb
Armament:	(defensive) 6 x AM-23 cannon in three positions. (offensive) conventional HE bombs up to the 20,000lb FAB-9000, nuclear weapons as available

Top left: **A versatile design, the Tu-16 was built in numerous specialised variants for reconnaissance, maritime surveillance (seen here in 1989), electronic intelligence gathering (ELINT), and electronic warfare (ECM).**

Above: **A further development, the Tu-16K-10-26, carried a single K-10S and two KSR-2 or KSR-5 AS-6 'Kingfish' missiles. Some were later converted into ELINT platforms, as illustrated.**

Below: **This Tupolev Tu-16, Bort 50 (1880302), was essentially a standard bomber version, which throughout its career served as a prototype for other versions. The airframe currently resides in Monino.** *Foxbat Files artwork by Andrey Zhirnov*

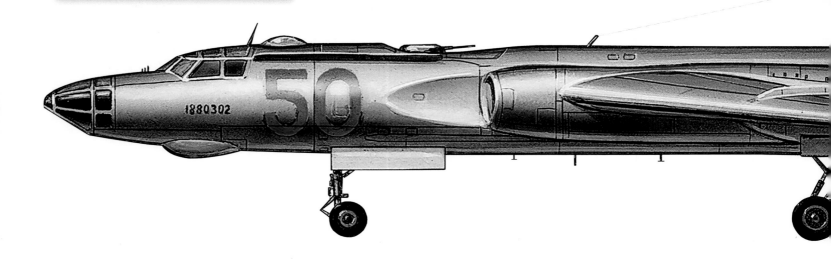

Tupolev Tu-95 'Bear'

Some aircraft prove impossible to replace. For the RAF it was the Canberra, and for the USAF the B-52. For the Soviets, it has surely been Tupolev's Tu-95, NATO codename 'Bear', whose origins can be traced back to 1951, but which remains in widespread front-line service to this day.

Tupolev's early choice of swept wings (35 degrees), swept tailplane and four turboprop engines for its big bomber might seem a strange one, but the need was for extreme range and the fuel economy of then-current jet engines simply did not meet the requirement. With its four Kuznetsov NK-12 engines, each

giving 12,000ehp for take-off and driving contra-rotating propellers (2 x 4 blades per engine), the Tu-95 looks – and sounds – unique. Your author remembers, when he was but a lad, reading the entry in a recognition journal for the Tu-95. Under 'distinguishing features' it stated simply 'The Bear is like no other aircraft'.

The first prototype flew from Zhukovsky on 12 November 1952 in conditions of unprecedented (even for the Soviet Union) secrecy. Flight testing continued but not without incident. On the 16th flight the gearbox on one engine failed totally and it was only the skill of pilot Aleksey Perelyot that ensured the aircraft was landed safely, such that the cause of the failure could be investigated. Just months later, Perelyot was not so lucky. On 11 May 1953 an engine fire developed leading to the No 3 engine parting

with the aircraft and a general fire developing. Perelyot died in an unsuccessful attempt to crash land. For this he was awarded Hero of the Soviet Union, while the senior engineer at the plant was charged with responsibility for the failings that led to the crash and was sentenced to death by a court martial (although

Below: **The 'baddest' Bear of them all, the Tu-95MS carries a powerful punch of up to 16 cruise-missiles, including six Kh-55, Kh-55SM or Kh-555s on a rotary launcher in the weapons bay.** *Foxbat Files photo by Dmitriy Pichugin*

a subsequent act of 'clemency' saved him from execution). Despite these mishaps, the type was ordered into production and the first aircraft off the line flew late in 1955.

Despite the apparent handicap of its not being pure jet-powered, the Tu-95 has a cruise speed of around 460mph and is credited with a combat radius of over 6,000 miles. The choice of a swept wing means that the main spar need not pass through the bomb bay which, as a result, is suitably vast and capable of carrying a variety of suspension units for

*Left: **Cold War foes. An RAF Lightning of No 5 Squadron intercepts a Tu-95KM 'Bear-C' as it approaches UK airspace, a scenario played out many times when tensions ran high between East and West. The 'Bear-C' was a modified and upgraded version of the Tu-95K, most notable for its enhanced reconnaissance systems.***
Foxbat Files Image Library

*Right: **As a Cold War behemoth surviving in an age of 'stealth', the Tu-95 is something of an anachronism, as testified by its rear gun turret, more akin to a World War 2 bomber.***
Foxbat Files photo by Dmitriy Pichugin

different weapons and roles. The Tu-95 has proved supremely adaptable. Early versions (Tu-95 'no suffix' and Tu-95M 'Bear-A') served as strategic bombers, armed with free-fall nuclear weapons, but not equipped with a flight refuelling probe. It appears, though, that the Soviet Air Force never mounted airborne alerts with 'Bears' carrying live nuclear weapons. Such alerts, although providing perhaps the ultimate nuclear deterrent, have always been costly in men and materials, while the Soviet

Command and Control system traditionally allowed their aircrews very little autonomy. Basing 'Bears' north of the Arctic Circle, however unpleasant the environment and however frugal the airfields, brought suitable and worthwhile strategic targets in North America well within range.

The Tu-95MR was an all-purpose reconnaissance aircraft suited to both photo (PHOTINT) and electronic (ELINT) tasks, with the bomb bay carrying racks of cameras, and with numerous 'lumps, bumps and aerials' mounted on the fuselage. An in-flight refuelling probe was also installed. Soviet 'Bears' regularly undertook long missions designed to probe Western air defences. Now with in-flight

refuelling, the aircraft's endurance was limited mainly by factors of crew fatigue. Taking off from an airfield on the Kola Peninsula, one can imagine a 'Bear' on a training sortie coming around the North Cape and soon afterwards being intercepted by Norwegian Starfighters who shadow it for a while. Later in its flight it approaches the vast UK Air Defence region, and RAF fighters – Lightnings or Spey Phantoms – are launched from Leuchars to assess its intentions. Somewhere well to the north of the Scottish mainland, the 'Bear's' captain announces to his crew: 'OK comrades, where's it to be today? Angola or Cuba?'

The final new-build production version, the Tu-95MS, was a specialised cruise-missile carrier, capable of carrying up to six Kh-55 subsonic missiles internally on a rotary launcher in the bomb bay and on under-wing pylons. 88 were built, NATO christening this variant 'Bear-H'.

The Russian front-line force of 'Bears' is diminishing, but money has been spent even in recent years on upgrades to the fleet, and no real replacement type has been identified. Few aircraft types have ever proved so good a return on investment.

*Below: **Polar Bear. An early Tu-95 pictured in suitable Arctic surroundings. The arrangement of the aircraft's contra-rotating propellers is particularly well illustrated.***
Foxbat Files Image Library

Tupolev Tu-95M 'Bear-A'

Crew:	9
Length:	151ft 5in (46.1m)
Wingspan:	164ft 2in (50.0m)
Height:	39ft 9in (12.1m)
Weight empty:	186,000lb (84,300kg)
Max. T/O weight:	401,200lb (182,000kg)
Max Speed:	565mph (910km/h)
Range:	8,200 miles (13,200km)
Powerplant:	4 x Kuznetsov NK-12M turboprops rated at 15,000hp
Armament:	(defensive) 6 x AM-23 cannon in three positions. (offensive) 12,000lb of bombs, free fall nuclear or HE

Above: **East meets West during the Cold War as a US Navy F-14A Tomcat of VF-51 keeps a close eye on a Tu-95 'Bear-G'. Although encounters with 'Bears' were, and still are, not uncommon, they were at their height in times of tension in the 1960s and 1970s. Quite remarkably the 'Bear' can claim to have been intercepted by every generation of jet fighter.** *US Navy via Foxbat Files*

Left: **The menacing shape of the Tu-95 'Bear' became even more threatening when it carried the large Raduga Kh-20 (NATO reporting name: AS-3 'Kangaroo') cruise missile armed with a nuclear warhead. The missile was initially intended for retaliation strikes against major targets in the US, however it proved unsuitable as a first-response weapon and was relegated to secondary strikes against targets.**
Foxbat Files Image Library

Main: **The immense range of the Tu-95 means that it can patrol far and wide and then 'loiter with intent'. Add air-to-air refuelling to the mix and the only limitation is the fatigue of its crew. Nearly 60 years after it first entered service, the Tu-95 made its combat debut on 17 November 2015, being employed for the first time in long range airstrikes as part of the Russian military intervention in the Syrian Civil War.** *Foxbat Files photo by Yevgeniy Kazennov*

Centre: **Tupolev Tu-95MS6 Sprut 'Bear-H', Bort 33 black, 37th Air Army, 22nd Guards Heavy Bomber Air Division, 184th Guards Heavy Bomber Air Regiment, based at Engels AB, Russia. All 'Bears' now in Russian service are the Tu-95MS variant, built in the 1980s and 1990s.** *Artwork © Zaur Eylanbekov*

Bottom: **The Tu-95/Tu-95M was the early basic variant of the long-range strategic bomber and the only model of the aircraft never fitted with a nose refuelling probe. It was known to NATO as the 'Bear-A'.** *Foxbat Files artwork by Andrey Zhirnov*

Myasishchev M-4 and 3M 'Bison'

If there was a direct Soviet equivalent to the Boeing B-52 it was Myasishchev's M-4. This four-engined jet bomber design was intended to give the Soviet Air Force the ability to bomb the continental USA, but in the event the M-4 proved to have insufficient range to make the full out-and-return flight.

First flight was on 20 January 1953. The aircraft came into public view in July 1955 at an air show at Tushino in July 1955, when a relatively small number of M-4s made more than one pass over the airfield to give the impression that the type was already

Above left: **The Soviet's answer to the B-52, the 'Bison' was a beast of an aircraft, with impressive dimensions. However it was badly underpowered and its role as a bomber was short-lived.**
Foxbat Files Image Library

Left: **The Myasishchev 3MD 'Bison' quickly became an endangered species and sightings by the West were rare. In the early 1960s, the 'Bison-C', with a specialised search radar, was introduced, but by this time, many of the original M-4s had been converted to M-4-2 fuel tankers for aerial refuelling. Later, 3Ms were converted to 3MS-2 and 3MN-2 tankers as well.**
Foxbat Files Image Library

Below: **The Myasishchev 3MD variant of the 'Bison' was built from the outset as a missile carrier. Depicted is '30 Red' (c/n 6302831) the only surviving example of 11 built. It currently resides at the Central Russian AF Museum at Monino.** *Foxbat Files artwork by Andrey Zhirnov*

in widespread service. Taken with other intelligence assessments and 'authoritative' articles in the American aviation press, this gave rise to American fears of a 'bomber gap' existing between US and Soviet forces.

The aircraft had a 'bicycle' undercarriage, with main gear legs in front of and behind the bomb bay, and balancing outriggers in fairings at the wing tips. This was a massive aircraft with a 165ft wing span which looked every inch a capable strategic bomber, but it was underpowered and poor fuel economy severely limited range. The type was allocated the NATO reporting name 'Bison', the M-4 becoming the 'Bison-A'. In fact, this variant never entered full-scale service and production soon switched to the much improved Myasishchev 3M, which first flew on 27 March 1956 and went into full production later that year. This version was given the code name 'Bison-B'. Re-engined and with armament reduced, the 3M got closer to the original design range.

While the aircraft never made a name for itself as a bomber, many M-4 and later 3M were converted as flight-refuelling tankers, a role in which they remained until the early 1990s. Total production of all variants is believed not to have exceeded 100 aircraft.

Myasishchev M-4 'Bison-A'

Crew:	8
Length:	154ft 10in (47.2m)
Wingspan:	165ft 7in (50.5m)
Height:	46ft 3in (14.10m)
Weight empty:	175,700lb (79,700kg)
Max. T/O weight:	400,135lb (181,500kg)
Max Speed:	588mph (947km/h)
Range:	5,030 miles (8,100km)
Powerplant:	4 x MikulinAm-3a turbojets
Armament:	(defensive) 9 x NR-23 cannon in three positions. (offensive) Typically 19,840lb of bombs, free fall nuclear or HE. Up to 4 x cruise missiles carried externally

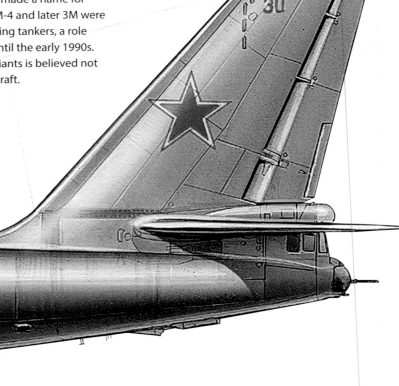

★ Tupolev Tu-22 'Blinder'

Tupolev's Tu-22 was developed to meet the perceived need in the early 1960s to replace the Tu-16 with a supersonic aircraft. Detailed design began in 1955, with the aim of producing a medium-range bomber with the ability to strike targets in Europe and Asia.

Below: A true child of the sixties, the futuristic Tu-22 certainly looked the part, though its handling characteristics did not live up to the image. The 'Blinder' was gradually phased out of Soviet service in favour of the more-capable Tupolev Tu-22M.

First flight of the prototype took place from Zhukovsky on 21 June 1958 and series production was approved shortly afterwards, the type supplanting the Tu-16 on the line at Kazan. First public showing was at Tushino in July 1961, when 10 aircraft overflew the assembled 'Soviet Air Forces Day' crowds. It is said the type was initially allocated the NATO reporting name 'Bullshot', surely by someone with a sense of humour, but that this was later changed to 'Blinder' as being 'more appropriate'. This may be apocryphal, but it's the sort of story you really want to believe.

With a futuristic streamlined design with two large afterburning turbojets sitting podded at the tail, the Tu-22 proved to have a disappointing performance. Initial production was of two versions. The Tu-22B 'Blinder-A' was a bomber, armed primarily with free-fall bombs, which entered service in September 1962. Pilots never liked it, not only for its flying characteristics – it was criticised for being heavy and tiring to fly – but also for the restricted forward view through the sharply-pointed windscreen. In the event, the 15 aircraft built served mainly for training. The Tu-22R was the

reconnaissance version, 'Blinder-C', and carried a comprehensive camera fit in the bomb bay as well as chaff dispensers in the rear of the undercarriage pod, although it retained a bombing capability. Later modifications gave this variant IR linescan equipment. The Tu-22K was the specialised missile carrier and proved to be the major production variant. Initial armament was a Kh-22 stand-off missile, carried semi-recessed into the bomb bay. The Kh-22 (otherwise known as the AS-4 'Kitchen') could fit a nuclear warhead and was designed for anti-shipping duties, with the US Navy's Sixth Fleet very much the sort of target its designers had in mind. The test programme of Tu-22K and Kh-22 was far from successful, but series production of both aircraft and missile was already under way and service introduction took place in

1965. Some 76 Tu-22Ks were built in a total production run of over 300.

Despite its failings and its unpopularity, the Tu-22 lasted in service through the 1990s, although primarily in the reconnaissance role. Its replacement would be a new aircraft, again from the Tupolev stable, which would prove far more successful.

Bottom left: **The only Soviet combat use of the 'Blinder' occurred in 1988, during the Soviet war in Afghanistan. Radar-jamming Tu-22PD aircraft covered Tu-22M bombers operating in Afghanistan near the Pakistan border, protecting the aircraft against Pakistani air defence activity.**

Below: **Early Tu-22s (such as Bort 32, 5050051) did not feature a refuelling probe. This aircraft is now on display at Monino.**
Foxbat Files artwork by Andrey Zhirnov

Tupolev Tu-22K 'Blinder-B'	
Crew:	3
Length:	136ft 6in (41.6m)
Wingspan:	77ft 5in (23.6m)
Height:	32ft 8in (10.0m)
Weight empty:	106,000lb (48,100kg)
Max. T/O weight:	207,000lb (93,900kg)
Max Speed:	940mph (1,510km/h)
Range:	3,000 miles (4,800km)
Powerplant:	2 x Dobrynin RD-7M turbojets rated at 24,000lb dry and 36,400lb in afterburner
Armament:	(defensive) 2 x R-23 cannon in rear fuselage. (offensive) Kh-22 stand-off weapon

★ Tupolev Tu-22M 'Backfire'

Big and menacing, the supersonic, variable-sweep wing, long-range strategic and maritime Tu-22M 'Backfire' bomber was intended to follow the Tu-22 'Blinder', a type which had singularly failed to replace the much earlier Tu-16 'Badger'.

There was a competition between the design bureaus of Tupolev, Myasischev, Sukhoi and Yakovlev, with some of the proposals featuring very large and complex aircraft offering strategic range. In the end, Tupolev won the day with the Tu-22M and the promise that the new aircraft was based on the company's earlier Tu-22. In fact even a cursory look at the new design, with its variable geometry wings and two NK-144 (later NK-22) turbojets now installed totally within the fuselage, revealed that commonality between the two was minimal. A degree of area-ruling was evident in the contours of the fuselage to limit high-speed drag, the four crew members were seated in a pressurised crew compartment and the engine intakes were fitted with a movable ramp to control the shock wave in the intake duct. While the variable geometry 'swing wings' were primarily to improve short field take-off performance, this was – unlike the Tu-22 before it – a Mach 2 aircraft.

First flight by the prototype was on 30 August 1969. Production aircraft designated Tu-22M1 started coming off the Kazan line, which had previously built the Tu-22, from 1971. Unlike the earlier aircraft, the Tu-22M was primarily a missile carrier, standard armament initially being a single Kh-22 semi-recessed into the bomb bay. The new aircraft was welcomed by its crews; handling was good and the view from the cockpit vastly improved. American intelligence assessments of the performance – and particularly the range – of the Tu-22M were wide of the mark, considerably over-estimating the type's fuel capacity and hence its range. In fact, with a single Kh-22 its realistic unrefuelled combat radius was no more than 1,500 miles.

Service introduction of the Tu-22M was not without its problems. Engine time between overhauls was at best 50 hours and this fact led to an edict to pilots to 'take it easy' with engine thrust to limit turbine temperatures in an effort to prolong engine life. The Tu-22M2 'Backfire-B', the definitive production standard aircraft, entered service with both the air force and naval aviation regiments. While the former used

the aircraft in the strategic bomber role, naval aviation saw it primarily as a counter to US Navy battle groups.

A comprehensive weight-reduction programme, improved avionics and developed NK-25 turbojets gave rise to the final production variant, the Tu-22M3 'Backfire-C'. With the Kh-22 now becoming less effective, a new stand-off weapon was introduced as the Kh-15. With a nuclear or conventional warhead, the Kh-15 had the capability to make its final diving approach to its target at Mach 5, making it far more difficult to intercept. Maximum bomb load of the Tu-22M3 was 12 tons carried internally or up to 24 tons with the addition of under-fuselage racks and under-wing pylons, while the bomb bay could carry a rotary launcher for six Kh-15 air-to-surface missiles. The Tu-22M3 was, numerically speaking, the major production variant in a total run that approached 500 examples and continued into the mid-1990s ie well beyond the end of the Cold War. Some continue in Russian service to this day.

Above: **Big and menacing, significant numbers of the Tu-22M3 'Backfire-C' remain in service with the Russian Air Force, such as these examples taxying out at Ryazan Dyagilevo in an impressive show of strength.** *Alexander Beltyukov*

Left: **A Russian AF 'Backfire-C' departs from its base at the start of another long-range mission. During the Cold War, the Tu-22M was operated by the Soviet Air Force (VVS) in a strategic bombing role, and by the Soviet Naval Aviation (Aviacija Vojenno-Morskogo Flota, AVMF) in a long-range maritime anti-shipping role.** *Foxbat Foxbat Files photo by Yevgeniy Kazennov*

Tupolev Tu-22M3 'Backfire-C'

Crew:	4
Length:	139ft 4in (42.5m)
Wingspan:	112ft 6in (34.3m) wings fully forward
Height:	36ft 3in (11.0m)
Weight empty:	128,000lb (58,050kg)
Max. T/O weight:	277,800lb (126,000kg)
Max Speed:	1,400mph (2,250km/h)
Range:	4,200 miles (6,760km)
Powerplant:	2 x Kuznetsov NK-25 turbofans rated at 31,500lb dry and 55,100lb in afterburner
Armament:	(defensive) 1 x GSh-23 23mm cannon in rear fuselage. (offensive) Kh-15 or Kh-22 stand-off weapons, up to 24 tons of free-fall bombs carried internally and on pylons

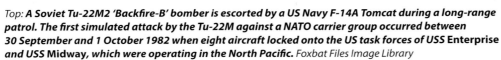

Top: **A Soviet Tu-22M2 'Backfire-B' bomber is escorted by a US Navy F-14A Tomcat during a long-range patrol. The first simulated attack by the Tu-22M against a NATO carrier group occurred between 30 September and 1 October 1982 when eight aircraft locked onto the US task forces of USS** Enterprise **and USS** Midway, **which were operating in the North Pacific.** *Foxbat Files Image Library*

Above: **The Tu-22M suffered from widespread maintenance issues during its service with the Soviet forces. These stemmed from poor manufacturing quality.** *Foxbat Files Image Library*

Right: **Carrying a Raduga Kh-22 anti-ship missile under its port wing, a Tu-22M3 returns from a mission. The 'Backfire' was first used in combat in Afghanistan in December 1987, but more recently the bomber has played an important part in Russia's air campaign in Syria, operating from its home airfields and from Iran's Hamedan Airbase.** *Foxbat Files photo by Sergey Krivchikov*

Below: **Tupolev Tu-22M2 'Backfire-B' bomber, Bort 42 red, 43rd Combat Training and Flight Crew Training Centre, Dyagilevo AB, Ryazan, mid 1980s.** *Artwork © Zaur Eylanbekov*

★ Tupolev Tu-160 'Blackjack'

Although essentially outside the 'Cold War' parameters of this issue, mention must be made of the Tu-160, the Soviet Union's only truly strategic supersonic bomber to enter service. Featuring variable geometry wings, it resembles in many ways a B-1B Lancer on steroids, but is an altogether larger aircraft.

While the first prototype flew on 19 December 1981, the type's progress into full operational service was slow and it was only in summer 1987 that a front-line unit started its work-

up. The Tu-160 'Blackjack' is primarily a missile carrier equipped with nuclear-tipped cruise or supersonic stand-off missiles. Total production did not exceed 40 aircraft, this figure including prototypes, although in 2015 it was announced that an updated version will be put back into production as the Tu-160M2 fitted with new engines, new radars and new avionics. Capable though this aircraft undoubtedly is, the lateness of its arrival in service meant that it had only a limited effect on the outcome of the Cold War.

Above: ***Viewed head-on, the undoubted influence of the Rockwell B-1B Lancer on the Tu-160's design is all too apparent, but there the similarity ends. The Tu-160 is much larger (about 30%) and much faster than the B-1B, with a maximum take-off weight of over 606,000lb and top speed greater than Mach 2.05.***
Foxbat Files photo by Yevgeniy Kazennov

Right: ***A 'Blackjack' returns to terra firma after a mission from Engels AB. Dwarfing the B-1B Lancer, the Tu-160 is the heaviest combat aircraft ever built.***
Foxbat Files photo by Yevgeniy Kazennov

Tupolev Tu-160 'Blackjack'

Crew:	4
Length:	177ft 6in (54.10m)
Wingspan:	189ft 9in (55.7m) wings fully forward
Height:	43ft 0in (13.10m)
Weight empty:	242,505lb (110,000kg)
Max. T/O weight:	606,260lb (275,000kg)
Max Speed:	Mach 2.05
Range:	7,643 miles (12,300km)
Powerplant:	4 x Samara NK-321 turbofans rated at 30,865lb dry and 55,115lb in afterburner
Armament:	Two internal bays for 88,185lb (40,000kg) of ordnance including two internal rotary launchers each holding 6 × Raduga Kh-55SM/101/102/555 cruise missiles (primary armament) or 12 × AS-16 'Kickback' short-range nuclear missiles

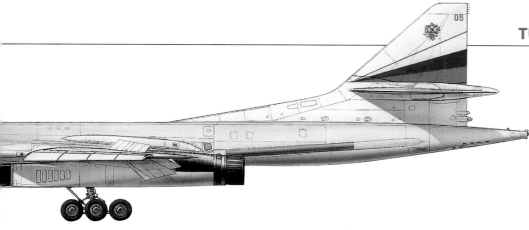

Left: Shown as it looked in the early 2000s, this 'Blackjack' belonged to the 121st GvTBAP and is still based at Engels AB. Along with the other Tu-160s it is scheduled to go through a series of upgrades to its internal and weapons systems. Foxbat Files artwork by Andrey Zhirnov

Far left: Arguably the most powerful aircraft ever put into production, a Tu-160 thunders into the sky as it departs Engels AB, home of the 'Blackjack'. Nineteen Tu-160s were also delivered to the 184th Guards Heavy Bomber Aviation Regiment at Priluki (Ukraine). These were left at the Ukrainian base after the break up of the USSR in 1991 and, after protracted discussions between Ukraine and the Russian Federation, eight were returned to Russia in 1999. Foxbat Files photo by Yevgeniy Kazennov

Left: A Tupolev Tu-160 launching a Kh-101 cruise missile against targets in Syria in November 2015, watched from a discreet distance by a Sukhoi Su-30SM.

Below: The Tu-160's primary armament has always been long-range cruise missiles like the Kh-55MS, of which it can carry a dozen. More recently however, the Russians have used the conventional version Kh-555 version of the cruise missile against targets in Syria alongside much more advanced and stealthy Kh-101 cruise missile. Foxbat Files photo by Yevgeniy Kazennov

Vickers Valiant

The origins of the Vickers Valiant, the first (in every sense) of Britain's three V-bombers, can be traced back to 1946. The British government, fully aware of the significance that World War 2 had been ended by the dropping of two atom bombs, realised that it needed to develop its own nuclear weapons and to have the means to deliver them over long distances. While scientists wrestled with the physics to produce a viable bomb of a suitably small size (all things are relative), Britain's aircraft industry started refining designs for four-jet bomber aircraft to deliver them a decent distance into the Soviet Union, which was by then emerging as the likely enemy in any future European war.

Specification B35/46 (ie bomber specification 35 of 1946) was issued to industry, requiring an aircraft capable of Mach 0.875, a range of 3,350 miles (London to Moscow is 1,560 miles!) and the ability to reach 50,000ft. With such an ambitious level of performance, it was considered that enemy fighters would be unable to get anywhere near to effect an interception, so no defensive armament was specified. Planning for the first British atom bomb (or 'special weapon' as it was euphemistically referred to), envisaged a casing 24ft in length and 5ft in diameter. Safety considerations, including aerodynamic heating, required it to be stowed internally, which necessitated the provision of a huge bomb bay.

Right: The Vickers Valiant became the RAF's first strategic nuclear bomber when it entered service in 1955. Embedded in the big wing were its four Roll-Royce Avons.

Avro tendered its Type 698, which would become the Vulcan, while Handley Page offered an equally futuristic design as the HP80, which would be built as the Victor. Vickers at Weybridge came up with a somewhat less ambitious – but still extremely advanced – four-jet design as the Type 660, which would later be christened Valiant. Sir George Edwards, Vickers' Chief Designer, is quoted as saying that he aimed to make the Valiant an 'unfunny aircraft' of straightforward design which would be ready for squadron service earlier than either of the other two. A revised (ie less ambitious) specification was issued as B9/48 for a 'medium range bomber' to accommodate it, this being one of those rare cases where a ministry specification was written around an aircraft manufacturer's offering, rather than the other way around.

In the event, all three designs were built, as the Valiant, Vulcan and Victor – Britain's legendary trio of V-bombers. How Britain could justify building three different designs of V-bomber when the total requirement would prove to be less than 350 remains one of life's unanswered questions, but together they

brought Britain into the atomic age and all three served the RAF well.

Three Valiant prototypes were ordered and construction got under way at the company's Foxwarren experimental site, with final assembly at its nearby test airfield at Wisley. WB210, the first of the three, took to the air on 18 May 1951, its pilot being 'Mutt' Summers who, just 15 years before, had made the first flight of the prototype Spitfire. The Valiant appeared at the 1951 SBAC show at Farnborough, where it wowed the crowds with its fighter-like performance. Given the high priority accorded to the programme, 25 production Valiants had already been ordered in April 1951.

Powered by four Rolls-Royce Avon turbojets buried in the wing root, the Valiant also had provision for the fitting of a Super Sprite Rocket under each inner wing to provide a yet more sprightly (sorry!) take-off performance. The pressure cabin in the forward fuselage housed the five crew members, with two pilots in

Vickers Valiant B1

Crew:	5
Length:	108ft 3in (33m)
Wingspan:	114ft 4in (34.8m)
Height:	32ft 2in (9.8m)
Weight empty:	75,881lb (34,420kg)
Max. T/O weight:	175,000lb (79,400kg)
Max Speed:	560mph (900km/h)
Range:	4,500 miles (7,250km)
Powerplant:	4 x Rolls-Royce Avon RA 28 rated at 10,000lb
Armament:	21 1,000lb HE bombs/ Blue Danube atom bomb

ejection seats (Martin-Baker Mk 3A) but no such provision for the three rear crew members. This design feature (ie design failing) was repeated in the two following designs of V-bombers; as a result, rear crew members had a significantly reduced chance of surviving a catastrophic situation in the air.

The initial version, the Valiant B1, was a pure bomber, designed for the strategic nuclear role but perfectly capable of dropping conventional iron bombs if required. The Valiant was the aircraft on which RAF Bomber Command learned and perfected its new role of nuclear deterrence as the Medium Bomber Force (MBF) started its build-up. The first UK atomic bomb named Blue Danube was delivered to the RAF at the end of 1953, although the initial front-line Valiant unit, No 138 Squadron, did not form until 1 January 1955. By the close of 1956, production of the Valiant had allowed the RAF to reach its planned strength of seven front-line squadrons. These were based at four 'Class 1' airfields, but dispersal plans would see the force spread across the UK in flights of two or four aircraft in times of political tension, thus increasing survivability.

Above: **A stunning portrait of the Vickers Valiant prototype, WB210. At the Farnborough air show in September 1951 WB210 made a lasting impression with its performance, taking off and climbing steeply like a fighter and exhibiting extreme (for a bomber) manoeuvrability. However, tragedy was to strike on 12 January 1952 when WB210 crashed in Hampshire following a fire in the wing. All the crew escaped save the co-pilot Sqn Ldr B. Foster, who died when his ejection seat hit the tailplane on egress.**

Quick Reaction Alerts (QRA) were established in 1962 to provide fully-armed aircraft with crews at 15-minute readiness to launch, with each V-bomber squadron providing one (later two) aircraft. These, plus no-notice alerts and long-distance Ranger flights to test the crews' self-sufficiency, honed the V-Force into a formidable deterrent.

Valiant production totalled 104 aircraft. Not all were pure bombers. The B(PR)1 was a photo reconnaissance variant, the BK1 introduced the option of mounting flight refuelling gear in the bomb bay, while the B(PR)K1 was capable of all three roles – the true multi-role Vickers Valiant.

Valiant 'firsts' included the dropping of the first Blue Danube in Operation 'Buffalo'

at Maralinga, South Australia on 11 October 1956. Operation 'Musketeer', the ill-fated British Suez campaign of October/November 1956, saw the Valiant tasked as an iron bomber, and 24 aircraft undertook missions to drop 1,000lb bombs onto Egyptian airfields and defence installations until a halt was called to the British intervention.

Increasing deliveries of the more advance Victor and Vulcan allowed the Valiant progressively to be assigned a tactical role under NATO control from the start of 1960. This Tactical Bomber Force (TBF) commitment meant having aircraft at 15-minute readiness with US-built Mk 28 tactical nuclear weapons. With the increasing effectiveness of Soviet air defences, TBF Valiants started practising low-

level target approaches from 1963, now using parachute-retarded Mk 43 nuclear weapons.

The low-level environment took its toll on the Valiant's structural integrity. B(PR)1 WP217 suffered a major in-flight wing failure on 6 August 1964. The crew landed safely, but examination of the fleet showed fatigue problems affecting both front and rear spars in other RAF examples. All Valiants were grounded late in 1964 while an extensive and probably expensive rebuild plan was discussed with Vickers. Then, in what some consider a shameful and short-sighted decision, HQ Bomber Command announced on 26 January 1965 that the type was to be permanently withdrawn from service. The RAF's Valiant era had lasted just 10 years.

Above left: **Valiants of No 232 OCU lined up at RAF Gaydon in 1956. Of the V-bomber triumvirate, the Valiant was the most conventional in design.**

Left: **Cold War warriors – a Valiant crew sprint to their waiting bomber during an alert. A pressurised crew compartment contained the five crew members. The two pilots sat on Martin-Baker Mk3A ejection seats, while the three rear crew members were rearward-facing and, in time of emergency, had to bail out through a side entrance hatch.**

Top: **A Valiant scramble being re-enacted at Farnborough. For many years, the Valiant could claim to be the only V-bomber to have dropped bombs in anger, four squadrons having taken part in Operation 'Musketeer', the Suez campaign in 1956. Only late in its career did the Vulcan achieve the same distinction, attacking Port Stanley airport in the Falkland Islands in 1982.**

Right: **A Vickers Valiant blasts off from its birthplace at Brooklands, Weybridge. Although the Valiant was very much a 'pilot's aircraft', it was at its most temperamental during take-off.**

Above: *An early case of buddy-buddy refuelling. The Valiant carried its main fuel tankage in wings and fuselage, but could be fitted with underwing fuel tanks of 1,500 gallon (6,820lt), each. The tanks themselves could not be jettisoned.*

Left: *As well as its bomber duties, the Valiant could also operate as a tanker with a flight refuelling hose drum unit fitted in its bomb bay.*

Below left: *When it first entered service, height and speed protected the Valiant from attack. Only the Valiant of the three V-bombers has the distinction of dropping nuclear weapons, the type having been used extensively in British trials in the southern hemisphere through the 1950s. A large bomb bay could accommodate a single Blue Danube 'special weapon' with a yield of 15 kilotons. In the conventional bombing role, the Valiant could carry 21 1,000lb (454kg) bombs and was used in this way during the Suez crisis of 1956.*

Right: *Vickers Valiant B1, WZ395 of No 49 Squadron, RAF Marham, circa 1964. By 1963 the increasing sophistication of Soviet air defences meant that RAF Valiants would have to make low-level approaches to their target. An appropriate grey/green camouflage scheme was introduced in 1964. Valiant B1 WZ395 was one of a very few of the type to be finished in this tactical camouflage scheme before fatigue cracks, brought on by the low-level flights, caused the rapid grounding of the fleet.*
Rolando Ugolini/Airlinerart

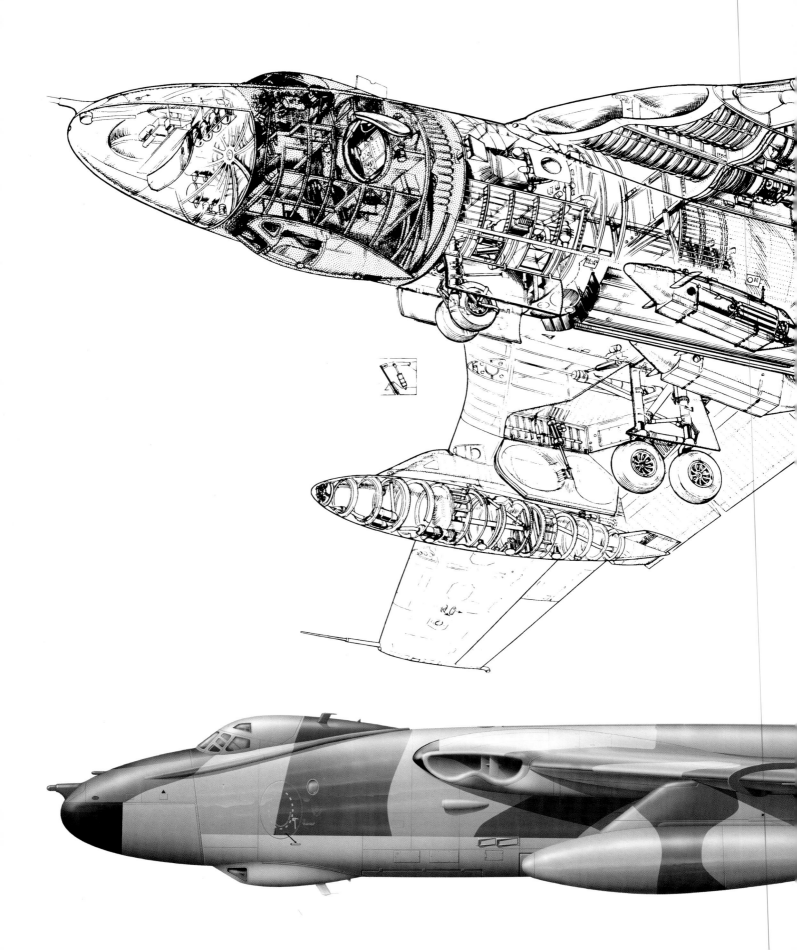

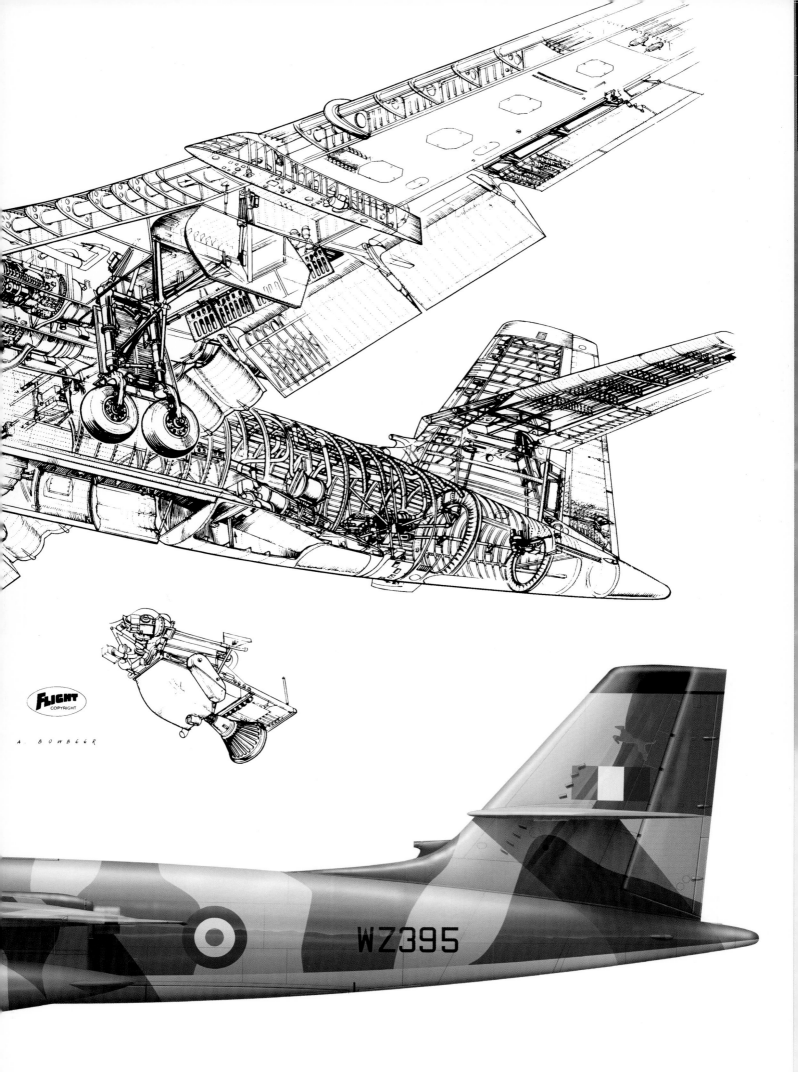

FLIGHT
COPYRIGHT

A. BOWBEER

WZ395

⊙ Avro Vulcan

VX770

VX770

There wasn't a 'best' of the three V-bombers – but if there was, the Vulcan has the strongest claim to such a title. Avro's delta-winged design was produced in greater numbers (134 production aircraft), proved more adaptable to changes of role and armament, and was used for longer in its original bomber role than either of the other designs.

The Vulcan was created by a team under the leadership of Roy Chadwick and featured a massive delta wing (a 'pure' delta shape with

Top left: V-bombers unite as a Vulcan takes on fuel from a Valiant tanker. Nine RAF squadrons operated the Vulcan, which became the backbone of RAF Bomber Command and served in the bomber role until 1982, and as a flight refuelling tanker for two years beyond that.

Centre left: Vulcan B1 XA912 of No 101 Squadron, RAF Finningley. Rolando Ugolini/Airlinerart

Left Avro Vulcan B2 XL321 with Blue Steel missile, No 617 Squadron, Scampton Wing, circa 1969. Rolando Ugolini/Airlinerart

straight wing leading edges in the prototype aircraft) containing four turbojets buried in the wing root, fed by long slit air intakes. Also housed within the wing were the eight-wheel bogie main undercarriage legs, fuel tanks and retractable air brakes. The engines were always planned to be Bristol Olympus, although prototype VX770 fitted four Rolls-Royce Avons.

VX770 made its first flight from Woodford on 30 August 1952, piloted by the inimitable R. J. 'Roly' Falk, Avro's chief test pilot whose trademark was to fly in a lounge suit rather than a flying suit. Just three days later at the Farnborough show he displayed the Vulcan's impressive manoeuvrability, flying it solo and with the benefit of just three hours on type.

The second prototype, VX777, was more representative of the intended production Vulcan and fitted four Olympus Mk 100 engines. Ordered into production as high priority to strengthen the RAF's Medium Bomber Force, 45 Vulcan B1s were built. Initially, two front-line squadrons – Nos 83 and 101 – were formed alongside 230 Operational Conversion Unit (OCU).

Above: The Avro Vulcan prototype, VX770, showing off its pure delta planform.

While very early aircraft featured the pure delta wing, a 'cranked' leading edge was found to offer improved handling characteristics and was introduced on the production line and then retrofitted.

By late 1957 the Vulcan B1 was well established in service and current thinking was that the type's altitude performance and manoeuvrability would ensure its survivability over hostile territory. Avro was also planning the Vulcan B2, with more powerful Olympus engines, increased span and electronic countermeasures (ECM) equipment in an enlarged tail cone. The B2 was to be the major production variant, with 89 examples built, the first delivery to the RAF being on 1 July 1960.

As a stopgap measure, 29 Vulcan B1s were rebuilt as the B1A with the ECM fit and bulged rear fuselage of the B2, but eventually all squadrons standardised on the B2. Nine RAF squadrons flew the Vulcan – Nos 9, 12, 27, 35, 44, 50, 83, 101 and 617.

Avro Vulcan B2

Crew:	5
Length:	99ft 11in (30.4m)
Wingspan:	111ft (33.8m)
Height:	27ft 1in (8.2m)
Weight empty:	99,630lb (45,190kg)
Max. T/O weight:	204,000lb (92,530kg)
Max Speed:	645mph (1,040km/h)
Range:	4,000 miles (6,440km)
Powerplant:	4 x Bristol Siddeley Olympus 201 rated at 17,000lb
Armament:	up to 21 1,000lb bombs, one Yellow Sun nuclear weapon, one Blue Steel stand-off weapon

*Right and below: **Vulcan production in full swing at Woodford. In May 1956 the Vulcan B1 was issued to the RAF's Vulcan Operational Conversion Unit, 230 OCU, at Waddington. Strangely, early production aircraft were delivered in an overall silver finish.***

*Left: **The mighty Vulcan, without doubt one of the most charismatic aircraft to ever take to the skies. After the naming of the Vickers Valiant, the Chief of the Air Staff, Sir John Slessor, decreed that Avro's and Handley Page's bombers should similarly be given names starting with 'V'. Thus the Type 698 became the Vulcan – and the legend of the 'V-bombers' was born.***

handed future control of the UK deterrent to the senior service and effectively ended all future lines of V-bomber development.

The Vulcan's role as part of the strategic deterrent ended on 30 June 1969, when responsibility for the UK's strategic deterrent passed to the Royal Navy's Polaris-armed submarines. In 1982 a Vulcan flew from Ascension Island to Port Stanley to attack the runway that was being used by Argentine forces during their occupation of the Falkland Islands. This incredibly long-range mission, which required the back-up of numerous Victor tankers, is pointed to by proponents of the Vulcan as the type's finest hour. The Valiant may have dropped bombs operationally in the Suez crisis, but the Vulcan took part in a war that Britain actually won!

The Vulcan was to soldier on in the tanker role (a hasty post-Falklands conversion) until 31 March 1984 when No 50 Squadron disbanded, marking the end of 27 years of RAF Vulcan operations.

The Vulcan's bomb bay could carry a single nuclear weapon or up to 21 1,000lb bombs. In parallel with the B2, Avro had been developing the Blue Steel stand-off weapon, a rocket-powered Mach 2+ nuclear-armed missile with a range of 100 miles. This weapon avoided the need to overfly defences in the target area and would deliver the warhead with a supersonic dash. In the event, 53 production examples were built and were issued to a number of Vulcan B2 and Victor B2 squadrons. The weapon proved difficult to 'match' to the carrier aircraft and temperamental and unreliable in service. Because of its size (10.7m in length and 17,000lb fully fuelled), the Blue Steel round was carried semi-externally in the bomb bay. Blue Steel became operational with No 617 Squadron in February 1963, but the decision later that year to re-role the Vulcan fleet to low-level attack, flying at 1,000 or even 500ft above the ground to avoid enemy radar and SAMs, rendered Blue Steel yet less effective.

Both Victor and Vulcan – as well as the VC-10 – were put forward as potential launch platforms for the Douglas Skybolt, a true air-launched ballistic missile with a range exceeding 1,000 miles. The UK government put all its faith for the UK strategic deterrent into Skybolt, selecting the Vulcan B2 as the initial launch platform before the programme was cancelled in December 1962. This was a hammer blow for the RAF. A hurried agreement was reached to allow Britain to purchase the American Polaris SLBM, but this decision

*Right: **In the Cold War, Britain's deterrent posture assumed just a four-minute warning of a Soviet attack. The requirement was for the V-bomber force to be able to launch within this time. The Vulcan proved well capable of achieving this, the procedure being honed in frequent readiness exercises.***

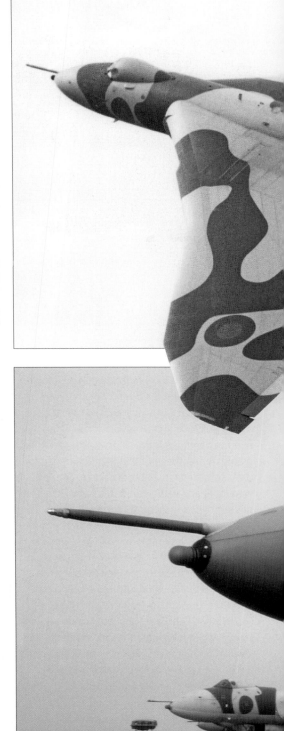

Top: *The front cockpit of the Vulcan with its fighter-like joysticks. The pilots sat on Martin-Baker 3KS ejection seats. The other three crew members faced rearwards and had swivelling seats to provide assisted exit in case of emergency. Entry to the cockpit was by an extending ladder in the lower forward fuselage.*

Above: *White wonder. The Vulcan B2 carrying the Blue Steel rocket-powered stand-off weapon. The Vulcan's great advantage over the Handley Page Victor was its adaptability. Its good ground clearance made it more suitable for the installation of the Blue Steel weapon, also produced by Avro, and introduced to some of the squadrons from late 1962.*

Top centre: *The Vulcan had a reputation for handling like a fighter, an impression heightened by the provision of a stick for the pilot rather than the more conventional yoke. Because of its QRA commitment, the Vulcan was fitted with a system that allowed all four engines to be started at the same time.*

Top right: *The usually quoted service ceiling of the Vulcan was 55,000ft, but an aircraft with no bomb load and minimum fuel could get to 60,000ft, an altitude at which the Vulcan still proved manoeuvrable and able to look after itself from any predatory fighters.*

Right: *The Vulcan saw out its final days in service at RAF Waddington in service with No 50 Squadron, whose aircraft are pictured here just prior to the last ever 'scramble' in 1984.* Allan Burney

◎ Handley Page Victor

Handley Page Victor B2(R)

Crew:	5
Length:	114ft 11in (35m)
Wingspan:	120ft (36.6m)
Height:	28ft 1in (8.6m)
Weight empty:	109,950lb (49,900kg)
Max. T/O weight:	223,000lb (101,150kg)
Max Speed:	645mph (1,040km/h)
Range:	3,800m (6,115km)
Powerplant:	4 x Rolls-Royce Conway 17 rated at 20,000lb
Armament:	35 1,000lb HE bombs, one Yellow Sun nuclear weapon, one Blue Steel stand-off missile

*Top: **The prototype of the futuristic-looking Victor V-bomber made its maiden flight on Christmas Eve 1952 from Boscombe Down. The aircraft was impressively displayed at the 1953 Farnborough Air Show, but a year later it was tragically lost following structural failure of its tail.***

*Right: **The Handley Page final assembly line of the Victor. The first production aircraft took to the air in early 1956 and the type received operational status in November 1957 with No 10 Squadron.***

*Far right: **Scramble! Scramble! RAF aircrew of No 15 Squadron sprint towards their Victor B1, XH594, during a training drill. No doubt it was a matter of pride for the pilot to win the race!***

Handley Page's Victor was, in every sense, the last of the V-bombers. It was the last to fly in prototype form, the last to enter squadron service and the last to leave front-line RAF service, although by that time as a flight refuelling tanker. It was, though, surely the most futuristic of the designs, with a crescent wing form which had three different degrees of sweep on the leading edge, the sweep angle decreasing towards the tip, and a flight deck canopy faired in completely with the forward fuselage.

Prototypes WB771 and WB775 were constructed in the experimental shop at Cricklewood, as the main factory at Radlett was at the time busy producing Canberras for the RAF. WB771 was then partially dismantled and moved by road to A&AEE Boscombe Down for its first flight, the fuselage being covered by tarpaulin and disguised as a boat with the name 'Geleypandhy' on the side. This strange name was, thanks to a signwriter's error, actually an anagram of 'Handley Pyge'. It remains unclear how effective this ruse might have been in confusing Soviet intelligence.

First flight by WB771 was on Christmas Eve 1952, with Sqn Ldr Hedley Hazelden at the controls. Flight testing continued at Boscombe Down, but WB771 was tragically destroyed in a crash at Radlett on 14 July 1954 after the tailplane broke up at low level. Fifty Victor B1s were ordered for the RAF (XA917-922, XA923-941, XH587-594, XH613-621, XH645-651, XH667) and the first entered service with No 10 Squadron at Cottesmore in April 1958. Like the other V-bombers in the Mk 1 form, the Victors were primarily tasked with delivering a free-fall nuclear weapon, although up to 35 1,000lb iron bombs could alternatively be carried internally.

Like the other V-bombers it had a crew of five in a pressurised compartment. Early design studies envisaged ejector seats for all five crew members, but the final layout deleted this provision for the three rearward-facing system operators.

Plans were drawn up in the late 1950s to produce a higher-flying, larger Victor as the B2, again in the belief that the aircraft could remain invulnerable to Soviet defences for a few more years. The B2 was to be powered by Rolls-Royce Conway bypass engines (turbofans) of 17,000lb (later 20,000lb) thrust rather than the Armstrong Siddeley Sapphires of the B1. Thirty four B2s were built and the type went on to serve with Nos 100 and 139 Squadrons of the Wittering Wing from early 1962. With the advent of Blue Steel, 21 B2s were returned to Radlett for a quite comprehensive conversion to carry the new weapon. The new aircraft, designated B2(R) (for retro fit) or simply B2 (Blue Steel) were most easily recognised by the over-wing fairings or 'Kúchemann carrots' – shock bodies that also provided space for chaff dispensers. Nine other B2s were converted to the specialist strategic reconnaissance role under the designation B(SR)2 and served with No 543 Squadron at Wyton until 1975. Victors also provided two generation of RAF flight refuelling tankers, as redundant B1s and then B2s were converted to the tanker role, serving until late 1993.

The Victor was the most technically advanced of the V-bombers and the one with the highest performance; there is a reasonably well-documented case of a B1 going supersonic, when HP test pilot Johnny Allam exceeded the speed of sound over the Home Counties in XA917 on 1 June 1956. It proved less suited than the Vulcan to the Blue Steel role, not least because the very limited ground clearance under the fuselage complicated loading the weapon, and was built in smaller quantities than the other types.

Overleaf: **The crescent wing of the Victor is shown to advantage in this rare angle on a pair of K2s basking in the tropical heat of Ascension Island in 1982, shortly after the Falklands conflict. The Victor was the last of the V-bombers to be retired, the final aircraft being removed from service on 15 October 1993.** *Allan Burney*

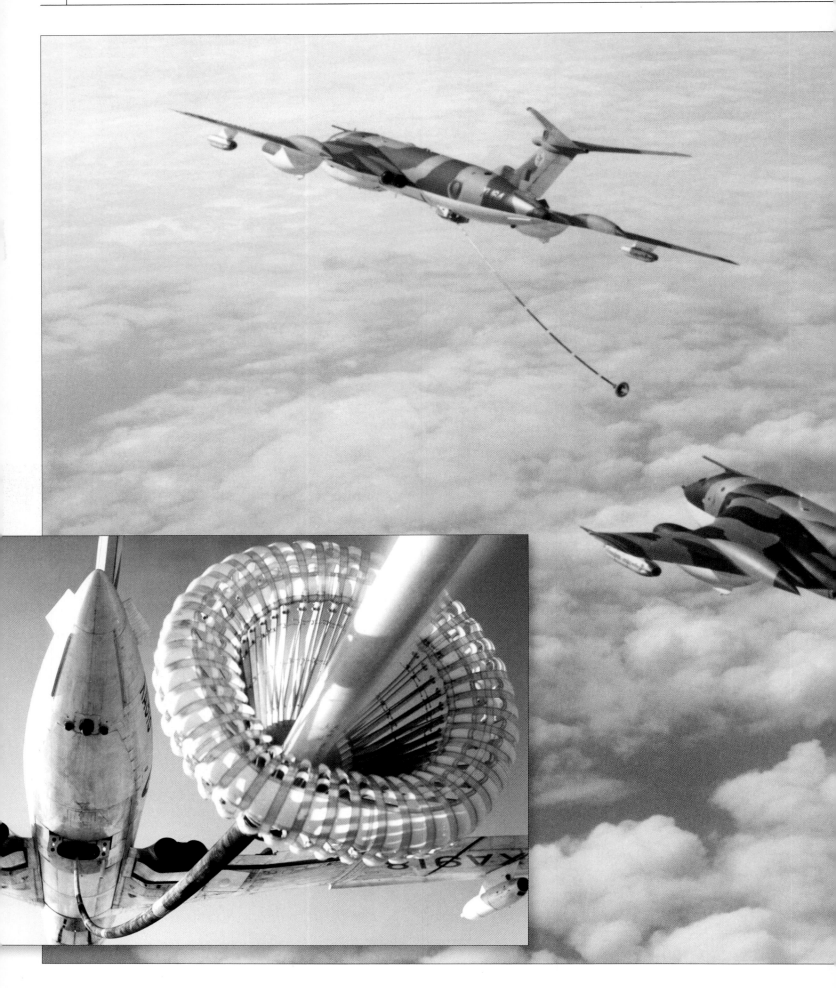

Below: **Looking like something straight out of the pages of a 'boy's own science fiction comic', the Victor was very much a product of the 1950s.**

Above: **A Victor B2 carrying out trials with the big Blue Steel stand-off nuclear missile. While assigned to the nuclear delivery role, the Victor was finished in an all-over anti-flash white colour scheme, designed to protect it against the damaging effects of a nuclear detonation by reflecting heat away from the aircraft.**

Left: **When the V-bombers were assigned to the low-level approach profile in the 1960s, the Victors were repainted in green/grey tactical camouflage to reduce visibility to ground observation; the same scheme was applied to subsequently converted tanker aircraft, as seen here.**

Far left: **The Victor established a successful second career for itself as an air tanker. As such it played a significant role in the Falklands crisis, providing refuelling support to its V-bomber compatriot, the Vulcan. Each Vulcan mission required the support of 12 Victor K2 tankers of Nos 55 and 57 Squadrons on the outbound leg, and a further two Victors on the return leg.**

The prototype B(I)8 VX185 – previously the record-setting sole B5 – up from Farnborough during the 1954 SBAC show and fitted with: A new forward fuselage with teardrop canopy on the port side; a ventral pack with 4 x 20mm Hispano cannon; one external hardpoint under each wing for up to 1,000lb (454kg) of bombs or unguided rockets; and LABS (Low-Altitude Bombing System) for delivery of nuclear bombs. Tip-tanks were added shortly afterwards.

⊙ English Electric Canberra

The English Electric Canberra was very much the mainstay of the RAF's light bomber force in the early and mid-1950s, with 24 squadrons operational at the close of 1954.

With the first of the V-bombers about to enter RAF squadron service, the Canberra air and ground crews represented a huge pool of experience in the operational employment of jet bombers. Indeed, it was from this light bomber force that many of the first V-bomber crews would come.

The Canberras, though, had only a conventional role at this time. It was not until 1958 that the Canberra squadrons with RAF Germany (RAFG) acquired a nuclear capability. The first mark of Canberra to be modified to drop nuclear weapons was the B(I)8 which then equipped three RAFG squadrons. Since no suitable British nuclear weapon existed, these Canberra units were issued with the American Mk 7 supplied to the UK under 'Project E' agreements. As with the V-bombers in the UK, RAFG Canberra B(I)8 and B(I)6 squadrons held a permanent QRA, typically with each squadron providing two aircraft and two crew on a 24-hour stint. The weapons remained under American control, with an American presence on the RAF bases to act as custodian. In practice, these arrangements worked well and the RAFG medium range strike force (where 'strike' meant 'nuclear') continued to fly the Canberra until the Buccaneer came in as replacement from early 1971.

Canberra B(I)6

Crew:	3
Length:	65ft 6in (19.96m)
Wingspan:	64ft (19.51m)
Height:	15ft 8in (4.77m)
Weight empty:	21,650lb (9,820kg)
Max. T/O weight:	55,000lb (24,948kg)
Max Speed:	Mach 0.88
Range:	810 miles (1,300km)
Powerplant:	2 x Rolls-Royce Avon RA7 Mk109 turbojets
Armament:	8,000lb (3,628kg) payload of bombs, type-approved for Mk7, B28, B57 or B43 nuclear weapons, Red Beard or WE177A nuclear bombs.

◎ Blackburn Buccaneer

The Buccaneer is often portrayed, perhaps unfairly, as 'the aircraft the RAF didn't want'. Through the mid-1950s and the 1960s, the air marshals always had their sights set on a supersonic design to replace the Canberra and saw the Buccaneer as a subsonic attack aircraft too lightly equipped to meet RAF requirements. Worse, it had been designed for the Royal Navy! In the event, it would give great service to the Navy, and would go on to serve with the RAF for 25 years.

While the Buccaneer's time embarked in aircraft carriers is perhaps outside the scope of this publication, mention must be made of the Buccaneer's evolution. Designed to counter the growing threat of the Soviet Sverdlov class of cruisers, it was built to allow high speed attacks at low level using conventional or nuclear weapons. The Buccaneer first flew on 30 April 1958 but the initial production S1 variant was underpowered, especially since the design incorporated 'flap blowing' (or boundary layer control) to blast high pressure air from the engine compressor over the wings and flaps to increase lift and reduce the take-off and landing speed. The S1, powered by the de Havilland Gyron Junior, only served with the Royal Navy. As a naval aircraft, it had folding wings and a radome that hinged backwards to reduce the length to fit on carrier deck lifts. It also had an internal weapons bay and a novel rotating bomb bay door, with weapons being carried on the inside of the door itself.

The Buccaneer S2, re-engined with a military version of the Rolls-Royce Spey turbofan already in production for BEA's Trident airliner, was being pursued by Blackburns even before the S1 had entered service. With the Spey, the Buccaneer's performance was transformed. The Navy's first front-line S2 squadron was commissioned on 14 October 1965 and eventually three squadrons were re-equipped, flying from the carriers *Eagle*, *Hermes*, *Victorious* and *Ark Royal*.

It was in 1968 and following the cancellation of the F-111K for the RAF that the government finally saw reason and ordered a batch of 26 Buccaneer S2 for the RAF. A number of changes were made to accommodate a wider range of weapons, the RAF variant being designated S2B. In addition, some ex-Navy

*Above: **Flying from Lossiemouth in Scotland, the last RAF Buccaneers were retired in 1994.***

Buccaneers would later become available with the run-down of the carrier force and would then be transferred to the RAF. RAF Buccaneers went on to serve in two main roles. Two squadrons formed in the UK and were allocated maritime/anti-shipping (No 12 Squadron) and strike/attack (No 208 Squadron) roles. From 1983, both operated from RAF Lossiemouth and both were assigned the maritime role. Two squadrons also formed with RAF Germany (RAFG), based at Laarbruch and replacing the ageing Canberra B(I)8. These units (Nos 15 and 16 Squadrons) worked up to their NATO

declaration in the attack and strike (ie nuclear) roles and held a permanent two-aircraft QRA strike alert from 1973 until the type's withdrawal from RAFG early in 1984.

The RAF's Buccaneer force had its shares of highs and lows. Making a first appearance at the USAF's Red Flag exercise at Nellis AFB in 1977, RAF aircrews employed their standard tactics of high-speed, ultra-low flying (100ft and even down to 50) approach to their targets in the desert. USAF aggressor squadrons had no experience of countering such a threat, and it is said they claimed no 'kills' at all on Buccaneers

HS Buccaneer S2	
Crew:	2
Length:	63ft 5in (19.3m)
Wingspan:	44ft (13.4m)
Height:	16ft 6in (5.0m)
Weight empty:	30,000lb (13,600kg)
Max. T/O weight:	62,000lb (28,100kg)
Max Speed:	645mph at sea level (1,040km/h)
Range:	1,730 miles (2,800km)
Powerplant:	2 x Rolls-Royce Spey 101 turbofans rated at 11,030lb
Armament:	8 x 100lb HE bombs, 2 x WE177A tactical nuclear weapons (side-by-side in weapons bay), 3 x Martel or 4 x Sea Eagle ASM, 2 x AIM-9G/L Sidewinder AAM

throughout the exercise. It was during the Buccaneers' third Red Flag deployment in February 1980 that S2B XV345 crashed on the Nellis range following a catastrophic failure of the starboard wing. This came as a huge surprise to all concerned; aircrews had a complete faith in the aircraft, which they claimed was hewn from a solid block of metal and 'built like a brick shithouse'. All RAF Buccaneers were immediately grounded, although the RAFG QRA alert was maintained throughout what would prove to be a six-month grounding. The failure was found to result from airframe fatigue and a rebuild programme was put into place. This resulted in something over 50 of the RAF's pre-crash fleet

of 90 being returned to service, but a number of airframes were cannibalised in the process.

Perhaps the Buccaneer's finest hour was the first Gulf War of 1991, when the Lossiemouth Wing deployed 12 Buccaneer S2s to Muharraq, Bahrain for 'Desert Storm'. Their role was to provide laser designation ('spiking', with reference to the Pave Spike designator pod) for LGB-equipped RAF Tornados. In this they proved supremely successful, the Buccaneers and Tornados together employing LGBs to destroy high value targets such as bridges and even aircraft on the ground. For this deployment the Buccaneers were painted desert pink and had unofficial nose art and names applied, with

much reference to scantily-clad ladies and brands of Scottish whisky. 250 sorties were flown by the detachment, which styled itself the 'Sky Pirates', and RAF crews later reflected that this was 'the Red Flag scenario for real'.

The end for the RAF Buccaneer force came on 26 March 1994 at Lossiemouth, when a nine-ship formation overflew the airfield as the highlight of a 'farewell weekend' for crews and families. Taxiing back to the dispersal, the nine aircraft simultaneously folded their wings and shut down their engines. And it was all over.

⭐ Boeing B-29 Superfortress

Boeing's B-29 will always be remembered as being the first (and, we must hope, the only) aircraft ever to drop a nuclear weapon in anger. This aircraft, with its sleek fuselage, pressurised crew areas and remotely-controlled defensive gun armament, also bids fair to the title of most advanced bomber design to see service in World War 2.

A total of 3,970 examples came off four different production lines between 1942 and 1946, but the end of the war caused large scale cancellation of contracts for further aircraft and widespread withdrawal and scrapping of those aircraft already in service.

The B-29 still had an important place in the inventory when SAC was formed on 21 March 1946, and when the USAF was established on 18 September 1947. The B-29 remained the only aircraft capable of delivering the American atomic bomb, a number of aircraft having been modified to be compatible under the wartime Project Silverplate. With the end of the war the Silverplate aircraft had lost their significance and, as a result, many had been scrapped, converted or dispersed around the fleet. On the formation of SAC, great efforts were made to locate as many as possible of the Silverplate B-29s and to bring them to a common modification standard. The project name Silverplate was superseded by Saddletree in May 1947, and further B-29s were converted to make them nuclear-capable to provide a stopgap nuclear delivery system until the improved B-50 became available. As things panned out, the final B-29s in the USAF's nuclear strike force were not replaced until 1951.

Even then, the B-29 had many more years of service ahead of it with the USAF. Some 92 examples were modified by Boeing Wichita as flight refuelling tankers as the KB-29M, these using the British 'hose and drogue' system. The later KB-29P used the Boeing-developed flying boom system. The use of a rigid boom allowed a much higher fuel transfer rate and this method was adopted as standard for SAC use.

The RAF found itself, in the aftermath of World War 2, without any suitable long-range bomber, the Avro Lincoln now being very long in the tooth and the new, jet-powered Canberra some years off. As a result, 87 B-29s were ordered from the United States under MDAP (Mutual Defense Assistance Program), an announcement being made in January 1950. In RAF service they were to be designated Washington B1. Some of these aircraft came from active service USAF units while others were awakened from their cocooned existence in the desert. Several still bore evidence of American nose art. The first four were handed over to the RAF on 20 March 1950 at Andrews AFB, MD, and then flown to RAF Marham where they arrived two days later. Nine RAF squadrons employed the Washington, which served until 1954, by which time more modern British bomber designs were becoming available in quantity.

Above: **A deadly accurate B-29 raid on a North Korean airfield, demonstrating that despite its World War 2 vintage, the Superfortress could still deliver a devastating strike.**

Top right: **Capt Donald M. Covic makes a 'command decision' by flipping a coin, just like the artwork on his B-29 pictured during the Korean War.**

Right: **The long slender wing of the B-29 was a thing of beauty.**

Below: **B-29A Superfortress 44-61835, Dragon Lady,** *as it looked in 1951 when assigned to SAC's 19th Bomb Group in Japan for Korean War duty. A World War 2 veteran, it bombed North Korea and shot down five MiGs, but crashed in the Pacific in late 1951 killing 10 of its 12 crew.*
Artwork © Zaur Eylanbekov

Boeing B-29 Superfortress

Crew:	11
Length:	99ft 0in (30.18m)
Wingspan:	141ft 3in (43.06m)
Height:	27ft 9in (8.45m)
Weight empty:	74,500lb (33,800kg)
Max. T/O weight:	133,500lb (60,560kg)
Max Speed:	357mph
Range:	3,250 miles (5,230km)
Powerplant:	4 x Wright R-3350-23 and 23A Duplex-Cyclone turbosupercharged radial engines
Armament:	(defensive): 8 or 10 x 4.50in (12.7mm) Browning M2/ANs (offensive): 20,000lb (9,000kg) payload

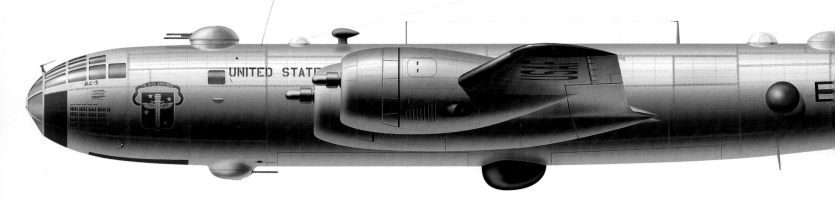

UNITED STATES AIR FORCE
5718

★ Convair B-36 Peacemaker

No aircraft better symbolises the Cold War bomber force of USAF Strategic Air Command (SAC) than Convair's giant B-36. Conceived in the early years of World War 2, the B-36 was designed with a 10,000-mile range to give it the ability to attack targets in Japan or Germany while operating from air bases on US soil. This required a large aeroplane and the B-36 was just that, with a 230ft wing span and six (later 10) engines.

Emerging from Convair's Fort Worth plant in the summer of 1946, the B-36 revealed itself as unlike any previous bomber. With six Pratt & Whitney R-4360 Wasp Majors driving pusher propellers, it had a design bomb load of 76,000lb – almost four times that of the B-29.

First flight of the XB-36 prototype 42-13570 was on 8 August 1946, with an eight-man Convair test crew. Difficulties arose during early flights, with engine cooling and propeller-induced airframe vibration causing much head scratching by Convair engineers. The USAF was by then in two minds as to whether the B-36 was really what SAC really needed but, with the Cold War hotting up and an increasingly urgent need for a true strategic bomber capable of delivering nuclear weapons, the initial 100-aircraft order for the B-36A placed back in August 1944 was allowed to stand.

First production B-36A was 44-92004, which flew on 28 August 1947. As deliveries to SAC got under way, the 7th Bomb Wing at Carswell, TX – a military base literally 'across the field'

from Convair's Fort Worth plant – received its initial aircraft, soon at the rate of one a week. The operational work-up was long and hard. By 1949, B-36 training sorties were routinely lasting 24 hours and the longest B-36 flight of all, in January 1951, was of 51 hours. On 12 March 1949, a 7th BW B-36A made a 9,600 mile out-and-back flight from Carswell without refuelling. Later, on 16 January 1951, six B-36s from Carswell landed at RAF Lakenheath to make the type's first appearance in England. They would later become a more familiar sight over the UK, thrashing their way at high altitude and seemingly taking an age to pass from horizon to horizon.

The type would go on to be built in several versions and to equip 10 USAF Wings. The B-36D was developed with four podded

*Left: **The last Peacemaker, Convair B-36J-10-CF 52-2827, comes to the end of the assembly line at Fort Worth, TX, in August 1954. The B-36 was in USAF service as part of Strategic Air Command from 1948 to 1959, but never fired a shot or dropped a bomb in anger.***

*Bottom left: **Convair B-36H-25-CF Peacemaker, 51-5718 of the 42nd BS, 11th BG, 8th AF, Carswell AFB, TX, Spring 1953.** Artwork © Zaur Eylanbekov*

*Right: **An idea as to the immense size of the B-36 was gained when the prototype was parked next to a B-29 Superfortress, then the biggest aircraft in the US inventory.***

*Below: **The prototype XB-36, 42-13570, takes off on its maiden flight, showing its giant single tyres. Production aircraft had a four-wheel main gear instead.***

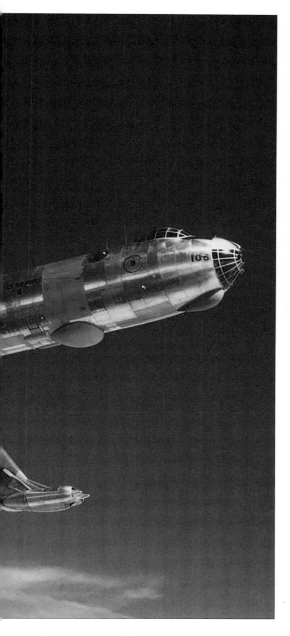

Above: *'Six turnin', four burnin'. This Convair RB-36D-5-CF, 49-2686, was a reconnaissance version of the mighty Peacemaker. In late 1952 during the Korean War, six 5th Strategic Reconnaissance Wing RB-36Ds were deployed to the 91st Strategic Reconnaissance Group at Yokota AB, Japan. This was the first introduction of the RB-36 to the Korean theatre. While not employed in any combat missions over North Korea, these RB-36s conducted high altitude aerial reconnaissance over Chinese Manchurian and Soviet east Asian targets.*

Left: *The B-36 was employed in a variety of aeronautical experiments throughout its service life. The FICON project involved a modified B-36 (called a GRB-36D 'mothership') and the RF-84K, a fighter modified for reconnaissance. The GRB-36D would ferry the RF-84K to the vicinity of the objective, whereupon the RF-84K would disconnect and begin its mission. Ten GRB-36Ds and 25 RF-84Ks were built and saw limited service in 1955–1956.*

General Electric J47 turbojets, two per side, mounted under the wings. Thus equipped, the aircraft had better take-off performance (and increased warload) as well as higher speed over the target area. The RB-36D was a dedicated reconnaissance version of the B-36D, with the bomb bays given over to cameras, photo flashes, extra fuel and a new pressurised crew compartment. The final production variant was the B-36J, 33 examples of which were built with the last coming off the production line on 14 August 1954. These were characterised by white-painted 'anti flash' undersurfaces, this feature underlining the aircraft's nuclear role.

Even with its new complement of 10 engines, the B-36 was a lumbering beast that became increasingly vulnerable to the latest generation of Soviet fighter aircraft. To give the type a few more years of relative invulnerability, a number of B-36Ds were modified to 'featherweight' configuration by removing much of the defensive armament. These aircraft are said to have been capable of cruising at 50,000ft.

In its time, the B-36 was a fearsome weapon, which surely did much to check Soviet thoughts of territorial expansion during the Cold War. The B-36's four large bomb bays, which were sized to carry the largest (43,000lb) conventional bombs, also ensured the aircraft were capable of carrying internally any of the early US atomic weapons. The Mk 7 atomic bomb was over 15ft in length and the later Mk 17 hydrogen bomb – ironically nicknamed the 'runt' – over 24ft.

Project Gem was initiated in 1947 to modify the B-36 for atomic weapons carriage as the US nuclear stockpile was built up. It was its versatility that made the B-36 such

Above: *Cockpit details of the B-36, complete with six throttle levers. Beginning with the B-36D, Convair added a pair of General Electric J47-19 jet engines suspended near the end of each wing. Consequently, the B-36 was configured to have 10 powerplants, six radial propeller engines and four jet engines.*

Convair B-36J Peacemaker

Crew:	13
Length:	162ft 1in (49.4m)
Wingspan:	230ft (70.1m)
Height:	46ft 9in (14.2)
Weight empty:	166,165lb (75,370kg)
Max. T/O weight:	410,000lb (186,000kg)
Max Speed:	411mph (660km/h)
Range:	10,000 miles (16,100km)
Powerplant:	6 x Pratt & Whitney R-4360 radials, 4 x General Electric J47 turbojets
Armament:	(defensive) 2 x 20mm cannon in tail (offensive) a variety of A-bombs and H-bombs, conventional bombs to 72,000lb

a valuable part of the SAC arsenal. Boeing's B-52 was, though, only a few years behind and offered a vastly improved, all-jet level of performance. B-36 operations were wound down progressively from 1956, and the final example was retired early in 1959. Just 385 had been manufactured, but the type was hugely important in the development of SAC's deterrent posture.

★ North American B-45 Tornado

Deserving its place in any review of Cold War bombers, the B-45 Tornado also justifies its mention as America's first jet bomber. Designed in 1944 by the team of North American's 'Dutch' Kindelberger, the XB-45 was a straight-wing, four-jet design with classic tricycle undercarriage. The pilot and co-pilot sat under a fighter-style cockpit canopy, while the bombardier was seated in the nose and the tail gunner in his own isolated position in the rear fuselage.

First flight of prototype 45-59479 was on 17 March 1947 at Muroc (now Edwards AFB). Two further prototypes flew soon afterwards, but the flight test programme did not always go to plan. 45-59479 was written off in a crash landing following a landing gear malfunction, partial flap failure and the loss of number 4 engine. Test pilot Albert Boyd might well have reflected that this was not his day, although the crew did emerge from the aircraft unscathed.

With more advanced, swept-wing bomber designs coming along, North American had to fight for production orders for the B-45. The

fitting of the GE J47 turbojet to later production B-45As (from 47-024) made the type viable enough to be issued to front-line units, and the 47th Bomb Wing was selected for re-equipment. Many of the 96 B-45A produced (47-001 to 47-096) served with the 47th, which moved across the Atlantic to install itself at Sculthorpe, Norfolk, in June 1952. With the B-45's limited range, the aircraft was assigned a tactical role, to employ atomic weapons against enemy airfields, troops, vehicles and communications and to slow any Soviet attack. Training missions continued unabated in the work-up to the unit's operational declaration. Inert, cement-filled 'shapes' were loaded in to B-45 bomb bays and released over the North Sea to simulate live weapons releases. The Mark 5 might have been a smaller, tactical atom bomb but it still measured 11ft in length and weighed upwards of a ton. Aircrew recalled that, immediately after weapon release, the aircraft suddenly gained 2,000ft. While the 47th BW's nuclear mission was officially secret, B-45As were sent to a number of RAF airfields for the 'At Home' days in September 1953 to show the flag.

From January 1958, re-equipment of the 47th BW with the Douglas B-66 got under way and the B-45A was fully retired later that year. Not all B-45s were bombers; further examples were built as – or converted to – RB-45C reconnaissance aircraft. These aircraft operated with SAC and TAC (Tactical Air Command) units in the States, in Europe and in Japan. A small number were also very temporarily 'transferred' to the RAF, such that they could take part in a number of highly secret 'Ju Jitsu' reconnaissance overflights of the Soviet Union from April 1952. These were undoubtedly high-risk missions. The aircraft wore RAF markings and were flown by RAF crews. Had an RB-45C been brought down over the Soviet Union, the USAF could have claimed that 'it isn't one of ours', while the RAF could equally have protested that it was demonstrably not an operator of this type. However impeccable the logic of this argument, the fact remains that the successful interception of an RB-45C on one of these missions would have had very serious political repercussions. Fortunately, it never happened.

Left: The XB-45 prototype of the Tornado releases its payload of bombs during early trials. Over 130 test flights were flown by the three prototype aircraft.

*Right: **A North American B-45C Tornado, 48-001. The type played an important part of the nation's nuclear deterrent in the early 1950s, but was quickly superseded by the Boeing B-47.***

*Bottom: **A B-45A of the 47th BW at RAF Sculthorpe in February 1955. Nuclear-capable B-45s began reaching the UK in May 1952, and deployment of the 40 aircraft was completed by mid-June.***

*Left: **Apart from being the first operational jet bomber flown by the USAF, the North American B-45 Tornado was also the first multi-jet engined bomber in the world to be refuelled in mid-air. Taken in June 1951, the official caption for this photograph reads: 'This is how the fast RB-45C appears during in-flight refueling (sic) from the blister of the KB-29 tanker.'***

North American B-45A Tornado

Crew:	4
Length:	75ft 4in (22.96m)
Wingspan:	89ft 0in (27.14m)
Height:	25ft 2in (7.67m)
Weight empty:	45,694lb (20,726kg)
Max. T/O weight:	110,000lb (49,900kg)
Max Speed:	570mph (920km/h)
Range:	1,000 miles (1,610km)
Powerplant:	4 x General Electric J47-GE-13 turbojets
Armament:	(offensive) 22,000lb bomb load (defensive) 2 x 0.5in (12.7mm) M3 guns

★ Boeing B-50 Superfortress

The Boeing B-50 was a development of the company's earlier B-29 and was originally designated B-29D. Appearances can be deceptive, though, and the B-50 was in fact a significantly new design with only a 25% commonality with the earlier aircraft.

New 28-cylinder, four-row Pratt & Whitney R-4360 engines gave 60% more power than the B-29's R-3350s, the airframe structure was constructed of a new, lighter aluminium, while a more obvious external distinguishing feature was the taller fin and rudder. The B-50 was born

into a political and military climate where the war had just ended, literally thousands of B-29s (and many other types) were being scrapped or put out to grass and the defence budget was being reeled back from its record wartime level. It is in this context that the re-designation from B-29D to B-50A should be seen, this allowing the manufacturer to present it as an 'all new' aircraft. One attraction it did have to the nascent SAC was that it was a purpose-built atomic bomber, intended to be capable 'as it came off the production line' of delivering any weapon in the US nuclear arsenal. In fact,

the almost manic security imposed by the US Atomic Energy Commission with regard to sharing information on any aspect of the US nuclear programme made Boeing's task of ensuring this compatibility all the more difficult.

There was no prototype B-50 as such, with all the type's new features already having been trialled and tested on a number of B-29s. Thus the first B-50A (46-2) off the Seattle line was a true production aircraft, which flew on 25 June 1947. 370 further B-50s of all marks would follow, with production extending into 1953. The B-50B and B-50D were improved variants

Above: A fine study of Boeing B-50D 48-096 as it cruises along the Pacific West coastline. This aircraft was later converted to become the mothership for the Bell X-2 rocket planes.

with higher gross weight. The continuing development of atomic weapons in the US arsenal required the B-50 – now the spearhead of the USAF nuclear-capable bomber force – to receive the necessary modifications to remain compatible. These were implemented under the on-going Saddletree programme, the changes affecting the bomb racks, electrical connections and bomb bay heating.

Five USAF Bomb Wings flew the B-50 in the nuclear role, the first being the 43rd BW at Davis-Monthan AFB, AZ, which took delivery from June 1948. The B-50 was essentially a stop-gap measure until the B-47 became available but, in the event, continued in the role until late 1955. Many B-50s were converted to flight refuelling tankers as KB-50J and KB-50K by Hayes Industries. Fitted with a three-hose hose and drogue system, these tanker KB-50s were primarily used to refuel the jet fighters of Tactical Air Command. SAC was, by this time, totally committed to the flying boom system.

Boeing B-50D Superfortress

Crew:	8-10
Length:	99ft 0in (30.18m)
Wingspan:	141ft 3in (43.05m)
Height:	32ft 8in (9.96m)
Weight empty:	84,714lb (38,426kg)
Max. T/O weight:	173,000lb (78,471kg)
Max Speed:	394mph (634km/h)
Range:	2,394 miles (3,853km)
Powerplant:	4 x Pratt & Whitney R-4360-35 28 four-row air-cooled radial piston engine, 3,500hp (2,600kW) each
Armament:	(offensive) 20,000lb (9,100kg) internally, 8,000lb (3,600kg) externally. (defensive) 13 x .50in (12.7mm) M2 Browning machine guns

⭐ Boeing B-47 Stratojet

Like the B-36, Boeing's B-47 Stratojet had its genesis in World War 2. With the growing realisation that jet engines represented the future of bomber aircraft, the USAAF canvassed ideas around the American aircraft industry. Boeing, whose B-29 was surely the most advanced heavy bomber of the War, responded with an early project which resembled a B-29 with four of General Electric's new jet engines in underwing pods. This design, though, offered insufficient improvements in performance and a complete rethink was required.

Overall: A B-47 take-off was always a thunderous affair, but when the bomber used JATO (jet assisted take-off) pods, the earth literally shook. Although it never saw combat as a bomber, the Stratojet was a mainstay of SAC's bomber strength during the late 1950s and early 1960s.

By October 1945, Boeing had come up with a 'clean sheet' proposal for a six-jet aircraft, the Model 450. This had a highly swept wing with two podded engines mounted side-by-side on a pylon under the inboard wing and a single podded engine well outboard. The main undercarriage was of bicycle type with two main gear legs, one behind the other on the fuselage centreline. Between the two was the all-important bomb bay, sized to accept the atomic weapons then being developed and, it was hoped, those that would follow. The pilot and co-pilot sat under a fighter-style cockpit canopy while the navigator/bombardier's position was forward of the pilots and lower in the fuselage. Unlike the British V-bombers, most marks of B-47 offered all crew members the luxury of an ejection seat, although the navigator/bombardier's fired downwards.

Boeing B-47E Stratojet

Crew:	3
Length:	107ft 1in (32.6m)
Wingspan:	116ft (35.4m)
Height:	28ft (8.5m)
Weight empty:	78,600lb (35,650kg)
Max. T/O weight:	200,000lb (90,700kg)
Max Speed:	600mph (965km/h)
Range:	4,700 miles (7,600km)
Powerplant:	6 x General Electric J47 rated at 7,000lb
Armament:	(defensive) 2 x 20mm cannon in rear fuselage. (offensive) A wide variety of US free-fall nuclear weapons ('special weapons')

*Above: **The XB-47 prototype was rolled out on 12 September 1947 and made its maiden flight on 17 December piloted by test pilots Robert Robbins and Scott Osler. Sadly, during an early high speed test flight the canopy flew off killing pilot Scott Osler. The co-pilot was uninjured and was able to recover the aircraft back to base.***

Boeing received a contract to construct two prototypes as the XB-47. The first of these was completed in record time and made its first flight on 17 December 1947. Eager to enter the jet bomber age, SAC placed an initial production order for the B-47A and the first aircraft was handed over to the 306th Bomb Wing on 23 October 1952. This unit, at MacDill AFB, FL, had a primary training role but further Wings followed, the second being the 305th BW that was also based at MacDill.

The pace of Boeing's B-47 deliveries allowed further Wings to re-equip through the early and mid-1950s, the production total eventually reaching over 2,000. The J47- powered B-47A was essentially a service test variant and was quickly succeeded in production by the B-47B, of which almost 400 were built. The B-47E, with uprated J47s and increased all-up weight, was the main production variant with over 1,500 built by Boeing, Lockheed and Douglas.

The B-47 rapidly achieved a reputation as a demanding aircraft to fly. It was generally agreed to have been under-powered, and to make possible maximum-weight take-offs

*Right: **Radical, sleek and fast, the B-47 had a fighter-like light touch to the controls, an impression enhanced by the large bubble canopy. In fact the aircraft was so clean aerodynamically that in a rapid descent into the landing pattern, the rear landing gear had to be deployed to act as an airbrake to slow it down. On landing a drag chute was deployed.***

Left: **The B-47's reliability and serviceability were regarded as good, but it was always useful to get a second opinion when inspecting its General Electric J47 engines. The first production batch was fitted with J47-GE-11 turbojets, and these were gradually upgraded to the J47-GE-25A of the definitive 'E' model.**

Below: **B-47E-125-BW Stratojet of the 380th Bomb Wing, Plattsburgh AFB, New York, shown as it looked in 1964 during deployment to RAF Brize Norton.**
Artwork ©
Zaur Eylanbekov

Above: **At the end of a long sortie, a Stratojet crew relax with a cigarette. Presumably the aircraft was not being refuelled at the time. Flying the Stratojet was a challenge. It was sluggish on take-off and fast on landing. If the pilot landed at the wrong angle, the B-47 would 'porpoise', bouncing fore-and-aft. If the pilot did not lift off for another go-around, instability would quickly cause the bomber to skid onto one wing and cartwheel. However, improved training led to a good safety record.**

Top: **The honour of being the 1,000th Stratojet produced by Boeing fell to B-47E 52-609. The B-47 formed the backbone of SAC into 1959, when the B-52 began to assume nuclear alert duties. B-47 production ceased in 1957.**

Above: **The three man Stratojet B-47E crew consisted of the aircraft commander, co-pilot, and a navigator/bombardier, the latter seen here using the K bombing system.**

Left: **The awesome and rather frightening sight of 13 Stratojets powering overhead, leaving heavy smoke trails in their wake.**

from airfields at high altitudes or in high ambient temperatures racks of JATO bottles could be fitted to the rear fuselage to boost take-off performance. So streamlined was the design that a ribbon-type brake parachute was employed to slow the aircraft for landing, the pilot streaming it on – or sometimes even before – touchdown. The aircraft's range was nowhere near that of the B-36 that preceded it or the B-52 that followed. Fortunately, SAC was, at the time, building up its fleet of KC-97 flight refuelling tankers and the B-47 had a suitable

*Below and bottom: **Always a sight and sound to behold, a Stratojet blasts off from terra firma aided by JATO bottles to provide added power permitting heavier payloads, increased range, shorter take-off runs, or a combination of these.***

receptacle for the Boeing-designed boom in the forward fuselage. At high altitude, the B-47 pilot could find himself in 'coffin corner'. This occurred at the point in the flight envelope where low-speed stall and high-speed buffet came together. Pull back on the control column and the aircraft would start to stall, push forward and it would encounter high-speed buffet. Getting out of such a situation required careful handling by the pilot.

With the B-47's limited range, overseas deployments became more regular. 'Reflex Action' deployments of three-week duration brought SAC B-47s to bases in the UK, Spain and North Africa, where they held a permanent alert, ready to launch towards targets in the Soviet Union at 15 minutes' notice. In the UK, the airfields concerned included Brize Norton, Upper Heyford, Greenham Common and Fairford, where Reflex activity continued until early 1965.

Early in its service career the B-47 operated primarily at high altitude, but improved Soviet radars and defences forced a rethink in the late 1950s to train in low-level flying and weapons delivery involving the Low Altitude Bombing System (LABS) manoeuvre. With this method, the aircraft ran in at low level before pulling up steeply into a half loop, 'tossing' the nuclear weapon towards the target in the climb before rolling out and heading for home. Provided, of course, there was still a home to head for.

Numerically speaking, the B-47 was the most important bomber type in the SAC inventory. Withdrawal started as early as 1959, but it was not until end-December 1967 that the last SAC B-47 was retired. Most were flown to the boneyard at Davis-Monthan AFB, AZ, where they were reduced to produce.

★ Boeing B-52 Stratofortress

Despite the first aircraft having flown 64 years ago (first flight of the YB-52 49-231 was 15 April 1952) and the fact that the production line closed down after the last aircraft (B-52H 61-040) was delivered in October 1962, the Boeing B-52 remains today very much in service with the USAF.

Of the 744 examples delivered, around 80 are still in front-line use with Bomb Wings at Barksdale, LA, and Minot, ND, while the projected current out-of-service date (OSD) has been pushed back to 2040. With the type already qualifying for its 'long service' award, today's B-52H looks externally very much like the YB-52 of 1952, save the fact that the current aircraft has eight P&W TF33 turbofans which give more power, better economy and, most noticeably, far less smoke than the earlier J57 turbojets.

In broad outline, the B-52 shares many design features with the company's B-47. Both have

swept wings, podded under-wing engines and a tandem undercarriage arrangement ('quadricycle' in the case of the B-52) that requires the pilot to perform 'flat' take-offs without the ability to rotate. Early model B-52s had the tall fin and rudder, but on the final B-52G and H models the fin height was considerably reduced.

Designed as a nuclear bomber, the B-52 today retains that capability but has developed into a highly capable carrier of all kinds of weapons. The B-52G was the sixth major production variant; the B-52A was only used on flight test duties. This variant had a beefed-up structure, a significant increase in fuel capacity and, most importantly, was the first to have a stand-off weapons capability. Two GAM-77 (later AGM-28) Hound Dog supersonic missiles could be carried, one under each wing. The first production Hound Dog (named, incredibly, after the song covered by Elvis Presley) was

handed over to Gen Thomas Power, C-in-C of SAC, on 21 December 1959. The missile's range of some 700 miles and its ability to fly a variety of attack profiles gave the B-52 a far better chance of attacking heavily defended targets.

The B-52H, the final production variant and the only one still in service, was similar to the B-52G but was fitted with TF33 turbofans offering 17,000lb of thrust each. Even without in-flight refuelling, the B-52H could go a long way. This was demonstrated, to the Féderation Aéronautique Internationale as a record and to the Soviet Union as a salutary reminder, by the 12,532-mile unrefuelled flight of B-52H 60-0040 from Kadena, Okinawa to Torrejon, Spain on 10 December 1962.

SAC (motto 'Peace is our profession') came into being on 21 March 1946 with the mission of creating and maintaining a nuclear strike force able to operate in all conditions and to provide nuclear deterrence against the

emerging Soviet threat. It would go on to control two of the three elements in the US nuclear 'triad' – manned bombers and ICBMs. B-52s were the cornerstone of this deterrence, with fully-armed aircraft being put on ground alert, ready to launch within 15 minutes and backed up by KC-97 tankers, from 1 October 1957. The aim was to have a third of SAC's bombers on ground alert at all times. The 15 minutes allowed was determined by the amount of warning of attack that planners expected to have before Soviet missiles started impacting defence installations in the continental US.

This readiness was extended to having nuclear-armed B-52s in the air on a constant airborne alert from early 1961. Operation 'Chrome Dome' involved a number of aircraft taking off from their home bases and taking either the Western route over Alaska, the Northern route over Canada and Greenland or the Southern route over the Atlantic, over Spain

*Above: **The giant Boeing B-52 Stratofortress is the longest-serving warplane in the history of aviation, still in action over 60 years after its first flight. The B-52's official name Stratofortress is rarely used; informally, the aircraft has become commonly referred to as the BUFF (Big Ugly Fat Fella [polite version]).***

and into the Mediterranean. The aircraft were fully armed and ready to attack their assigned targets on receipt of the correct, authenticated orders. Apart from that, it was a case of flying long missions lasting 24 hours or more on vast orbits. One 'Chrome Dome' sortie on the Southern route gave rise to the USAF's worst nuclear accident when, on 17 January 1966, a B-52G from Seymour Johnson AFB, NC, collided with a KC-135 tanker while refuelling off the coast of Spain. Four B28 hydrogen bombs were released and both aircraft were destroyed. The result was a vast search and a costly clean-up operation.

The ground nuclear alert held by SAC B-52s was stood down in September 1991 in the new spirit of détente. Subsequently, around 350 early model (pre-B-52H) aircraft, which had been in store at Davis-Monthan AFB or recently retired in the case of the B-52G fleet, were most visibly broken up in the early 1990s under the terms of the Strategic Arms Limitation Treaty (SALT).

ECM on the B-52 has improved greatly over the years, while other stand-off weapons such as AGM-69 SRAM (Short Range Attack Missile) and AGM-86 ALCM (Air Launched Cruise Missile) have been introduced to allow the B-52 to attack targets in a high-threat environment. The Douglas GAM-87 Skybolt air-launched ballistic missile (see section on the Avro Vulcan) was designed for the B-52 and would have offered a stand-off range of over 1,000 miles. Test launches from a B-52 began in April 1962 but went badly and the whole programme was cancelled in November of that year.

Above: The XB-52 prototype featured the original tandem seating arrangement with a framed bubble canopy. Here the aircraft is seen taking off from Boeing Field, Seattle, in its typically nose-down attitude.

Left: The Boeing B-52 assembly line, highlighting the immense wingspan of the Stratofortress. Early production of the B-52 was shared between Boeing's Seattle and Wichita plants, but in 1957 it was decided to transfer all production to Wichita. Production ended in 1962 with 742 aircraft built, plus the original two prototypes.

Right: 'Ain't nothin' but a hound dog'. A B-52 looks menacing with a pair of GAM-77 Hound Dog stand-off nuclear missiles slung under its wings. Remarkably the missile was named after the song made famous by Elvis Presley.

Bottom right: B-52H 60-0021 of the 19th Bombardment Wing (BW), based at Wurtsmith AFB, Michigan, during the Cuban Missile Crisis of October 1962. The aircraft is armed with a pair of GAM-77 Hound Dog missiles.

Cold War warriors unite. Defying the test of time, a B-52 Stratofortress from Barksdale AFB, LA, takes fuel from a KC-135 Stratotanker assigned to the 100th Air Refueling Wing at RAF Mildenhall, England, in the skies near Spain. The KC-135 was designed and built specifically to deliver fuel to the B-52. Between them the aircraft can boast over 120 years of service!

Above: Rare beast. Only three of the 13 B-52As ordered were built and all were used by Boeing in its test programme. The remaining 10 were upgraded and delivered as B-52Bs, becoming the first examples to enter active service.

Left: B-52 crews sprint to their aircraft during a 'Scramble' drill, to hone their readiness on alert. Note the anti-flash white underside of the fuselage.

Below: Using typical Cold War propaganda, the original caption to this image reads... 'The eight-jet Boeing B-52, a huge hydrogen-bomb carrier, described as the most formidable aircraft in the striking force of the United States Strategic Air Command, is ready to replace the obsolescent B-36s of the 42nd Heavy Bomber Wing at Loring AFB in Maine, and by 1958 some 500 of the monster aircraft will be in service to discourage any possible enemy attacks or to retaliate if any should come.' The actual image shows Boeing B-52s on the pre-delivery flight line at Boeing's Seattle plant.

Boeing B-52H Stratofortress

Crew:	5
Length:	159ft 4 (48.6m)
Wingspan:	185ft (56.4m)
Height:	40ft 8in (12.4m)
Weight empty:	166,000lb (75,300kg)
Max. T/O weight:	488,000lb (221,350kg)
Max Speed:	630mph (1,010km/h)
Range:	8,800 miles (14,200km)
Powerplant:	8 x Pratt & Whitney TF33 turbofans rated at 17,000lb
Armament:	(defensive) 1 x M61 rotary cannon in rear fuselage. (offensive) 4 x GAM-87 Skybolt ballistic missiles. 2 x AGM-28 Hound Dog cruise missiles, up to 70,000lb of ordnance

Below: **An amazing photograph that demonstrates the strength of the B-52. On 10 January 1964 a Boeing test crew were flying over a mountainous stretch of Colorado when their B-52H was hit by turbulence. Pilot Chuck Fisher climbed to 14,300ft in hope of smoother air, but the aircraft was struck by turbulence so strong that it sheared off the aircraft's vertical tail fin. Fisher told the crew to prepare to abandon ship. He descended to 5,000ft where they would bail out, but the B-52 continued to fly without significant impediment. Fisher landed it in one piece – minus the tail – at Blytheville AFB in Arkansas. Not surprisingly he said 'The B-52 is the finest airplane I ever flew'.**

Left: **Pratt & Whitney J-57 turbojets powered early versions of the B-52, but in 1961 the B-52H introduced the cleaner burning and quieter Pratt & Whitney TF33-P-3 turbofans with a maximum thrust of 17,100lb.**

Below: **Some things never change. The trademark smoky take-off of a B-52 Stratofortress as water is injected into its engines to increase thrust.**

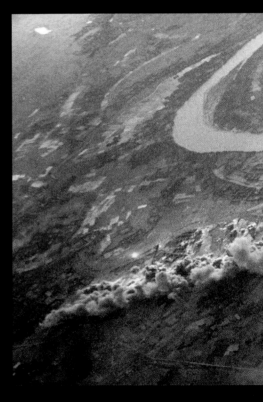

Below: **B-52G 57-6516 of the 63rd Bombardment Squadron (Provisional)/72nd BW (Provisional), Andersen AFB, Guam, 1972.**

VIETNAM VET

The B-52's first combat mission, Operation 'Arc Light', was flown by B-52Fs on 18 June 1965, when 30 bombers of the 9th and 441st BS struck a communist stronghold in South Vietnam. It was an inauspicious start as two B-52s collided, which resulted in the loss of both bombers and eight crewmen. The bomber went on to play a crucial but sometimes controversial role in the conflict, which ended with Operation 'Linebacker II', the 'Eleven-Day War' of 18-29 December 1972. In that effort against military and industrial targets in the Hanoi-Haiphong area of North Vietnam, B-52D and B-52G models flew 729 sorties against 24 target complexes delivering 300,000lb of bombs. After years without a loss, 15 B-52s were shot down by Soviet-supplied SA-2 'Guideline' surface-to-air missiles. The 'eleven days of Christmas' is credited by many with bringing North Vietnam to the negotiating table and ending the war on 27 January 1973.

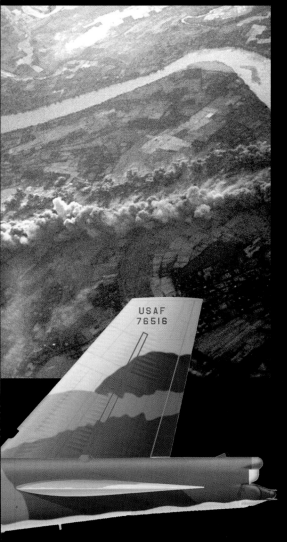

★ Convair B-58 Hustler

In the late 1940s, the USAF knew it would eventually need a new bomber type to replace the B-47, even though that aircraft had yet to enter service. It liked the idea of a jet-powered supersonic design and Mach 2 capability was deemed desirable. Several US manufacturers responded with proposals but the delta-winged MX-1626 (which later became the MX-1964) design from Convair was selected in December 1952.

The proposed aircraft was small for a bomber but, Convair argued, the one nuclear weapon that it would be capable of delivering carried as much destructive power as all the bombs dropped by the USAAF 8th Air Force during World War 2.

Delta-winged and with four podded, under-wing GE J79 turbojets, the type would be designated B-58A Hustler in USAF service. Just three crew – pilot, navigator/bombardier and defensive systems operator – were needed. Only the pilot had any real view on the outside world, but all three had individual escape capsules to give a good chance of surviving ejection at Mach 2 or at 70,000ft. Unlike most every bomber up to that time, the B-58 had no bomb bay. Rather, a 57ft-long, streamlined, finned pod was carried under the central fuselage. The MB-1C pod, the initial version, contained fuel tanks front and rear, an equipment bay and a large thermonuclear weapon. The fuel was used by the aircraft in

getting to its target; the pod with the bomb could then be released to make its free-fall descent to its objective, the fins imparting a slow spin as it descended. The later TCP (two-component pod) had two separate sections. The lower part of the pod was a pure fuel tank and could be jettisoned en route once empty, while the upper component housed further fuel and a Mark 53 nuclear weapon which could remain on the under-fuselage pylon until over the target.

The B-58A entered USAF service from August 1960, when the first examples were delivered to the 43rd Bomb Wing at Carswell, TX. This unit would later move to Little Rock AFB, AK, while a second Wing was formed

when the 305th BW at Bunker Hill AFB, IN, received its first aircraft in May 1961. Both Wings had transitioned from the B-47. Soon after the B-58 entered service, the type started setting speed records to underline the fact that the USAF had its first supersonic bomber. In Operation 'Heat Rise', a 43rd BW aircraft flew from Los Angeles to New York and return in 4hrs 41min, averaging 1,045mph. The B-58 was normally speed-limited to keep the external airframe temperature to 115°C to ensure the structural integrity of the aluminium honeycomb panels used in its construction, but for this record attempt Convair engineers agreed an increase to 125°, to allow speeds of up to 1,400mph. Skin temperature sensors were installed to ensure temperatures kept

Below: **Appropriately named the Hustler, the highly aerodynamic Convair B-58 was the first operational bomber capable of Mach 2 flight.**

within these limits, and this was the explanation behind the project name 'Heat Rise'. This two-way trans-continental dash set a number of records and saw the crew receive several awards including the Bendix and Mackay Trophies. The USAF subsequently received over 10,000 complaints and demands for compensation for damage from people under the flight path. Evidently the SAC PR machine still had some way to go to persuade the entire US population that the sonic boom was indeed 'the sound of freedom'.

The Hustler was never easy to fly and crews were hand-picked from the USAF community. High speeds and high angles of attack were required for both take-off and landing, maintaining a safe centre of gravity during acceleration or deceleration was challenging and the loss of an engine in supersonic flight could pose serious problems. Alongside the record flights, B-58s were involved in a number

of crashes. Perhaps the most public were two losses of aircraft having made the trans-Atlantic flight to attend the Paris air show at le Bourget. In 1961, 59-2451 'The Firefly' crashed performing low-altitude aerobatic manoeuvres, while four years later 59-2443 'Bye Bye Birdie' undershot when landing.

Although originally seen as a replacement for the B-47, in the event the B-58 only ever equipped two Bomb Wings and just 116 examples were produced. By 1970, after only 10 years, the B-58 fleet had been quietly retired and the remaining aircraft flown to the desert boneyard at Davis-Monthan AFB. This decision was taken primarily on financial grounds. The B-58 was expensive to maintain and to operate and, with just two Wings equipped, was but a minor type in the USAF's inventory. SAC protested and argued for an extension to 1974, when the FB-111A would be established in service, but to no avail.

Convair B-58A Hustler

Crew:	3
Length:	96ft 9in (29.5m)
Wingspan:	56ft 10in (17.3m)
Height:	29ft 11in (9.1m)
Weight empty:	55,560lb (25,200kg) without MB-1 pod
Max. T/O weight:	176,900lb (80,240kg)
Max Speed:	Mach 2 - 1,320 mph (2,120km/h) at altitude
Range:	4,400 miles (7,080km)
Powerplant:	4 x General Electric J79 turbojets rated at 9,700lb dry and 15,600lb in afterburner
Armament:	(defensive) M61 rotary cannon in rear fuselage. (offensive) Under-fuselage MB-1 or TCP pod with Mark 39 or Mark 53 nuclear weapon

*Left: **The Convair B-58 production line. Well shown are the three self-contained crew compartments in tandem arrangement.***

*Below left: **Convair testing a novel ejection capsule that made it possible to eject at an altitude of 70,000ft (21,000m) at speeds up to Mach 2 (1,320mph). A protective clamshell would enclose the seat and the control stick, allowing the pilot to continue to fly even 'turtled up' and ready for immediate egress. In an unusual test programme, live bears and chimpanzees were successfully used to test the ejection system!***

*Above right: **Instead of an internal bomb bay, the Hustler carried its payload in a large streamlined external pod, which gave the aircraft an even more aggressive appearance.***

*Right: **The sleek lines and delta wing of the Convair B-58 prototype. Serial number 55-660, was completed in late August 1956 and took to the air three months later.***

*Below: **A rare colour image of the second Convair B-58 prototype, 55-0661. A difficult and protracted flight test programme involving 30 aircraft continued until April 1959.***

Above: **The B-58 could never be accused of being subtle, but then very few aircraft of that era were. The large engine cowlings housed four General Electric J79-GE-1 turbojet engines, while the large centreline pod concealed its deadly nuclear weapon.**

Right: **The 'front office' of the Convair B-58 Hustler with standard flying instruments to the left and the four-banks of engine instruments to the right.**

Top right: **The introduction of highly accurate Soviet surface-to-air missiles forced the B-58 into a low-level penetration role that severely limited its range and strategic value. This led to a brief operational career between 1960 and 1970 when the B-58 was succeeded by the smaller, swing-wing FB-111A.**

Centre right: **The Hustler was a thirsty beast and relied heavily on air-to-air refuelling to extend its range. The B-58 set 19 world speed records, including coast-to-coast records, and one for the longest supersonic flight in history. In 1963, it went from Tokyo to London (via Alaska), a distance of 8,028 miles (12,920km) in 8hrs 35min, averaging 938mph (1,510km/h).**

Right: **Convair B-58A-30-CF Hustler 61-2053, 305th Bomb Wing, Bunker Hill AFB, IN, late 1960s.**
Artwork © Zaur Eylanbekov

⭐ General Dynamics FB-111

The F-111 programme was instigated in the early 1960s when the US Secretary of Defense directed the US Navy and the USAF to adopt a single aircraft design to meet their widely differing needs under the TFX programme.

The aircraft featured variable geometry ('swing wings'), afterburning turbofan engines and terrain-following radar for low-altitude, terrain-hugging approach to the target. Suffice to say that the F-111's development programme encountered numerous problems, that the US Navy pulled out as its version was clearly unsuited to the requirement for a carrier-based interceptor, and that the aircraft was late in coming into service with the USAF.

Although nuclear-capable, the original F-111 was essentially a tactical aircraft. As such, it served with Tactical Air Command units in its F-111A/D/E/F versions from summer 1967. In a later development and as an interim measure to replace the B-58A Hustler, the FB-111A was ordered in 1966. With longer wings (from the cancelled US Navy F-111B), a lengthened fuselage and increased fuel tankage, the FB-111A achieved what can just be considered strategic range – around 3,300 miles with high altitude cruise. The FB-111A could carry nuclear armament and in particular the AGM-69 SRAM nuclear stand-off weapon, mounting two internally and four on under-wing pylons.

The FB-111A served with two SAC Wings – the 509th at Pease AFB, NH and the 380th at Plattsburg AFB, NY – from 1971. Although plans were initially for 200+ FB-111As, in the event only 76 were built, and the type – like the B-58 Hustler it replaced – never became a major player within SAC. All had been retired by 1991.

General Dynamics FB-11A

Crew:	2
Length:	75ft 6in (23.01m)
Wingspan:	70ft 0in (21.33m), 34ft (10.36m) fully swept
Height:	17ft 0in (5.18m)
Max. T/O weight:	114,000lb (51,709kg)
Max Speed:	Mach 2 – 1,320 mph (2,120km/h) at altitude
Range:	3,350 miles (5,391km)
Powerplant:	2 x Pratt & Whitney TF30-P-7 turbofan engines
Armament:	Boeing – AGM-69A SRAM with W6 warhead

Left: Sun glints of the canopies of this pair of FB-111s with wings in the forward position.

★ Rockwell B-1 Lancer

If we take the accepted end of the Cold War as 1991, the year the Soviet Union finally collapsed, the B-1 Lancer (often referred to as the 'Bone' (B-One)) only took its place in the USAF arsenal for the final five years of this period.

The original B-1A was developed by Rockwell as a strategic bomber capable of Mach 2 at altitude and Mach 0.85 at low level. Its design included a number of features then in vogue – swept wings to allow operation from shorter runways than those usable by the B-52 and an ejectable crew capsule (rather than individual ejector seats) to improve the crewmembers' chances of surviving an ejection at altitude.

*Below: **The prototype of the Rockwell B-1A Lancer revealed a well-proportioned curvaceous airframe that blended in to the variable-sweep wings. Serialled 74-0158, it first flew on 23 December 1974.***

Four prototypes were ordered, the first (74-0158) taking to the air on 23 December 1974.

For reasons both of programme cost and the B-1A's increasing vulnerability to a new generation of Soviet defences, the programme was cancelled in 1977 before a production decision was taken. The aircraft re-emerged, albeit in a slightly different form, in 1981 following Ronald Reagan's installation as US president, and a contract for 100 of the 'new' B-1B was announced in January 1982.

Numerous changes to the design were made to suit the B-1B for the low-level penetrator role now envisaged. The maximum speed requirement was lowered to Mach 1.25 and emphasis was put on reducing the radar cross-section and improving the avionics and ECM suite. Two B-1A prototypes were modified to include systems and equipment intended for the new variant, and the initial production B-1B

(82-0001, christened 'Leader of the Fleet') made its first flight on 18 October 1984. Progress from that point onwards was fast. Deliveries to the first operational unit, the 96th Bomb Wing, at Dyess AFB, TX, began in June 1985, Initial Operational Capability (IOC) was achieved on 1 October 1986 and the 100th and final aircraft was handed over on 2 May 1988.

While initially serving as a nuclear bomber, the B-1B was switched to a non-nuclear role in the mid-1990s. In the first six months of Operation 'Enduring Freedom' in 2001/2, eight B-1Bs dropped almost 40% of the total tonnage delivered by coalition forces. The type is today the true multi-role bomber in the USAF inventory, capable of delivering a wide variety of conventional munitions, both guided and unguided. Various modification and upgrade programmes are under way to extend the B-1B's service life towards 2040.

Above: The cockpit of an early B-1 was highly advanced for its time.

Right: The first Rockwell B-1 nearing completion and revealing the extensive use of aluminium and titanium in its construction.

Below: The sleek shape of the Rockwell B-1A with wings in fully-swept position. Unlike the B-1A, the B-1B cannot reach Mach 2+ speeds; its maximum speed is Mach 1.25 (about 950mph or 1,530km/h at altitude), but its low-level speed increased to Mach 0.92 (700mph, 1,130km/h).

Rockwell B-1B

Crew:	4
Length:	146ft (44.5m)
Wingspan:	136ft 8in at minimum sweep (41.7m)
Height:	33ft 7 in (10.2m)
Weight empty:	190,000lb (86,200kg)
Max. T/O weight:	477,000lb (216,370kg)
Max Speed:	820mph (1,320km/h)
Range:	7,400 miles (11,900km)
Powerplant:	4 x General Electric F101 turbofans
Armament:	Up to 84 Mk 82 500lb HE bombs, a variety of cruise missiles (SRAM, ALCM, ACM)

The B-1B entered service in 1986 with the USAF Strategic Air Command (SAC) as a nuclear bomber. In the early 1990s, it was converted to conventional bombing use and first served in combat during Operation 'Desert Fox' in 1998 and again during the NATO action in Kosovo the following year. The B-1B has supported US and NATO military forces in Afghanistan and Iraq. The B-1B is expected to continue to serve into the 2030s and possibly beyond.

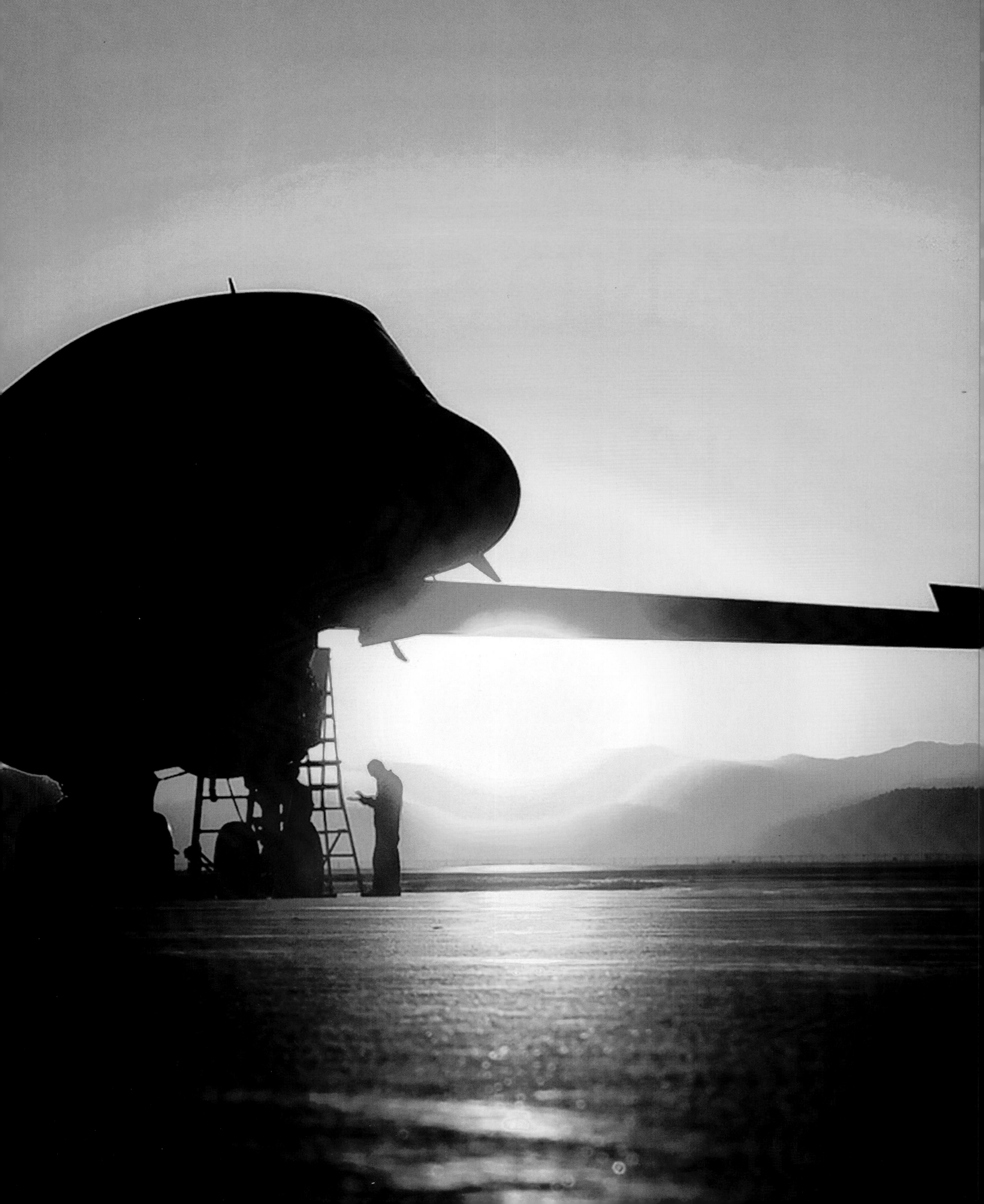

Left: *Nobody could have imagined that this 1940s technology jet would still be going strong 60 years later.* USAF
Below: *It is though!* USAF

EDITOR: Jerry Gunner
With thanks to: Greg Spahr for the use of his archive and encyclopaedic knowledge and Lt Gen 'Buck' Shuler for his little nuggets of gold.

CHIEF DESIGNER: Steve Donovan
DESIGN: Lee Howson

PRODUCTION
Production Editor: Sue Blunt
Production Manager: Janet Watkins

ADVERTISING AND MARKETING
Advertising Manager:
Ian Maxwell
Advertising Group Manager: Brodie Baxter

Advertising Production Manager: Debi McGowan
Advertising Production Controller:
Danielle Tempest
Marketing Manager: Martin Steele
Marketing Executive: Shaun Binnington
Marketing Assistant: Deborah Stokoe
Commercial Director: Ann Saundry
Group Editor-in-Chief: Paul Hamblin
Managing Director and Publisher: Adrian Cox
Executive Chairman: Richard Cox

CONTACTS
Key Publishing Ltd
PO Box 100, Stamford, Lincs, PE9 1XQ
Tel: 01780 755131
Fax: 01780 757261

Email: enquiries@keypublishing.com
www.keypublishing.com

DISTRIBUTION
Seymour Distribution Ltd, 2 Poultry Avenue, London EC1A 9PP. Tel: 020 74294000

PRINTED BY: Warners (Midlands) plc, Bourne, Lincs
The entire contents of this special edition is copyright © 2012. No part of it may be reproduced in any form or stored on any form of retrieval system without the prior permission of the publisher.

KEY **PUBLISHER:** Key Publishing Ltd .
PRINTED IN ENGLAND

The Year of the
B-52

ON APRIL 15, 1952 the first flight of America's newest warplane – Boeing's enormous B-52 Stratofortress – took place from the company's airfield outside Seattle, Washington. Sixty years later the B-52, a utilitarian weapon of war, has acquired near-mythical status after a career spanning more than half of the 109 years of manned flight, with no end in sight – indeed, it seems more than likely that the last B-52s, built more than 50 years ago, will carry on till they've chalked up their century!

Because of its high-profile involvement in the Cold War – and the first war to be extensively televised, Vietnam – the B-52 attracted wide public attention. Stanley Kubrick's movie, Dr Strangelove, featured the bomber and since then popular culture has given its name to a drink, a hair-style and a rock group.

Boeing called the B-52 'Stratofortress', carrying on the Fortress theme that started with the B-17 Flying Fortress and moved on through the B-29 and B-50 Superfortresses. As a result of the carpet bombing of jungles during the Vietnam War it gained the monikers 'Monkeyknocker' and 'Coconutknocker'. Today it is known as the Buff, an acronym and an affectionate nickname: the letters stand for Big (no argument there); Ugly (many won't agree); and then we get the first big disagreement – the first 'F' means either Friendly (depending on whose side you're on) or Fat (although some versions look quite svelte). However, the last 'F' denotes either Fellow (which we use, being a polite publication) or another four-letter word, which we definitely will NOT use!

In these 108 pages we give the reader an insight into what has made the Buff such an icon. Conceived as a Cold War instrument of Armageddon, it morphed into a bomb-truck to devastate miles of jungle in Southeast Asia and then launched cruise missiles against Saddam Hussein and Milosevic. Today it continues to be a key part of America's nuclear deterrent and is acknowledged as one of the most important and versatile aircraft in the US Air Force's inventory. Air Force Global Strike Command, custodian of the Buff, has declared 2012 'The Year of the B-52'. Men and women yet to be born will go on to work with the Buff before the last one makes its way to a museum or the smelter.

Jerry Gunner,
Editor

Birth of the
BUFF

As the world emerged from the Second World War its leaders looked forward to a changed political reality where the Soviet Union and America and its allies were on opposite sides of the Iron Curtain. This led to the arms race which, as **Jerry Gunner** explains, brought about the B-52

HOW A SUPERFORTRESS GREW INTO A STRATOFORTRESS

STRATEGIC BOMBING has always been a controversial subject and there remains a large and vociferous cohort that maintains that bombing on its own can never achieve military victory. While that may be so, it is undeniable that aerial bombing has been part of warfare almost since the dawn of manned flight. German Zeppelin airships and Gotha bombers attacked Great Britain during the First World War. Britain's fledgling Royal Air Force used bombing in the 1920s

to try to subdue 'rebel tribes' in Iraq, with mixed results. It was the German Condor Legion in Spain during the Spanish Civil War that first resorted to the large-scale deployment of purpose-built bombers against civilians. And in the Second World War, large fleets of bombers were deployed by both Axis and Allied forces. By the end of that conflict it was the US that had the largest bomber fleet, comprising mostly Consolidated B-24 Liberators and a large number of Boeing

B-17 Flying Fortresses, of which nearly 12,000 were built. For the last year of the war, in the Pacific theatre of operations it fell to the B-29 Stratofortress, also designed by Boeing, to make history by decisively demonstrating that bombing could bring peace, albeit by deploying nuclear weapons, when B-29As from the 509th Composite Group used two atomic bombs to destroy two Japanese cities – first, Hiroshima on August 6, 1945; and then Nagasaki three days later.

Although far more people were incinerated by incendiary bombs dropped from B-29s on Japanese cities, which were largely made of wood, it was the nuclear weapons that induced Emperor Hirohito and his advisers to sue for peace.

Cold War
At the end of the Second World War it was apparent to the US that the Soviet Union harboured expansionist ambitions and was likely to be a potential foe – and

Above: *Although 13 B-52As were planned, in the event only three were built. Rolled out in March 1954 the first one didn't fly until August 5 of that year. The side-by-side seating arrangement led to the adoption of the cockpit arrangement familiar to this day in the B-1B, B-2A and B-52H.* Boeing

Left: *B-29-45-MO Superfortress 44-86292* Enola Gay, *perhaps the most famous individual warplane ever. Named after pilot Col Paul Tibbet's mother, it dropped the first atomic bomb to be used in anger on August 6, 1945 on the Japanese City of Hiroshima. B-29s formed the backbone of SAC when it was formed in 1948.* P Chinnery

although the 'Cold War' did not start in earnest for some time, plans were made to attack and defeat this erstwhile ally. Part of this preparation involved the creation of a credible strategic bombing force, Strategic Air Command (SAC), which was stood up less than a year after the end of the Second World War on March

21, 1946. Its first commander was General George Kenney, who had had a 'good war', ending up as chief of the US Far East Air Force. His experience in masterminding some of the US's most important operations against the Japanese had made him a talented commander and he was awarded his fourth star to make

full General on March 9, 1945, just two months before the Allied victory over Japan. But Kenney's tenure as chief of SAC was brief and, in the view of many, less than illustrious. He devoted his time to ensuring that America had an air force independent of the army (the USAF was formed as a separate entity on

September 18, 1947) and, partly because of this diversion, SAC failed to thrive, Kenney being faced with swingeing cuts and dwindling resources after the massive airpower expansion in wartime. The situation was set to change under the leadership of SAC's next and undoubtedly most famous commander. General

Curtis E LeMay.

Fewer than ten nuclear weapons were available when SAC was formed and there was no true strategic bomber capable of flying to, and back from, Moscow. Convair's remarkable B-36 Peacemaker, designed to carry a bomb load of 10,000lb (4,500kg) to Europe and fly back to the continental United States, was scheduled to enter service in 1948, but this expensive project had its critics and its future was far from assured.

LeMay took over SAC from Kenney on October 19, 1948, determined to ensure that his command was capable of fulfilling the objective given to it in 1946 by General Carl Spaatz, commander of the then US Army Air Forces (USAAF), to be capable of "intense and sustained combat operations employing the latest and most advanced weapons". Prior to assuming his new responsibility, LeMay had been involved in organising the Berlin Airlift and undoubtedly the insight he gained into the mindset of the Soviet High Command during this period, spurred him on in his efforts to turn SAC into the most formidable fighting force the world had ever seen. He fought his corner

Below: 'Tex' Johnston takes YB-52 49-0231 into the air for the first time on April 15, 1952 at Seattle, Washington. Boeing

*Above: **Neither fish or fowl, the astounding B-36J Peacemaker had six Pratt & Whitney R-4360-53 Wasp Major radial engines and four General Electric J47 turbojets. It served with many SAC wings until being replaced by the B-47 and then the B-52.** 92nd USAAF - USAF Memorial Association.*
*Below: **Mainstay of SAC's fleet for many years was Boeing's B-47 Stratojet, of which more than 2,000 were built.** Key Collection*

tenaciously and ensured that the B-36, far from being cancelled, entered large-scale production. The Peacemaker stayed in service for most of the 1950s and bore the brunt of the responsibility for providing the US's nuclear deterrent during this time – indeed, until the first intercontinental ballistic missiles (ICBMs) came on stream at the end of 1959 there was no other 'big stick' to be waved at the Russians.

During SAC's first few years, most of its aircraft were B-29s; as many as 500 were active in 1948

when LeMay assumed command. The few B-36s operational at this time were not in use as bombers. A third type, and the first to be intended from the outset as a nuclear-capable bomber, was a derivative of the B-29, the Boeing B-50. This new designation was little more than a smokescreen to hide that fact that the bomber (still called the Stratofortress and originally given the designation B-29D) was not a new machine at all. A trials aircraft, Boeing B-29A-5-BN serial number 42-93845, was developed by Boeing to improve

the basic design and given the designation XB-44. It was fitted with a larger vertical stabiliser to handle the power produced by the more powerful 3,000hp Pratt & Whitney R-4360 Wasp-Major radial engines while its undercarriage was strengthened and flaps improved. The XB-44 first flew in May 1945, and although the end of the war led to the cancellation of thousands of B-29 models, the B-29D derivative (now named B-50 and marketed as a new aircraft) was reprieved. The first of 79 B-50As flew on June 25, 1947; the last one was retained by Boeing for further development as the YB-50C to serve as the prototype for a further incarnation, the proposed B-54. But the jet-age was dawning and the need for further piston-powered bombers was rapidly decreasing. Nevertheless, 336 B-50 bombers went on to equip six of SAC's Bombardment Wings. Being intended purely as a nuclear bomber meant it was never used in anger, although older B-29s were deployed for use in the Korean War.

SAC'S First Jets

Although, in terms of sheer numbers, LeMay's air-arm was well equipped, few of the aircraft had the range to carry a worth-

Above: *XB-52 49-0230 suffered damaged during pressurisation tests and the wings had to be repaired before it could take to the air so it became the second B-52 to fly, on October 2, 1952.* Boeing
Middle: *Another view of XB-52 49-0230 showing the original B-47 inspired tandem cockpit layout.* Boeing
Below *One of only three B-52As built, 52-0001 was used for tests throughout its career before eventually being scrapped at Tinker AFB, Oklahoma.* Boeing

while bomb-load to the Soviet Union or the means to counter the threat posed by the early MiG jet-fighters. Even before the end of the Second World War, Boeing had commenced working on yet another derivative of the B-29 – this time with jet engines.

In 1943 the USAAF was keen for American manufacturers to consider incorporating the new turbojet into their products and Boeing, along with other leading manufacturers, took up the challenge. Boeing's initial offering, the type 424, was a scaled-down B-29 powered by four jet engines. Wind-tunnel testing indicated that the engine

Above: *Boeing built the B-52 at both Seattle and Wichita, Kansas. The Seattle-built RB-52B nearest the camera, 52-8716, was destroyed when serving with the 93rd BW on November 30, 1956 when it crashed four miles North of Castle AFB, California and burnt out two minutes and 44 seconds into what appeared to be a routine flight. Ten souls onboard lost their lives.* Boeing

configuration was inefficient, which led to further refinements and changes. Of particular importance was German research material on swept-wing aircraft, which had become available to the Allies at the end of the war. (North American's B-45 Tornado, developed as a consequence of the same USAAF requirements, did not benefit from the German research and was never as successful as its Boeing counterpart – although it was the first jet aircraft to be refuelled in flight and was the Americans' first operational jet bomber.)

So it was that, in April 1946, the USAAF ordered two prototypes of what was now to be the six-engined Boeing 450, giving it the military designation XB-47. The first of two prototype Boeing XB-47-BO Stratojets, serial number 46-0065, took to the air on December 17, 1947, 44 years to the day since Wilbur and Orville Wright made the first successful powered, sustained flight in a heavier-than-air machine at Kitty Hawk, North Carolina. In some ways it could be said that the B-47 was to be nearly as important as that first practical aeroplane. ▶

Enter the BUFF

Such was pace of technical development that by 1958 the Stratojet's successor was rolling off the production lines to swell SAC's ranks even further. The factories – first at Boeing's home at Seattle, Washington, then additionally at Wichita in Kansas – were churning out B-52s.

It is difficult to separate the development of the B-52 from that of its predecessor, the B-47. Both stemmed from the same requirement, but the gestation period for the larger B-52 was longer, with its design going through several different phases. A significant step was made in September 1947 when the Heavy Bombardment Committee (HBC) was formed to determine exactly what kind of aircraft needed to be produced. Three months of deliberations bore fruit on December 8, 1947; the HBC had decided the new aircraft must have a top speed of 500mph (800km/h) and a range of 8,000 miles (13,000km) using newly-perfected air-to-air refuelling techniques. Many configurations were considered for the new bomber, from a machine that looked like a large B-29 to another that resembled what later came to be built in the Soviet Union as

As many as 2,032 B-47s of all variants would be built – and the technology embodied in the design, and the research needed to perfect it, were used not only in Boeing's military aircraft (notably the B-52) but also acted as a catalyst in the development of the Boeing 707 airliner. It is not a leap of the imagination to say that without the B-47, development of jet airliners would not have been as rapid. With the B-47, SAC became familiar with operating long-range jet bombers: within seven years of its entry into service in late 1951, no fewer than 28 Bombardment Wings and five Strategic Reconnaissance Wings were flying Stratojets.

Above: *The YB-52 shares ramp space at Seattle in May 1954 with an early B-47E.* Boeing
Below: *The rate of development in aviation in the immediate post-Second World War period was truly astounding. Here a pair of B-36Hs provide the backdrop for the XB-52 and the Northrop X-4 Bantam, used by the National Advisory Committee on Aeronautics, (the forerunner of NASA) to investigate the flight characteristics of semi tailless jets.* Key Collection

Seattle-built B-52C 54-2669 shows off the classic lines of the big Boeing bomber. Like many of its peers, it was flown to Davis-Monthan AFB, Arizona and inducted into MASDC on July 6, 1971. It lingered there until being scrapped in October 1993. Boeing

'IT IS NOT TOO GREAT A LEAP OF THE IMAGINATION TO SAY THAT WITHOUT THE B-47, DEVELOPMENT OF JET AIRLINERS WOULD NOT HAVE BEEN AS RAPID'

Above: *From little acorns mighty oak trees grow. Less than 17 years separated the first flights of the B-17 Flying Fortress and the B-52. Were the B-17 to have been in service as long as its descendant then it would still be serving today.* Key Collection

SAC MISSION

SAC's original mission statement was expressed by General Carl Spaatz, who was then Commanding General of the USAAF:
"The Strategic Air Command will be prepared to conduct long-range offensive operations in any part of the world, either independently or in co-operation with land and naval forces; to conduct maximum-range reconnaissance over land or sea, either independently or in co-operation with land and naval forces; to provide combat units capable of intense and sustained combat operations employing the latest and most advanced weapons; to train units and personnel of the maintenance of the Strategic Forces in all parts of the world; to perform such special missions as the Commanding General Army Air Forces may direct."

the Tu-95 Bear (itself a derivative of the Tu-4, a reverse-engineered copy of the B-29). These dated designs were overtaken both by advances in technology and the need for increased range and payload. In July 1948, Boeing was awarded a contract to build two turboprop-powered long-range bomber prototypes of the Boeing 464-35, to be designated B-52.

It was not until later in 1948 that the USAF's Air Materiel Command asked Boeing to investigate powering the new machine with the increasingly reliable, but still 'new technology', jet engine. Many in the air force and industry were sceptical: the jet engines available at the time were very thirsty – turboprop engines, however, were nearing the peak of their development and were readily available.

Boeing presented its latest plans to the USAF's chief of bomber development, Col Pete Warden, on October 21, 1948. Warden was not satisfied with the four-engine turboprop proposal and asked Boeing engineers Vaughn Blumenthal, Arthur Carlsen and George Schairer if they could adapt the design to incorporate jet engines. Undaunted, the Boeing team went back to their hotel and, having enlisted the help of their vice president of engineering, Ed Wells, tried again, this time putting four turbojets in place of the propeller engines.

Next morning, Warden was still no happier with the design and asked for a more radical solution to the problem of carrying a large bomb-load a long way at high speed. Back to the hotel, where the atmosphere must have been

electric with the Boeing team – now swollen by the addition of two more engineers, Maynard Pennell and Bob Withington – realising they were tantalisingly close to satisfying the requirement.

Over the weekend, another concept based loosely on the award-winning B-47, emerged. Plans were drawn up for a new aircraft incorporating a 185ft-wide wingspan swept back at the same 35° as its predecessor, but with four pairs of engines in wing-mounted pods. But the team didn't stop there. By the time they went back to Col Warden on the Monday morning, not only was there a neatly-presented 33-page booklet describing the new bomber and predicting performance figures that exceeded all requirements, but also a 14in

scale model of the new machine. The Colonel was impressed: "Now we have an airplane," he said. "This is the B-52."

The USAF quickly approved the proposal, which was effectively an entirely new bomber but with the same designation, B-52, as the two contracted aircraft. Amazingly, when the first one took to the skies less than four years later, it looked very like the aircraft described in the booklet and portrayed in the silver-painted balsa-wood model dreamt up by Boeing's engineers at the Hotel Van Cleve near the new Wright-Patterson Air Force Base in Dayton, Ohio. Not surprisingly, the story has gone down in Boeing history.

Getting the basic layout accepted was not the end of Boeing's problems; there was much work to be done on identifying a suitable powerplant.

By April 1949 a full-size mock-up of the jet had been completed and, while it was generally well received, fuel consumption was still a major concern. Early turbojets – including the Westinghouse J-40 originally intended for the B-52, and its replacement, the Pratt & Whitney J57-P-29W – were still gas-guzzlers and there were many in the USAF and Boeing who wanted to delay the project until more frugal engines be- ▶

Above: *Raison d'être: B-52Bs stand nuclear alert 'somewhere in America' in the 1950s. The undersides of the jets are painted white to reflect the heat and light from a nuclear explosion.* USAF

came available. Enter LeMay, SAC's new commander, who insisted that the new bomber come into service as soon as possible; and what the General wanted, usually, the General got. On February 14, 1951, Boeing was awarded a production contract for 13 B-52As. LeMay continued to monitor the design closely – it was he who insisted that, to improve crew co-operation and communication and reduce their fatigue, instead of continuing with the B-47-style tandem cockpit configuration used on both XB-52 pre-production aircraft, B-52s be fitted with side-by-side seating for pilot and co-pilot.

Even then the Boeing team was not totally confident it would be the sole supplier of the next generation of bombers – Convair had gone ahead with a development of its B-36 with eight jet engines to rival the Boeing product. In an effort to reduce costs, this project, designated the B-60, was to have 72% parts commonality with the B-36, at the time SAC's largest bomber. But development was more difficult than the engineers had hoped and only one prototype flew before the programme was cancelled in January 1953.

Above: *Despite the availability of the three B-52As and some B-52Bs the two prototypes continued to assist in the development programme for the B-52. YB-52 49-0231 is seen here.* Boeing

Cleared for Take-off

By 1952 the Cold War was getting icy, leading to an obsession with security. The US Air Force's insistence that the B-52's first flight should take place at night was a symptom of this, but Boeing couldn't see the sense in the proposal and made an official complaint to the Pentagon. After discussions between officials from both sides it was agreed that the big bomber should take to the skies for the first time in daylight. The second B-52 built, YB-52 serial number 49-0231, became the first to fly because the other prototype, XB-52

49-0230 had been damaged in ground tests.

The man chosen to be at the helm for the historic occasion was one of Boeing's top test pilots, Alvin M 'Tex' Johnston, a colourful character whose nickname reflected his penchant for wearing cowboy boots – even during test flights. (He later gained fame when, while demonstrating the prototype Boeing 707 to the public for the first time, he performed two 360° barrel rolls over Lake Washington in 1954.) Sitting in the right-hand seat, representing the USAF, was Lt Col Guy M Townsend, a veteran of many wartime operations in the B-17 and B-29. Both men had flown many hours in the B-47.

April 15, 1952 was a warm, sunny Tuesday in Seattle. News of the impending flight had reached far and wide, and every available vantage point around the airstrip was lined with spectators who waited while the pilots ran through their checklists and tested the huge aircraft's controls. At 1045hrs local time, one by one the big jet's eight jet engines came to life and spooled-up with an

ear-piercing roar amid clouds of smoke. Eighteen minutes later the brakes were released and the monster trundled ponderously away from its parking spot to the active runway. Johnston stopped at the end to complete his final checks and then advanced the eight throttles to take-off power and released the brakes. The take-off run commenced at 1109hrs and a few seconds later the wings began to fly. A few more seconds after that, the undercarriage gave up its hold on the runway and the first of 744 B-52s soared into the blue.

Johnston and Townsend stayed overhead the Seattle area for about 40 minutes, checking the functionality of the landing gear, flaps and ailerons before climbing to 25,000ft and heading east to land at Moses Lake field, Washington, shortly to be renamed Larson Air Force Base, for two more hours of tests before landing there at 1400hrs. The two hours, 51 minutes mission had been the longest first flight in Boeing's history and, according to Johnston, the jet had performed exactly as the engineers had said it would. A legend was born. ✪

'THE TAKE-OFF RUN COMMENCED AT 1109HRS AND A FEW SECONDS LATER THE WINGS BEGAN TO FLY. A FEW MORE SECONDS AFTER THAT, THE UNDERCARRIAGE GAVE UP ITS HOLD ON THE RUNWAY AND THE FIRST OF 744 B-52S SOARED INTO THE BLUE'

Right: *For a long time, B-52s engaged on airborne nuclear alert missions like Chrome Dome flew around in circles waiting for orders to unleash Armageddon.* Boeing

The XB-52 operated out of Wright-Patterson with its two outboard pods replaced by single J-75 engines. Greg Spahr collection

B-52 from A to H

XB-52 [1], YB-52 [1], B-52A [3]

XB-52	serial 49-0230
YB-52	serial 49-0231
B-52A	serials 52-0001 - 0003

BOB ARCHER DETAILS THE DIFFERENT MODELS OF THE STRATOFORTRESS

THE INITIAL B-52 design was changed many times to incorporate emerging innovations while at the same time attempting to satisfy the requirement for a strategic bomber with a truly intercontinental range. Before becoming head of Strategic Air Command (SAC), the legendary General Curtis E LeMay was briefly deputy chief of staff for research and development in the USAF. His senior positions in both organisations made him fully aware of the precise needs of SAC, and he was able to provide Boeing with guidance in relation to this, its Model 464 long-range bomber design.

In 1949 the air force authorised one experimental XB-52 and a single prototype YB-52. The adoption of turbojet engines for the new bomber was controversial because of the poor fuel efficiency of this new form of power; but its potential was recognised and the decision made to make the B-52 jet-powered. A letter of contract was issued in June 1946 enabling the company to go ahead with initial design work. After alterations to increase speed and range, the air force acknowledged the merits of the more conventional design of the B-52 over the 'flying wing' proposed by Northrop Corporation – including the cavernous B-52's capacity to provide more options for radar and armament installation. Moreover, Air Materiel Command's (AMC) engineering division at Wright Field, Ohio, was in favour of the B-52 and the Air Staff also believed the Boeing design would be easier to maintain than the flying wing.

In March 1948, the Secretary of the Air Force, William S Symington, notified Boeing that the contract would be modified to incorporate relevant changes. The following month, Boeing presented its Phase II proposal for the design, development, construction and testing of two XB-52s; they were given the company designation Model 464-35. The proposal received USAF endorsement in July 1948. But, despite having received the go-ahead, the air force was still evaluating new and emerging technologies. Boeing engineers were well aware of these developments and were able to counter every obstacle thrown in the path of their project. At a meeting held at Wright Field on October 21, 1948, Boeing engineers were informed by senior AMC personnel that the project needed a reappraisal. In particular, AMC was adamant that Pratt & Whitney J-57 turbojet engines should be installed. So the ever-resourceful Boeing engineers spent the weekend at a nearby hotel, applying the experience from their B-47 programme to a redesign of the 464. On Monday, October 25, a 33-page report and a hand-carved wooden model were presented for the new Model 464-49. The revised design featured eight J57 engines mounted in four pylons – the extra weight involved being more than compensated for by the increased power. Still, reservations remained as the new technology was unproven. In particular, it was believed the B-52 would have less range than the 4,000-mile (6,400km) reach of the B-36. Boeing was convinced that a more extensive redesign would solve the problem and that this, the Model 464-67, would have similar range to the B-36 (although this would not be achieved until production aircraft entered service in the mid 1950s). While other manufacturers were also proposing heavy bombers, the air force and, in particular, General LeMay favoured the B-52, and on March 24, 1950 the board of senior officers approved the design.

The plan for two XB-52s was altered to a single example for experimental purposes; this, along with a YB-52 prototype, was funded in the 1949 fiscal year. Having spent years and millions of dollars developing a world-beating bomber, and while construction of the first few machines was under way, another issue emerged: USAF Headquarters decided that ▶

Above: *In this cutaway of the XB-52 cockpit we can see on the upper deck, from front to back, that the Pilot and Co-Pilot both have ejection seats. Behind them is a non-ejector seat for an observer. The Navigator and Radar-Navigator sit below, side by side in downward-firing ejector seats. Behind the navigators is a toilet, and along the starboard side of the lower deck is stowage for food, water, survival equipment, etc.*

The YB-52 was greeted by crowds of onlookers keen to see America's new bomber when it taxied out for the first time on April 15, 1952. Key collection

reconnaissance – and photography in particular – should be the primary mission for the new jet, with strategic bombing a secondary role. To enable both missions to be conducted satisfactorily, Boeing proposed installing a multi-purpose pod in the bomb bay to house reconnaissance equipment; this could be removed quickly to convert the aircraft back to bomber configuration, with bomb racks replacing the recce pod when necessary. The Air Staff dictated that all aircraft be designated as RB-52s, although a requirement to be able to carry out bombardment operations would be retained.

Following its maiden flight on April 15, 1952 the YB-52 was officially accepted by the USAF on March 31, 1953, but retained by Boeing at Seattle for company testing. It made a total of 345 flights, accumulating 738 hours before, in January 1958, it was handed over to the air force and donated to its museum at Wright-Patterson AFB, Ohio.

However, this pioneering jet was subsequently scrapped. Many published accounts say that they fell victim to the campaign to divest the nation of surplus military equipment initiated by the wife of US President Lyndon B Johnson. However, it wasn't until his 1965 State of the Union Address that President Johnson announced the clean-up initiative that his wife had championed and we have photo evidence from early 1964 that the XB-52 and YB-52 were already in the fire pits of Wright-Patterson AFB; their scrapping had begun long before the First Lady's beautification campaign began.

Meanwhile, the experimental XB-52 49-0230 first flew on October 2, 1952, almost one year later than planned. Because of the hold-up, only six hours of Phase I testing was carried out by this aircraft. Phase II flight testing destined to be solely carried out by the XB-52 was also delayed, but was completed by March 15, 1953. The test duties were shared between the manufacturer and the air force at the Wright Air Development Center at Wright-Patterson AFB. Eventually the XB-52 joined this unit permanently, and had its four outboard J57s replaced with a pair of J75 engines to become the only Stratofortress to intentionally fly with six engines fitted (a bonus of having pairs of engines mounted in pods was that in the event of a fire the pod was likely to melt its mounting pylon, the engines dropping off, thereby saving the aircraft). The XB-52 was also eventually scrapped at Wright-Patterson. The B-52A incorporated many changes to the XB and YB-52. New, more powerful J57-P-1W engines fitted with water injection to boost

The clean lines of the type are perhaps even more streamlined when coupled with its original B-47-inspired fighter type cockpit configuration. Key collection

Both prototypes were used for testing throughout their careers. Here is a previously unpublished image showing the YB-52 carrying the 1,000 US gallon external fuel tanks as used on the B-52B and the shortened vertical stabilizer as used on the B-52G and H. Greg Spahr collection

Above: *A fine shot of the YB-52A landing on Rogers Dry Lake bed.*
Below: *The YB-52 was cannibalized to keep the XB-52 in operation and eventually put on display at the NMUSAF as Wright-Patterson AFB. Unfortunately, this historic machine was removed from display in 1965 and towed to the base fire pit and destroyed. Some of it lingered into the early 1970s.* Both Greg Spahr collection

take-off were installed and a 360-US gallon (1,362 litre) tank was mounted in the rear fuselage to accommodate the water. Further improvements included electronic countermeasures equipment, a chaff dispenser system and a four-barrel 0.50-calibre tail gun. A pair of 1,000-US gallon (3,785 litre) fuel tanks were fitted beneath the wings, extending range even further. Although 13 B-52As were intended to be used as test and development aircraft, USAF hierarchy decided that it could not afford the luxury of such a large number and the order was cut to three in 1952. Those three B-52As never entered squadron service, and spent their careers as test-beds. The other ten were delivered as B-52Bs and all of them were involved in testing, indeed two of them were tested to destruction, but seven were indeed brought up to nearly full B-52B specification under Project Sunflower in 1956 and 1957, and delivered to SAC to join the main bomber force..

Air Force Chief of Staff General Nathan F Twining attended the B-52A roll-out ceremony on March 18, 1954. Aircraft serial number 52-0001 was accepted by the USAF two months before its first flight on August 5, 1954. The two remaining aircraft were delivered during August and September. The three

jets flew with Air Force Systems Command (AFSC) at Edwards AFB, California, until being retired, starting in 1960. The first two were scrapped, but 52-0003, redesignated as an NB-52A, was retained for test programmes associated with the North American X-15 project, a research aircraft that to this day holds the world record for the highest speed ever achieved by a manned rocket-powered aircraft. The X-15 was designed to provide technical information on hypersonic aeronautics in preparation for manned space-flight. The NB-52A received modifications by North American technicians to accommodate the X-15. These included having a 6ft x 8ft (1.82m x 2.43m) section removed from the starboard wing-flap to house the

X-15's wedge tail; a pylon to carry the X-15 was suspended beneath the wing between the inboard engines and the fuselage. The NB-52A performed the mother-ship mission at Edwards AFB, with the first true flight involving separation of the X-15 taking place on June 8, 1959. A second 'B' model was redesignated as a NB-52B and joined the programme to ensure X-15 launches were less affected by serviceability issues caused by only having one 'mothership' or the X-15.

S/N 52-0003 participated in 59 of the 199 X-15 flights before the programme ended in 1968. This NB-52A, which was named 'The High and the Mighty One', was retired to storage at Davis-Monthan AFB, Arizona, on October 15, 1969 before being transferred to the adjacent Pima Air Museum where it remains to this day.

The designers of the B-52 learned much from the development of the B-47 Stratojet, which had seen delays and deficiencies – Boeing and the air force were determined such problems would not occur with the Stratofortress. Design work included 670 days of wind tunnel testing along with a further 130 days of aerodynamic and aero-elastic evaluation. Many parts were thoroughly tested before installation, and improvements highlighted by the YB-52 development programme ▶

Above: *Only three B-52As were built and they spent their lives as test aircraft. 52-0002 is pictured visiting China Lake NAS, California, in the 1950s.* Greg Spahr collection
Below: *52-0003 went on to have a long and illustrious career at Edwards AFB, but images of her when first delivered to the Air Force Flight Test Center at Edwards AFB are rare. Of note are the fuel tanks on the wings and, of course, the now familiar side-by-side seating arrangement mandated by General Le May. She exhibits the white and black calibration marks between the wings as worn by the prototypes, but unlike them her chin markings are black.* Greg Spahr collection

were incorporated into the B-52B design. This resulted in written test reports after flights to test the innovations integrated in the test aircraft that generally stated nothing more alarming than "no airplane malfunctions were reported", a testament to the good work of the engineers. Nevertheless, the B-52B development programme was lengthy. Several aircraft intended to spearhead the type into SAC service were instead diverted to the test programme before joining operational Bombardment Wings (BWs). However, the aircraft was considered outstanding by the Wright Air Development Center's commander, Major

General Albert Boyd, who declared the B-52 to be one of the finest airplanes yet built, and announced, with tongue in cheek: "We need to discover how we accidently developed an airplane that flies so beautifully!"

Above: *By the 1960s NB-52A 52-0003 was wearing the more garish colour scheme she sported for the rest of her service life. She is seen carrying one of her more high-profile loads, the X-15 rocket-plane. Astronaut Neil Armstrong, the first human to set foot on the moon, was also one of the test pilots launched in an X-15 from beneath the NB-52A.* Key collection

B-52B

B-52B [23] RB-52B [27]
B-52B   serials 53-0373 to 0376; 53-0380 to 0398
RB-52B   serials 52-0004 to 0013; 52-8710 to 0716; 53-0366 to 0372; 53-0377 to 0379

Wing	Location	Years
22nd BW	March AFB, California	'63 - '66
93rd BW	Castle AFB, California	'55 - '65
95th BW	Biggs AFB, Texas	'59 - '66
99th BW	Westover AFB, Massachusetts	'58 - '59

Above: *Of the three X-15s built, 56-6670 was used from beginning to end of the test series that ran from June 8, 1959 to October 24, 1968. NB-52A 52-0003 was used to launch her at high altitude before she rocketed to the edge of space.* Key collection
Left: *Astronaut Neil Armstrong, the first human to set foot on the moon, was also one of those launched in an X-15 from beneath the NB-52A.* Key collection

B Model

THE INTRODUCTION of nuclear bombs to SAC Bomb Wings necessitated safety measures being taken to enhance aircrew survivability – and because the underside of the bomber could be scorched by the detonation of a nuclear weapon, commencing with the 'B' model, the aircraft's undersides were painted by the manufacturer with special white heat-reflecting paint before being delivered to the air force.

Despite what has frequently been asserted in the past, only the first 15 B-52s (XB-52, YB-52, B-52A, and service test RB-52Bs 52-0004 through to 52-0013) were delivered without this treatment. The first production B-52Bs were fitted with the K-3A bomb-sight, the same as installed on the B-36. It was replaced by the MA-6A radar-optical bombing/navigation system in those jets during a modification programme and it became the standard system for the 'B' model. B-52Bs could, as

"WE NEED TO DISCOVER HOW WE ACCIDENTLY DEVELOPED AN AIRPLANE THAT FLIES SO BEAUTIFULLY!"

Above: *Fashion gives the game away as much as anything, but this rare colour image of RB-52B 52-0005, taken during an air-show at Edwards AFB, would have been taken in the first few months after delivery to the air force when she was used for trials at Edwards by AFFTC. Today she is preserved at the former Lowry AFB, Colorado.* Greg Spahr collection

Above: *93rd BW RB-52B 52-8715 in flight in the 1950s. The clear panels for the oblique cameras mounted in the belly are just visible. The SAC sash around the fuselage was later moved to the nose.* Greg Spahr collection

The B-52 fleet was flown by SAC from 1955 until the Command was inactivated in 1992. The number of B-52s operational in the SAC inventory was as follows:

Year	Qty	Year	Qty	Year	Qty
1955	18	1968	579	1980	343
1956	97	1969	505	1981	344
1957	243	1970	459	1982	300
1958	380	1971	412	1983	262
1959	488	1972	402	1984	262
1960	538	1973	422	1985	261
1961	571	1974	422	1986	233
1962	639	1975	420	1987	260
1963	636	1976	419	1988	258
1964	626	1977	417	1989	248
1965	600	1978	344	1990	222
1966	591	1979	343	1991	178
1967	588				

stated, be fitted with a capsule for reconnaissance operations, which required that the crew be increased to eight from six.

The original September 1952 order for 43 RB-52Bs was reduced by ten aircraft in a May 1954 amendment. These ten were instead to be constructed as RB-52Cs alongside a further 25 of the variant, bringing the order book up to three B-52As, 17 RB-52Bs (fiscal year 1952), 33 RB-52Bs (fiscal year 1953) and 35 RB-52Cs. On January 7, 1955, the USAF issued a significant amendment to the entire programme by reversing the Air Staff directive of October 1951 and changing the B-52's primary role back to strategic bomber – relegating

the reconnaissance capability to a secondary duty. The decision resulted in the 50 RB-52Bs and 35 RB-52Cs being redesignated as B-52Bs and B-52Cs respectively. Furthermore, 23 of the 50 RB-52Bs were modified to eliminate the reconnaissance capability altogether.

Operational B-52 deliveries to SAC were due to begin in April 1953. But the demands of the Korean War changed US priorities, leading to a 15-month slippage: revised delivery schedules arranged for B-52s to be delivered between April and December 1954 although additional procurement authorised in April 1953 had extended deliveries to April 1956.

The USAF accepted its first Stratofortress in August 1954 but another delay (this time for 90 days) caused by cracks in landing gear forgings resulted in the final deliveries of 'B' models not taking place until August 1956. The first aircraft to be accepted by SAC, 52-8711, joined the 93rd Bombardment Wing at Castle AFB, California, on June 29, 1955. The 93rd BW was flying conventional and nuclear bombardment missions with the B-47 but assumed responsibility for aircrew training on the new type. The unit was declared combat-ready on March 12, 1956. The majority of 'B' models produced were operated by the 93rd BW, some of which had initially been flown

for development work before joining SAC. The sheer size of the aircraft and its eight engines called for radical changes in the infrastructure and management of maintenance and spares holdings. The first B-52 operations encountered all manner of problems and the constantly changing delivery schedules did nothing to improve the situation. The Buff's vast wingspan with its small outrigger-wheels, plus its enormous gross weight, required changes to be made to runways, taxiways and parking ramps, all of which took time and money. Furthermore a shortage of spare parts, ground support equipment and components such as bomb racks and electronic counter-measures systems only added to the problems. ▶

Above: *Anonymous B-52B 52-0010 on the ramp at Wright-Patterson AFB in the early 1950s. After it was retired in 1966 it was tested to destruction.* Greg Spahr collection

Above: **Three B-52Bs of the 93rd Bomb Wing after their record-setting round-the-world non-stop flight.** USAF

To enable technicians to transition to the B-52 as smoothly as possible, many personnel were selected from B-47 units to bring multi-engine jet bomber experience to the new Stratofortress organisation. The first crash involving a B-52 occurred on February 16, 1956 when a 93rd BW example, B-52B 53-0384, suffered an alternator fault which caused a fire and resulted in the aircraft breaking up and crashing near Sacramento, California. Four

of the crew of eight were killed. All B-52s were grounded while Boeing rectified the problem.

Another potential problem (which SAC insisted should be overcome, almost before it became apparent) was the supply of routine maintenance items to flying units. This was allotted the highest priority to prevent B-52 spares being delayed in transit from manufacturer to end-user, and specialised supply channels were established to avoid the

usual logistic routes that were considered to be too slow and cumbersome, and to ensure a substantial spares holding could be in place ahead of aircraft arriving at each base. In addition, contractor maintenance teams of 50 specialists were formed at each B-52 base to identify and rectify maintenance issues immediately, rather than waiting until the aircraft could undergo a major overhaul at Air Materiel Command depots.

The USAF accepted delivery of the last B-52B in August 1956 by which time the 93rd BW had already converted to the B-52D model, their complement of the earlier machines having been redistributed elsewhere. But rather than being retired and placed in storage, small numbers of B-52Bs were assigned to seven Bomb Wings (the 91st, 92nd, 306th, 340th, 380th, 494th and 509th BWs) to act as 'bounce birds' for training locally. The remaining

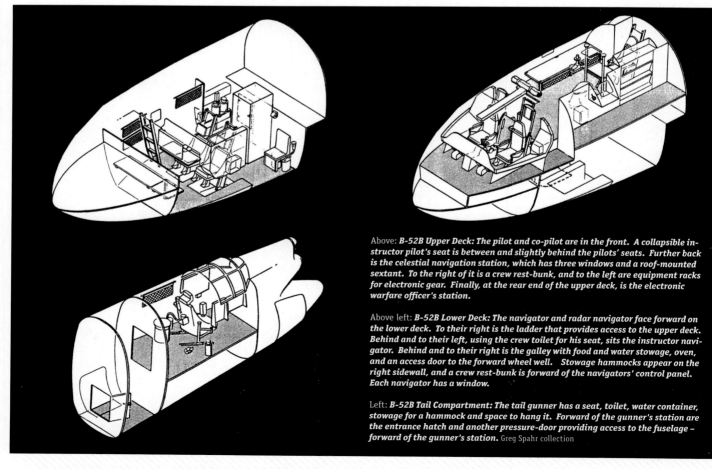

Above: **B-52B Upper Deck: The pilot and co-pilot are in the front. A collapsible instructor pilot's seat is between and slightly behind the pilots' seats. Further back is the celestial navigation station, which has three windows and a roof-mounted sextant. To the right of it is a crew rest-bunk, and to the left are equipment racks for electronic gear. Finally, at the rear end of the upper deck, is the electronic warfare officer's station.**

Above left: **B-52B Lower Deck: The navigator and radar navigator face forward on the lower deck. To their right is the ladder that provides access to the upper deck. Behind and to their left, using the crew toilet for his seat, sits the instructor navigator. Behind and to their right is the galley with food and water stowage, oven, and an access door to the forward wheel well. Stowage hammocks appear on the right sidewall, and a crew rest-bunk is forward of the navigators' control panel. Each navigator has a window.**

Left: **B-52B Tail Compartment: The tail gunner has a seat, toilet, water container, stowage for a hammock and space to hang it. Forward of the gunner's station are the entrance hatch and another pressure-door providing access to the fuselage – forward of the gunner's station.** Greg Spahr collection

Above: *B-52C 53-0399 spent its career as a test-bed with the Aeronautical Systems Command at Wright-Patterson AFB, Ohio, where this image was taken.* Greg Spahr collection

NB-52B

RB-52B 52-0008 was redesignated as an NB-52B after it underwent similar modifications to those made to NB-52A to enable it to be used for air-launching the X-15. As an NB-52B it performed 140 launches of different types of air-vehicles for the air force before the completion of those trials in 1968.

The programme to air-launch various research craft continued under control of the National Aeronautics and Space Administration (NASA) with the Dryden Flight Research Center at Edwards AFB, California. These included several types of the more unusual aircraft tested at Edwards AFB, including the so-called lifting bodies including Martin-Marietta's X-24A and Northrop's M2-F3 and HL-10. One of the most important tasks was to launch a demonstrator vehicle used to evaluate controlled flight without wings and precision landing without power – which tested the viability of gliding Space Shuttle landings. With the arrival of the Shuttle era, the NB-52B, now with its new identity of 'NASA 008', dropped Shuttle solid-rocket booster test vehicles in order to assess their booster recovery parachute system. During the early 1990s, the aircraft kicked up plumes of dust on Rogers Dry Lake's bed at Edwards AFB testing the Shuttle's new drag chute system.

NASA 008's long career ended as historically as it began, launching the last hypersonic X-43A scramjet-powered research vehicle on November 16, 2004 to reach nearly Mach 10, a record speed for air-breathing aircraft. The mother-ship was retired on December 17, 2004 and is now on permanent display near the north gate at Edwards AFB.

three BWs operating the B-52B began retiring the type in March 1965, some being transferred to Air Training Command for ground crew training. The remainder were retired in quick fashion and were stored at Davis-Monthan AFB by June of 1966. The first operational Stratofortress to be retired was B-52B 52-8714 which was transferred from the 22nd BW to Chanute Technical Training Center at Chanute AFB, Illinois, for use as a ground trainer. The closure of the base in 1993 resulted in the bomber being scrapped.

Record breakers and history makers

During the 1950s and first half of the 1960s, four SAC bases in England (RAF Brize Norton, Fairford, Greenham Common and Upper

Above: *Carefully, assiduously following the check-list, technicians install B61 'Silver Bullet' nuclear bombs in the bomb-bay of a B-52.* Greg Spahr collection

The mission tally for the NB-52B with NASA

Launched craft	Missions	Launches
North American X-15	161	106
Northrop M2-F2	13	13
Northrop M2-F3	34	27
Northrop HL-10	37	26
Martin-Marietta X-24A	31	25
Martin-Marietta X-24B	49	36
F-15 Remotely Piloted Research Vehicle (RPRV)	41	27
F-15 Spin Research Vehicle (SRV)	32	26
Shuttle Re-usable Booster/Drop Test Vehicle (SRB/DTV)	22	14
Drones for Aeroelastic Structures Testing (DAST)	13	5
F-111 Parachute Test Vehicle (PTC)	57	57
Highly Manoeuvrable Aircraft Technology (HiMAT)	40	26
Orbital Sciences Pegasus	13	6
X-38 Crew Return Vehicle	21	8
X-43A Hyper-X	6	3

Heyford) hosted B-47s deployed to the UK on a rotational basis to stand alert. B-52s from all Bomb Wings occasionally visited these bases, but only one B-52B model is known to have made the trip to England – 53-0397 of the 93rd BW, which arrived at Upper Heyford from Castle AFB on January 17, 1961 and stayed for the weekend.

It had been one of five similar aircraft to take-off from Castle on January 16, 1957 under the command of Major General Archie J Old Jr, flying 53-0394 'Lucky Lady III'. Three of the five jets flew non-stop around the world with the help of in-flight refuelling from KC-97s; one aircraft, 53-0397, was an air-spare which deliberately left the formation near Casablanca, Morocco while another aborted the mission and diverted to Goose Bay, Canada, when its in-flight refuelling receptacle iced over. The 24,235-mile (39,002km) flight was completed in 45 hours 19 minutes. This, the first non-stop circumnavigation of the globe by jet aircraft, was conducted to demonstrate SAC's ability to deploy nuclear weapons anywhere on the planet.

The 'Lucky Lady' series of flights serve as an indicator of the advances made in aviation in the post-World War Two period. 'Lucky Lady I' was a B-29A that made a circumnavigation of the globe in 15 days in July and August 1948. A year later, the man who went on to command the lead aircraft in a 1961 non-stop circumnavigation (Operation Power Flite), Lt Col James H Morris, was co-pilot of B-50A 'Lucky Lady II', serial number 46-0010, when it made the first non-stop round-the-world flight. It would be less than 12 years until the B-52s made their own contribution to the long-distance record book. ▶

Seen at Westover AFB, Massachusetts with B-36 Peacemakers in the background, B-52C 54-2665 was a new addition to the unit when the picture was taken. Greg Spahr collection

B-52B 52-0013 had the distinction of being the first Stratofortress to deliver a live nuclear weapon. In an operation called Redwing Cherokee, it dropped a bomb with a yield of 3.8 megatons at 05:51hrs local time above Namu Island in Bikini Atoll on May 21, 1956. The operation was designed to provide the Department of Defense with valuable data on high-yield air-bursts as well as sending a clear message to the Soviet Union that the United States had the capability to deliver hydrogen bombs by air. The target area was directly over Namu Island, but the crew mistook the observation post on another island as their targeting beacon and launched the weapon incorrectly. The bomb detonated four miles away from the target, resulting in almost all the data being wasted. Nevertheless this important aircraft has been preserved at the National Atomic Museum, Albuquerque, New Mexico.

The reconnaissance-capable RB-52B featured a multi-purpose pressurised pod installed in the bomb bay, manned by a crew of two who were provided with downward-pointing ejection seats. Each pod was capable of a variety of missions and several different cameras could be installed, including one for vertical photography and another for mapping. Electronic recording data was also fitted. No further B-52 models were equipped with the reconnaissance system because the tasks were handled effectively by other aircraft types such as the RB-47 and RB-50.

B-52C

B-52C [35] B-52C serials 53-0399 – 0408; 54-2664 – 2688

Wing	Location	Years
42nd BW	Loring AFB, Maine	'56 - '57
99th BW	Westover AFB, Massachusetts	'56 - '66

Below: **Stunning rare colour study of 'C' model 54-2668.** Greg Spahr collection

C Model

OF THE eight production versions, the B-52C was the produced in the fewest numbers; gross weight was increased to 450,000lbs (204,116kgs). Larger, 3,000-US gallon (11,356 litre) under-wing tanks were fitted to increase range and the water injection system was improved.

The first flight of a B-52C, 53-0400, the second 'C' model built, took place in March 1956 with deliveries beginning in June. All 35 of the variant were delivered to the 42nd Bomb Wing at Loring AFB, Maine. However, the type's tenure at Loring was short; the B-52D started joining the Wing in December and the now unwanted B-52Cs were transferred to the

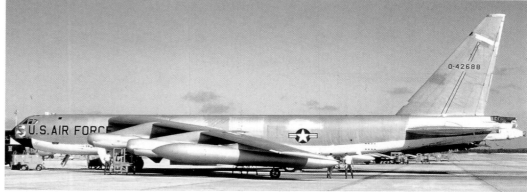

Above: **: Early in their careers B-52Ds were all painted in the silver-grey and white nuclear colour scheme.** Greg Spahr collection

99th Bomb Wing at Westover AFB, Massachusetts.

From the outset, B-52s were fitted with guns for self-defence. Four 0.50 calibre machine guns installed in the extreme rear of the fuselage were controlled by the A-3A Fire Control System (FCS) which was fitted to all B-52As, some 'B's and all 'C's except the last one built, 54-2688, which benefited from the B-52D's MD-9 FCS, the first such system to work satisfactorily. The first eight Wichita-built B-52Ds, 55-0049 to 55-0056, also came off the production line with the older A-3A system before the factory changed to the MD-9. The MD-5 FCS, based around two M-24A-1 20mm cannon, was fitted to 33 RB/B-52Bs but provided few advantages over the original system, and the last few 'B' models reverted to the A-3A.

The arms race extended to avionics: technical developments invented on one side of the Iron Curtain were quickly countered by their opponents on the other side – and the new technology predictably suffered teething problems. In particular, the bombing/navigation system on early B-52s was unreliable, and contractors strove to solve the difficulty of ensuring weapons' accuracy, crucial for nuclear armaments. Automation was increasingly introduced to reduce human error and to enhance defensive systems.

As the B-52D dedicated bomber version of the Stratofortress entered service in large numbers, the B-52C became surplus to requirements. Small numbers

Above: *Seen before it was deployed to Southwest Asia, B-52D 55-0061 was shot down during Linebacker II with the loss of the entire crew.* Greg Spahr collection

were assigned to more than a dozen Bomb Wings to be used as training aircraft – or 'bounce birds' – removing some of the training burden from the B-52D fleet and reducing wear and tear on the more sophisticated jets. These units were each assigned a small number of 'C' models, ranging from one up to half a dozen. Among the Wings involved were the 7th BW at Carswell AFB, Texas; 17th BW at Wright-Patterson AFB, Ohio; 22nd BW at March AFB, California; 28th BW at Ellsworth AFB, South Dakota; 70th BW at Clinton-Sherman AFB, Oklahoma; 91st BW at Glasgow AFB, Montana; 92nd BW at Fairchild AFB, Washington; 93rd BW at Castle AFB, California; 96th BW at Dyess AFB, Texas; 306th BW at McCoy AFB, Florida; 454th BW at Columbus AFB, Mississippi; 484th BW at Turner AFB, Georgia; and the 509th BW at Pease AFB, New Hampshire. As mentioned above, the 99th BW kept some of its B-52Cs up until 1971 for training. The B-52C was phased out within a short time, the final example, 53-0402, arriving for storage with the Military Aircraft Storage and Disposal Center (MASDC) at Davis-Monthan AFB, Arizona on September 29, 1971. MASDC change its title to Aerospace Maintenance and Regeneration Center (AMARC) in 1985 and again to 309th Aerospace Regeneration and Maintenance Center (AMARG) in May 2007. For the purposes of this publication, it will generally be referred to as D-M throughout. ▶

Above: *As it says on the nose, 55-0049 was the first B-52D to be built at Boeing's Wichita plant. In 2012 it was announced that the factory is to close.* Key collection
Below: *Wearing its Vietnam war-paint, this B-52D receives attention on the ramp. The enormous engine cowlings caused many lasting injuries to those unfortunate enough to have to open and lift them.* Key collection

D Model

DESIGN OF the B-52D began in December 1953 and it was intended from the outset to be a nuclear bomber. The Cold War was intensifying, and USAF leaders did their best to ensure that SAC was more than capable of defeating the Soviet Union, even to the extent of exaggerating the pace of Soviet bomber development to justify accelerated US production. While the US had a significant lead in the number of aircraft and nuclear weapons available, it suited the USAF leadership to allow politicians and the general public to believe the Soviets enjoyed numerical and technical parity, if not supremacy. Because this came to be seen as fact, politicians, who held the purse strings, were persuaded to make available substantial sums of money to build up the SAC armada. The B-52D was the first Stratofortress version to be ordered into large-scale production and, to increase the rate of manufacture, Secretary of the Air Force Harold E Talbot authorised a second plant to build the aircraft in Wichita, Kansas.

Three separate contracts were placed for the B-52D. The first, for 50 aircraft, placed on August 31, 1954, was followed by another for 69 aircraft on November 29, 1954 before the final order for 51 on October 26, 1955 (although some of these were actually completed to B-52E standard). The first B-52D, 55-0049, a Wichita-built aircraft, completed its maiden flight on June 4, 1956 while the first to be built in Seattle, 55-0068, took to the skies on September 28, 1956. Both aircraft were assigned to test programmes for a short time but production continued unabated with new

B-52D

B-52D [170] B-52D serials 55-0049 to 0117; 55-0673 to 0680; 56-0580 to 0630; 56-0657 to 0698

Wing	Location	Years	Wing	Location	Years	Wing	Location	Years
2nd BW	Barksdale AFB, LA	'65 - '92	97th BW	Blytheville AFB, AR	'60 - '92	4039th SW	Griffiss AFB, NY	'60 - '63
5th BW	Travis AFB, CA	'59 - '68	319th BW	Grand Forks AFB, ND	'82 - '87	- designation later changed to 416th BW		
17th BW	Beale AFB, CA	'75 - '76	320th BW	Mather AFB, CA	'68 - '89	4126th SW	Beale AFB, CA	'60 - '63,
19th BW	Robins AFB, GA	'68 - '83	366th Wing	Mountain Home AFB, ID	'92 - '94	- designation later changed to 456th SAW		
28th BW	Ellsworth AFB, SD	'71 - '77	379th BW	Wurtsmith AFB, MI	'77 - '92	4135th SW	Eglin AFB, FL	'59 - '63,
39th BW	Eglin AFB, FL	'63 - '65	380th SAW	Plattsburgh AFB, NY	'66 - '71	- designation later changed to 39th BW		
42nd BW	Loring AFB, ME	'59 - '94	397th BW	Dow AFB, ME	'63 - '68	4137th SW	Robins AFB, GA	'60 - '63
43rd SW/BW	Andersen AFB, Guam	'83 - '90	416th BW	Griffiss AFB, NY	'63 - '92	- designation later changed to 465th BW		
68th BW	Seymour Johnson AFB, NC	'63 - '82	456th SAW/BW	Beale AFB, CA	'63 - '75	4241st SW	Seymour Johnson AFB, NC	'59 - '63
72nd BW	Ramey AFB, PR	'59 - '71	465th BW	Robins AFB, GA	'63 - '68	- designation later changed to 68th BW		
92nd SAW/BW	Fairchild AFB, WA	'70 - '86	4038th SW	Dow AFB, ME	'60 - '63,			
93rd BW	Castle AFB, CA	'66 - '67	designation later changed to 397th BW					

Above: *The GBU-15 unpowered guided bomb was used as an anti-shipping missile by B-52Ds from the late 1970s.* Greg Spahr collection

Above: *As many as 12 Mk84 500lb bombs could be carried on the Multiple Ejector Racks mounted on stub-pylons on each wing of the B-52D.* Greg Spahr collection
Below: *56-0703 was the fifth 'E' model to be produced in Wichita. She carries the name 'The Untouchables' under the cockpit.* Greg Spahr collection

B-52E 57-0096 captured just before landing. Greg Spahr collection

aircraft emerging from the factories every few days. Following the completion of evaluation, deliveries began to operational Bomb Wings – firstly the 42nd BW at Loring AFB, Maine, followed by the 93rd BW at Castle AFB, California, which again assumed the crew training role. By the end of 1956, SAC had almost 100 B-52s in service, 40 B-52Bs, 32 B-52Cs and 25 B-52Ds. However, while this number was impressive, there was a shortage of combat-configured aircrews: only 16 with the 42nd BW and 26 with the 93rd. LeMay and his successor at SAC, General Thomas S Power, set about rectifying the deficiency. Extra training courses were arranged and Air Training Command (ATC) was authorised to create a specific training Wing equipped with Convair T-29D 'Fly-ing Classrooms' exclusively for SAC bombardier navigators – the 3535th Navigator Training Wing at Mather AFB, California. Less than two years after the problem was identified, SAC had more than 400 combat-ready crews flying 380 B-52s; this was in addition to the many hundreds of B-47s and a small number of B-36s, which collectively numbered SAC's bomber fleet at more than 1,000. (The ATC's specialised commitment to SAC later reverted to navigator training for all the armed services.)

Despite the B-52's several years of production, the 'D' model experienced some of the same technical problems as earlier versions. These included malfunctioning of the water injection system which was resolved after investigation at SAC bases revealed that the pumps used continued to operate even when the tanks were empty; fixes were quickly applied. In addition, the fuel system was prone to icing and fuel tanks leaked.

One unforeseen problem was caused by the sheer number of aircraft located at each base. As B-52s continued to enter service, the quantity of aircraft placed a huge strain on base infrastructure. Each Bomb Wing was usually composed of three squadrons of 15 aircraft each. Added to this was a single squadron of KC-97 or, increasingly, KC-135 tankers numbering between 15 and 20 aircraft. While those aircraft on alert were usually maintained on ground readiness, they were occasionally launched to maintain crew proficiency – add routine training sorties to the mix and it's easy to see that the bases were very busy. Plus the gross weight of the heavy bombers and tankers ▶

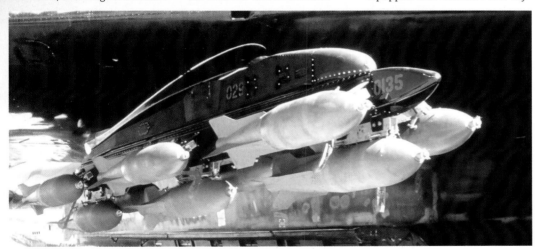

Above:: *Close-up of a Heavy Stores Adapter Beam mounted on a stub-pylon on a B-52D. Nine bombs could be carried on it.* Greg Spahr collection

Below: *Despite its increasingly important role employing conventional weapons, the 'D' model was still capable of carrying out its original nuclear-strike mission using the B28 weapon.* Greg Spahr collection

Star of the show at a 1950s' air show at Wright-Patterson AFB was 'E' model 57-0028. Greg Spahr collection

placed considerable strain on the taxiways and runways which had mostly been constructed to accommodate the lighter B-47.

One solution implemented during the late 1950s was to disperse the aircraft in smaller packages to a number of satellite airfields. With 60 or more aircraft at some bases, the airfields were obviously prime targets for a pre-emptive strike by the Soviet Union, so the dispersal of some squadrons made sound tactical sense. Some of these new, smaller entities, known as Strategic Wings, were located at fighter or transport bases where the B-52s, which tended to spend lengthy periods on pre-flight checks adjacent to the runway, could disrupt the core business of the facility.

Keeping the Buff out of harm's way

An organisation as large as SAC was never going to retain its advantage by standing still. Every time it gained the initiative, the Soviet Union countered with technological improvements of its own. Tactics improved and defences were bolstered, requiring the bomber crews to switch from high-altitude to low-level penetration. Soviet defences were known to be effective against high-flying targets, but less so in detecting those hugging the ground. B-52D crews began to practise egressing target areas at 500ft (152m) or lower, in all

Above: *One of the most colourful of the Stratofortresses was the NB-52E Control Configured Vehicle (CCV), 56-0632, which was operated by the Air Force Flight Dynamics Laboratory. It was retired to MASDC on June 26, 1974 and was scrapped there.* Key collection

weather conditions, day or night. The introduction of the North American AGM-28 Hound Dog cruise missile carrying a thermo-nuclear warhead gave crews the ability to launch from hundreds of miles away. An added bonus was that the missile was linked to the B-52's fuel system allowing its J52 engine to be used to give extra boost to the Buff during take-off. Meanwhile the addition of the McDonnell ADN-20 Quail decoy cruise missile enabled crews to confuse Soviet defences. Quails were designed to give a radar return very similar to that of the much bigger Buff, making it impossible for gunners and missile defences to know whether they were tackling a B-52

laden with nuclear weapons or a simple unarmed drone.

Other countermeasures carried by the early B-52s included the Sperry AN/ALQ-27 multiband automatic jamming and deception system, designed to counter all manner of detection systems including airborne and ground early warning radars as well as air-to-air and surface-to-air missiles (SAMs).

Vietnam stalwart

The deteriorating effectiveness of US forces in trying to halt the North Vietnamese infiltration of South Vietnam during the 1960s triggered a vast build-up of additional forces. Among the aircraft types ordered to bases

in South East Asia (SEA) were B-52Fs, which deployed to Andersen AFB, Guam in February 1965.

However, these were not very effective as the type was optimised for strategic nuclear bombing – operations in Vietnam were tactical, requiring the delivery of large numbers of conventional munitions. Invariably such sorties were aligned towards close air support, with US ground forces frequently being in the vicinity of the bombers' aiming points.

To rectify this problem, a programme was implemented in December 1965 to modify the B-52D with a so-called 'big belly' modification to allow the aircraft to carry more conventional bombs. The changes retained the capability to carry 24 x 500lb (227kg) or 750lb (340kg) bombs externally but the bomb bay was reconfigured to carry 84 (instead of 27) 500-pounders or 42 (instead of 27) 750lb weapons. All this added up to a massive 60,000lbs (27,215kg), a 50% increase over the B-52F. B-52Ds from the 28th BW at Ellsworth AFB, South Dakota, deployed to Andersen AFB, Guam, in March 1966 and the 484th BW at Turner AFB, Georgia, from April 1.

B-52Fs like 57-0139, pictured here, bore the brunt of the early Arc Light missions at the start of the Vietnam War. Greg Spahr collection

Whereas most aircraft deployed to SEA came under the Pacific Air Forces (PACAF) umbrella for day-to-day operations, those deployed by Strategic Air Command remained firmly under SAC control. Andersen AFB was a SAC facility, the 3rd Air Division having been established there on June 18, 1954 to administer deployed aircraft and personnel in the Far East.

Day-to-day operations at Andersen AFB came under the control of the 3960th Strategic Wing, formed originally as an Air Base Wing on April 1, 1955. SAC formed the 4133rd Bombardment Wing (Provisional) 'Black Eagles' on February 1, 1966 to oversee personnel rotated to the theatre of operations from bases in the USA.

The first combat operations flown by the Stratofortress over Vietnam, beginning in June 1965 with the B-52F, were code-named Operation Arc Light. The B-52D entered combat on June 18, 1965, a few days after the first jets arrived at Andersen AFB; their targets were sites suspected of housing Viet Cong and North Vietnamese in South Vietnam. Gradually, the list of targets requested by the commander of US forces in the region, General William Westmoreland, expanded as the North Vietnamese altered their tactics to escape the bombing and eventually encroached into another sovereign nation, Cambodia.

To reduce the long transit time to the target areas in SEA, the

Above: *Many B-52Fs were converted to deploy the Hound Dog stand-off nuclear missile.* Greg Spahr collection
Below: *Line up of Hound Dog-armed B-52Fs of the 93rd BW at its home base, Castle AFB, in the late 1950s.* Greg Spahr collection

The tail wasn't fixed in place until after a newly completed Buff was pulled from the final assembly hangar!
Key collection

Arc Light mission was shifted to U-Tapao Royal Thai Air Force Base (RTAFB), Thailand. The 4258th Strategic Wing was activated there on June 2, 1966 and B-52D units continued to rotate to the region from the USA for the rest of the war.

For political reasons, a huge list of potential targets, including vitally important industrial and military complexes, was off-limits to the bombers and remained untouched. This resulted in the 'big belly' B-52Ds delivering tonnes of munitions onto tiny targets, some of which had already been obliterated. Not only did this tactic fail to affect the enemy in any significant way, it was also very expensive for the Americans both in terms of resources and the morale of the crews who knew their efforts were frequently pointless.

In early February 1968, largely in response to the North Korean ▶

Above: *Note that these aircraft are in bare metal. Starting with B-52B 52-8710, all Boeing-Seattle aircraft were painted on the production line, but all Wichita-built aircraft rolled out of the factory in bare metal. The first B-52F flew in bare metal. Most Wichita aircraft were painted between roll-out and first flight.* Key collection

seizure of the US spy ship *Pueblo*, more B-52Ds were sent to South East Asia.

Peace talks were organised in Paris, but the North Vietnamese found numerous reasons to procrastinate. Eventually, the frustrated US Government authorised a huge increase in the number of B-52 missions. While not giving the bomber crews free-rein, Washington took a bolder approach and permitted an increase in the target lists available to local commanders. The strikes appeared to be influencing the North Vietnamese in Paris to look more favourably on US peace proposals but the talks

soon returned to stalemate when the bombing stopped. This lack of significant progress prompted President Nixon to order a second campaign of sustained bombing operations, launched in December 1972 – involving all the fighter and bomber assets stationed in the region.

But it was the imposing B-52s that captured the headlines. Andersen AFB held the largest number of aircraft with U-Tapao also supporting the campaign. Targets in North Vietnam, including the Hanoi and Haiphong areas, were pounded for the first time. Ten B-52Ds and six B-52Gs were lost

to enemy action, the US claiming that each one was downed by SA-2 Guideline SAMs, although the North Vietnamese claimed that at least two were shot down by MiG-21s. It is widely accepted by historians that the renewed campaign persuaded the North Vietnamese to sign the Paris Peace Accords on January 23, 1973 which led to the end of US involvement in Vietnam later that year.

Ironically, the most effective use of the B-52 in Vietnam was for tactical support of ground troops, a role it was never intended for. B-52s were called in to disrupt enemy troop concentrations and supply-areas with devastating effect. Raids were also flown against targets in North Vietnam, Cambodia and Laos, and General Westmoreland considered the B-52s essential to US efforts in Vietnam. Between June 1965 until August 1973, when operations ceased, B-52s flew 124,532 sorties which successfully dropped their bomb loads on target. Thirty-one B-52s were lost, 18 shot down by the enemy (all over North Vietnam) and 13 lost due to operational problems. With the end of hostilities in Vietnam, the B-52Ds returned home to the USA. Eighteen Bomb Wings and Strategic Wings flew the type, many deploying their aircraft for combat in South East Asia. The majority of B-52Ds were retired in late 1978 and 1982/1983.

E Model

B-52E

B-52E [100] B-52E serials 56-0631 to 0656; 56-0699 to 0712; 57-0014 to 0029; 57-0095 to 0138

Wing	Location	Years
6th BW/ SAW	Walker AFB, New Mexico	'57 - '67
11th BW/ SAW	Altus AFB, Oklahoma	'58 - '68
17th BW	Wright-Patterson AFB, Ohio	'63 - '68
70th BW	Clinton-Sherman AFB, Oklahoma	'63 - '68
93rd BW	Castle AFB, California	'57 - '58
96th SAW	Dyess AFB, Texas	'63 - '70
4043rd SW	Wright-Patterson AFB, Ohio	'60 - '63
designation later changed to 17th BW		
4123rd SW	Clinton-Sherman AFB, Oklahoma	'59 - '63
- designation later changed to 70th BW		

ONE HUNDRED B-52Es were ordered for manufacture at both Seattle and Wichita. The 'E' model was almost the same as the B-52D apart from more dependable electronics and a more accurate AN/ASQ-38 bombing and navigational system. Crew comfort was improved with the redesign of the navigator-bombardier station and the relocation of some instruments. The new bombing and navigational sight was not as accurate as expected and was

Above: *Four nuclear colour-schemed B-52Gs fly in salute over their new home, Barksdale AFB, Louisiana.* © ... Snohr collection

difficult to maintain – requiring major engineering modifications including the replacement of the main computer to ensure accuracy during low-level terrain avoidance sorties.

The first Seattle-built B-52E was flown on October 3, 1957 and the first Wichita example three weeks later. The 93rd BW at Castle AFB and the 6th BW at Walker AFB, New Mexico were the first two Wings to receive E-models, in December 1957. The type was also flown by six other Bomb Wings/Strategic Wings until retired for storage in 1969 and 1970.

Aircraft 56-0632 was assigned to a test programme from 1958, evaluating systems including more powerful engines and strengthened landing gear which were installed on subsequent B-52 models. Later in its career, 56-0632 was modified as an NB-52E and reconfigured for a specialised development project. Small swept canards were installed on the forward fuselage and a long, pointed nose probe attached. The wings were modified with enlarged control surfaces. Internally the conven-

Above: *Photographed shortly after it was delivered to the USAF, B-52G 58-0190 went on to have the unhappy distinction of being the 101st Buff to be lost when it burned out at Kelly AFB, Texas.* Greg Spahr collection

Below: *Wearing the colourful markings of the 2nd AF, this B-52G is equipped with an early EVS system and matching accessories – a camouflaged Hound Dog missile. Because the EVS comprised passive systems, undetectable by enemy defences, they could be used instead of the aircraft's navigation radar, allowing it to be turned off on low-level attack missions.* Greg Spahr collection

tional mechanical and hydraulic links to the control surfaces were replaced by electronic and electrical connections and various measuring equipment was installed. Test aircrew evaluated electronic flutter and buffeting suppression systems to help decrease aircrew fatigue and stress during low-level sorties. External sensors were attached for a programme identified as 'Load Alleviation and Mode Stabilization' (LOBE), which involved recording gusts and activating control surfaces to cut down on fatigue damage.

In 1973 the NB-52E was flown at 10 knots above the speed at which flutter would normally cause a Stratofortress to disintegrate: the canards reduced 50% of the horizontal and 30% of the vertical vibrations caused by turbulence during the tests, which were conducted jointly by the Air Force Flight Dynamics Laboratory at Wright-Patterson AFB, Ohio, and the Boeing Control Configured Vehicles programme. The aircraft was painted with a red scheme applied to the tail, forward fuselage, engine nacelles and wing leading edges. Tests were completed in June 1974 when the aircraft was retired to AMARC for storage.

Another B-52E used for testing was 57-0119, allocated to General Electric in 1965 to evaluate the TF-39 engine ahead of its being installed on the Lockheed C-5A Galaxy. The two J57s were removed from the inner port wing and replaced with the TF-39 – a high-bypass ratio turbofan engine which developed 43,000lbs of thrust, more than twice that of the J57s.

As expected, the arrangement created very different handling characteristics. This aircraft was also used to evaluate the TF-39's civilian version, the CF6, intended for use on the ▶

Above: *One of the first B-52Gs to receive the AN/ASQ-151 Electro Optical Viewing System (EVS) for safer low-level navigation. The right blister on the chin housed a steerable Hughes AN/AAQ-6 FLIR camera while the other an equally steerable Westinghouse AN/AVQ-22 low light-level television camera. Together they detected heat emissions and could provide a usable image by starlight.* Greg Spahr collection

Below: *B-52G 58-0175, which still lingers in the Arizona desert, is displayed with a GAM-72 Quail decoy. Although eight could be carried by each Buff, the usual load was four. They were carried at the back of the bomb-bay in a special module from which they could be dropped in flight to fly a pre-programmed profile.* Greg Spahr collection

McDonnell-Douglas DC-10-10, before being placed in storage at Edwards AFB, California in 1972.

Eight years later General Electric decommissioned and dumped the aircraft near Rogers Dry Lake within the base area. Its hulk, and that of derelict B-52B 53-0379, were photographed by a Russian satellite in 1991, prompting the Russians to insist that one of the airframes be rendered inoperative as part of the Strategic Arms Reduction Treaty. Aircraft 57-0119 was selected and later blown into three pieces with high explosives. There is some dispute about its designation - most sources state that it was designated as an NB-52E, but the prefix N signifies that the aircraft has been permanently converted, and it is unlikely that the USAF would have permitted General Electric to do that; usual practice was for the aircraft to be returned to USAF charge at the end of trials in the condition that it was received in. A more correct designation would be JB-52E.

In a similar vein, B-52E 56-0636 was bailed to Pratt & Whitney to test the JT9D turbofan engine for the Boeing 747; that machine was retired to D-M and scrapped.

Above: *An air-to-air front view of a B-52G from the 416th Bombardment Wing, armed with AGM-86B Air-Launched Cruise Missiles (ALCMs). This jet has the much-improved 'Phase VI+ ECM Defensive Avionics Systems' upgrade, installed under the 'Rivet Ace' programme. It comprised defensive counter-measures and jamming systems that account for the lumps and bumps on the nose and around the airframe.* USAF

B-52F

B-52F [89] B-52F serials 57-0030 to 0073; 57-0139 to 0183 66 more, 57-0074 to 57-0094 and 57-0184 to 57-0228 were cancelled and not built

Wing	Location	Years	Wing	Location	Years
2nd BW	Barksdale AFB, Louisiana	'63 - '65	designation later changed to 320th BW		
7th BW	Carswell AFB, Texas	'58 - '69	4228th SW	Columbus AFB, Mississippi	'59 - '63
93rd BW	Castle AFB, California	'58 - '78	designation later changed to 454th BW		
320th BW	Mather AFB, California	'63 - '68	4238th SW	Barksdale AFB, Louisiana	'58 - '63
454th BW	Columbus AFB, Mississippi	'63 - '66	- designation later changed to 2nd BW		
4134th SW	Mather AFB, California	'58 - '63			

F Model

THE B-52F was almost identical to the preceding version with the exception of slightly uprated J57 engines and minor improvements to the water injection system. Two additional tanks were installed in the wing to accommodate extra water. Additionally, alternators were fitted to the left hand engine in each pod in place of the air-driven turbines and alternators previously installed.

B-52Fs were built at both Seattle and Wichita with deliveries beginning in June 1958 to the 93rd BW at Castle AFB, California. Later in the year, the 7th BW at Carswell AFB, Texas, received the type, followed by the 4134th SW at Mather AFB, California (changed to 320th BW from February 1,1963) and the 4238th SW at Barksdale AFB, Louisiana (changed to 2nd BW on March 1, 1963).

Like most of the preceding versions, the B-52F also suffered from fuel leaks, caused primarily by clamps on flexible fuel couplings breaking and causing potentially catastrophic problems during flight operations. The faulty fixings were replaced by new aluminium clamps, but these proved little better and even the Boeing-developed stainless steel clamps that in turn replaced them failed to fix the problem; it was finally solved with a safety strap, retrofitted to the whole B-52 fleet at the end of 1958.

Visually, there were few clues to distinguish between the B-52F and the 'E' model. The main difference between the two, and

Above: **B-52G 58-0197 does its bit for global warming as it blasts away from the runway in 1991. It flew 17 Desert Storm missions with 4300 BW(P).** Glenn Sands collection

Above: *B-52G 59-2570 from the 42nd BW based at Loring AFB, Maine, powers away from RAF Mildenhall on August 25, 1986, with an AGM-84D Harpoon anti-shipping missile under the wing.* Bob Archer collection

a simple way to tell them apart visually, was the powerplants. Pratt & Whitney J57-P-43W turbojets, each with a maximum thrust of 13,750 pounds with water injection, were substituted for the Pratt & Whitney J57-P-19W turbojets of the earlier model. This amounted to an increase of nearly 2,000lbs thrust per engine. The new engines had large alternators mounted on the left side which gave the F model engine nacelles a distinctive bulge. The B-52F was the first Stratofortress version to be deployed to South East Asia for combat operations. The 2nd BW from Barksdale AFB, Louisiana, and the 320th BW from Mather AFB, California, deployed 30 aircraft to Andersen AFB, Guam, from February 11, 1965 with a similar number of KC-135 tankers deployed to Kadena AFB, Okinawa to provide fuel. Most if not all of the aircraft despatched

to the Pacific had been updated in the South Bay modification programme that gave these nuclear bombers the capability to drop large numbers of conventional weapons, 24 x 750lb (340kg) M117

Above: *The first effective non-nuclear stand-off missile for the B-52H was the AGM-142, known by its programme name of Have Nap. It is a licence-built version of the Israeli Popeye medium-range weapon. Three Have Naps and their guiding system could be carried on the two external pylons.* Lockheed Martin

Below: *A line-up of 416th BW B-52Gs at their home base, Griffiss AFB, New York, in the late 1980s.* Key collection

bombs, from racks mounted on the wings and another 27 carried internally. The 2nd BW aircraft rotated back to the USA in early May having been replaced by the 7th BW from Carswell AFB, Texas.

The B-52F carried out fewer than 1% of B-52 missions over Vietnam but those squadrons equipped with the type provided a valuable service by establishing operating procedures that were adopted by those who followed. Air-to-air refuelling procedures were changed to prevent a recurrence of the disastrous confusion on early Arc Light missions that resulted in the collision of two bombers and tactics, especially the use of the B-52s' own radar to identify targets, were devised and perfected ready for when the B-52D joined the fray in March 1966.

Fifteen B-52Fs were retired to MASDC in 1967 and 1968, followed by another batch between 1969 and 1973. The remainder, which had been flown by the training wing, the 93rd BW at Castle AFB, were flown into storage during the second half of 1978. ▶

G Model

B-52G

B-52G [193] B-52g serials 57-6468 to 6520; 58-0158 to 0258; 59-2564 to 2602

Wing	Location	Years	Wing	Location	Years	Wing	Location	Years
7th BW	Carswell AFB, TX	'69 - '83	306th BW	McCoy AFB, FL	'63 - '73	4047th SW	McCoy AFB, FL	'61 - '63
22nd BW	March AFB, CA	'66 - '82	307th SW	U-Tapao RTAFB, Thailand	'70 - '74	- designation later changed to 306th BW		
28th BW	Ellsworth AFB, SD	'57 - '71				4128th SW	Amarillo AFB, TX	'60 - '63
42nd BW	Loring AFB, ME	'57 - '59	340th BW	Bergstrom AFB, TX	'63 - '66	- designation later changed to 461st BW		
43rd SW	Andersen AFB, Guam	'72 - '83	376th SW	Kadena AB, Okinawa, Japan	'70	4130th SW	Bergstrom AFB, TX	'59 - '63
70th BW	Clinton-Sherman AFB, OK	'68 - '69	454th BW	Columbus AFB, MS	'66 - '69	- designation later changed to 340th BW		
91st BW	Glasgow AFB, MT	'63 - '68	461st BW	Amarillo AFB, TX	'63 - '68	4138th SW	Turner AFB, GA	'59 - '63
92nd BW/SAW	Fairchild AFB, WA	'57 - '71	462nd SAW	Larson AFB, WA	'63 - '66	- designation later changed to 484th BW		
93rd BW	Castle AFB, CA	'56 - '58	484th BW	Turner AFB, GA	'63 - '67	4141st SW	Glasgow AFB, MT	'61 - '63
96th SAW/BW	Dyess AFB, TX	'69 - '82	494th BW	Sheppard AFB, TX	'63 - '66	- designation later changed to 91st BW		
99th BW	Westover AFB, MA	'57 - '61, '66 - '72	509th BW	Pease AFB, NH	'66 - '69			

THE B-52G marked a radical improvement over the previous six versions of the Stratofortress. Among the changes were additional fuel tanks in the wings, making it the first B-52 with a so-called 'wet wing'; this offered a considerable increase in unrefuelled range. To boost thrust on take-off, a 12,000 US gallon (45,000lit) tank was installed that increased the capability and duration of the water injection system. The G-model also featured a vertical stabiliser some 7ft 4in (2.23m) shorter than that of previous models. With the new tail came a new gun system: instead of having a manned turret in the tail, four machine guns controlled by the AN/ASG-15 FCS were operated by a gunner from a station in the cabin with the rest of the flight crew.

Development of the B-52G was instigated against the backdrop of the troubled Convair B-58 Hustler which, had it been cancelled, would have left a gap in the US's strategic capability during the 1960s. This prospect led to calls to raise production of the B-52 to 20 aircraft per month, although lack of funding pegged the figure back to 15. However, intelligence suggested that Russian strategic bomber production was being cut, enabling the US to follow suit. Nevertheless, more B-52Gs were ordered than any other version. G-models began to enter service with the 5th BW at Travis AFB, California, on February 13, 1959,

the day after the final Convair B-36 Peacemaker was retired from SAC service, rendering it an all-jet bomber force. The B-52G was optimised from the outset for operations with both the Hound Dog nuclear missile and the Quail decoy. The 4135th Strategic Wing at Eglin AFB, Florida made the first SAC test-launch of the Hound Dog missile on February 29, 1960 and followed it on June 8 with a similar test with the Quail.

The B-52G weighed in 38,000lbs (17,236kg) heavier than its predecessor at 488,000lbs (221,353kg). The changes made to this model and the B-52H which followed, together with the need to fly more very low-level missions, had the potential to increase airframe fatigue. Between February 1962 and September

1964, steps were taken to reduce this risk by strengthening the wing structure. Both the B-52G and 'H were intended to remain in service for many years to come and, in 1970, the air force funded modifications to enable them to carry the Boeing AGM-69A nuclear warhead short-range attack missile (SRAM). Each bomber could carry 20 such missiles.

The 42nd BW at Loring AFB was the first unit to operate SRAM-equipped B-52Gs. Although not capable of carrying the same bomb load as the B-52D, the type was included in the build-up of forces in SEA with the first examples arriving at Andersen AFB, Guam on April 12, 1972. No fewer than 94 arrived in theatre before May 27, bolstering the 55 additional B-52Ds sent between February and April

1972, with G-models flying their first mission on April 18. When President Richard Nixon ordered Operation Linebacker II to begin on December 18, 1972, G-models were included in the dozens of B-52 sorties launched each night. Stiff North Vietnamese resistance brought down six B-52Gs, four coming down in the Hanoi area and the other two crashed in Thailand. A seventh B-52G was lost after take-off from Andersen AFB and crashed in the Pacific Ocean.

The losses to enemy air defences were of great concern to the USAF. If the North Vietnamese could knock down this number of aircraft in such a short time-span, how could B-52 crews penetrate the more formidable defences in place across the

B-52H 60-0048 prepares to land. The photo was taken before the aircraft received its modern wrap-around green camouflage and before the defensive General Electric six-barrel M61cannon in the tail was removed. USAF

Soviet Union? A range of sophisticated defensive systems were added to enhance the aircraft's survivability, including wideband receivers designed to scan enemy defences, while new jamming equipment was installed to frustrate enemy radar systems. The heart of the defensive package was the AN/ALR-20 receiver which displayed information on a small screen monitored by the electronic warfare officer. Chaff and flares were also carried as a means to defeat defence radars.

Twenty-five years after its first missions over South East Asia, B-52s played a major role in Operation Desert Storm during the Gulf War of 1991. B-52Gs were chosen to conduct the bombing offensive as the only other version remaining in service at the time, the B-52H, was dedicated to the nuclear role. The B-52G had dual conventional and nuclear capability, as instigated by SAC commander General John Chain in December 1987. For the Desert Storm deployments, four locations were selected for B-52 operations and aircraft began to arrive late in 1990. To coordinate operations with aircraft and personnel drawn from across the USAF, four provisional Bombardment Wings were formed:

801st Bombardment Wing (Provisional) at Morón Air Base, Spain, with aircraft from the ▶

Above: *Technicians at Andersen AFB, Guam install Mk62 Quickstrike naval mines onboard the last Buff built, B-52H 61-0040 in September 2010. USAF*
Right: *In effort to make the B-52 even more effective, new systems, like this Litening pod are constantly being integrated with the jet. This photo was taken when the pod was being trialled by 49th Test and Evaluation Squadron. USAF*
Left: *The four .50 calibre machine guns as used on earlier variants were still the main defensive armament for 'H' models, but the gunner controlled the weapons remotely from a station in the forward fuselage with the rest of the crew using the newer ASG-15 fire control system. Greg Spahr collection*
Far left: *Up to 20 AGM-69 Short-Range Attack Missiles (SRAM) could be carried by each Buff, six on each wing pylon and eight more on this rotary clip carried in the bomb-bay. Replacing the Hound Dog, this nuclear missile was in service from 1972. It was removed from the inventory on the orders of President George H W Bush in 1993. Greg Spahr collection*

2nd, 97th, 379th and 416th BWs.

806th Bombardment Wing (Provisional) at RAF Fairford, UK, with aircraft from 2nd, 379th and 416th BWs,

1708th Bombardment Wing (Provisional) at Jeddah/King Abdul Aziz International Airport, Saudi Arabia, with aircraft from 2nd, 42nd, 93rd, 379th and 416th BWs.

4300th Bombardment Wing (Provisional) at Diego Garcia, Indian Ocean, with aircraft from 42nd and 93rd BWs.

During the early morning of January 16, 1991, seven 596th Bomb Squadron, 2nd BW B-52Gs took off from Barksdale AFB, Louisiana, and headed toward the Persian Gulf. They flew a round trip of more than 14,000 miles (22,500km) and were airborne for 35 hours. Each aircraft was carrying five AGM-86C conventional air-launched cruise missiles which were fired against high-priority targets across Iraq in the opening salvo of the campaign. The mission was flown as Operation Senior Surprise, and was at the time the longest combat sortie in history. The entire operation remained classified for a year but, despite the secrecy, the Soviet Navy monitored the flight of the aircraft from spy ships in the waters around the Middle East. The mission was the first combat use of the Boeing AGM-86C conventional air-launched cruise missile (CALCM).

Strategic Air Command was disbanded on May 31, 1992. At the time only B-52G and H models remained in service. These, together with SAC's fleet of B-1Bs and B-2As, were absorbed into Air Combat Command along with other SAC operational assets: RC-135s, OC-135s, E-4Bs

Above: *The crew of the last Buff built, B-52H 61-0040, pose in front of their mount for Operation Persian Rug. On January 12, 1962 The eight men, from Minot AFB's 4136th Strategic Wing broke 11 world records and demonstrated to the world the unrivalled capabilities of the B-52 in a non-stop un-refuelled flight of 12,500 miles from Kadena, Okinawa to Torrejon, Spain. Fifty years later, and 60 years after the Buff's first flight SAC's successor, AFGSC has declared 2012 'The Year of the B-52'.* USAF

and U-2s and their direct training aircraft. SAC's KC-10As and various KC-135s all joined Air Mobility Command.

The prospect of hostilities in the Cold War gradually receded as nations in Eastern Europe sought to free themselves from control by the Soviet Union. The final hammer blow to Soviet hegemony took place on November 9, 1989 when East Germans breached the Berlin Wall, starting a chain of events that led to the elimination of the Russian presence outside Russia, the dismantling of the Warsaw pact and free elections across Eastern Europe – effectively ending the Cold War. These factors enabled the B-52Gs to be retired from 1989; by May 3, 1994, 140 of them had been consigned to the boneyard.

B-52H

B-52H [102] B-52H serials 60-0001 – 0062; 61-0001 - 0040

Wing	Location	Years	Wing	Location	Years	Wing	Location	Years
2nd Wing/BW	Barksdale AFB, LA	'92 - current	28th BW	Ellsworth AFB, SD	'77 - '86	379th BW	Wurtsmith AFB, MI	'61 - '77
			92nd BW	Fairchild AFB, WA	'86 - '94	410th BW	K I Sawyer AFB, MI	'63 - '94
5th BW	Minot AFB, ND	'68 -	93rd BW	Castle AFB, CA	'74 - '83	416th BW	Griffiss AFB, NY	'92 - '94
7th BW	Carswell AFB, TX	'82 - '92	96th BW	Dyess AFB, TX	'82 - '85	449th BW	Kincheloe AFB, MI	'63 - '77
17th BW	Wright-Patterson AFB, OH	'68 - '75	307th BW	Barksdale AFB, LA	'11 -	450th BW	Minot AFB, ND	'63 - '68
19th BW	Homestead AFB, FL	'62 - '68	319th BW	Grand Forks AFB, ND	'63 - '82	917th W	Barksdale AFB, LA	'93 - '11

The final B-52H was delivered 50 years ago in October 1962. Plans are in place to maintain the Stratofortress as an effective platform for weapons delivery for the next two decades, and possibly until the year 2050. Other strategic bombers have been produced subsequently, some of which have been retired, and others remain in service.

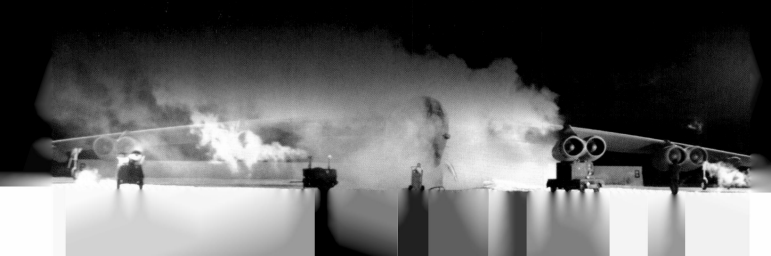

Below: *With temperatures dropping to as low as minus 25 degrees, Minot Air Force Base North Dakota is a good place for cold weather trials! This Buff was photographed on January 30, 2007 towards the end of tests to certify a mixture of synthetic and standard JP-8 fuel.* USAF

H Model

THE B-52H was the only version of the Buff powered by Pratt & Whitney TF-33-P-3 turbofan engines. The installation of the new powerplants offered a great improvement in range over the B-52G, with official figures suggesting an unrefuelled range in excess of 4,100 miles (6,598km).

Another advantage over the earlier J57 engine was its lack of reliance on a water injection system to provide extra power at take-off. The latest state-of-the-art electronic countermeasures equipment was fitted, with an enhanced fire control system, the AN/ASG-21. Self defence was improved with the installation of a single multi-barrel M-61 20mm Gatling gun mounted in the rear fuselage in place of the earlier four machine-guns.

The first B-52H, 60-0001, designated as YB-52H for early test flights before its delivery to Strategic Air Command (SAC), took to the skies of Seattle on July 10, 1960. When testing and evaluation was complete, 60-0001 was delivered to the 379th BW at Wurtsmith AFB, Michigan, on May 9, 1961, and six weeks later 20 B-52Hs were operational.

Minor problems with the TF-33 engine, including failure of turbine blades, high oil usage, and occasional flame-outs were investigated by the Oklahoma City Air Materiel Area, which was responsible for B-52 major over-hauls; it has since been re-named the Oklahoma Air Logistics Center at Tinker AFB, Oklahoma, and much B-52 maintenance is still undertaken there. Although the work was interrupted by the October 1962 Cuban missile crisis, when most B-52Hs were placed on alert, by the end of 1964, most problems had been resolved. The final B-52H serial 61-0040 was delivered to the 4137th Bomb Wing at Minot AFB, North Dakota, on October 26, 1962, nearly 50 years ago. That delivery marked the end of a production run of 744 bombers.

Many Bomb Wings were located in the central United States and had a degree of built-in protection (in the unlikely event of attack) provided by the significant land mass between the Atlantic and Pacific Oceans and the bomber's home stations. Air

Above: *This Buff, 60-0006, was important in that it trialled the early EVS system that so enhanced the abilities of the B-52. Sadly, it went on to be the 86th B-52 to be lost on operations when it crashed at Wright-Patterson AFB in 1974.* Greg Spahr collection

Combat Command (ACC) had assumed control of the strategic bomber fleet from SAC on May 31, 1992, and SAC was disestablished the following day, having become a casualty of the major reorganisation of the USAF's major commands that followed the collapse of the Soviet Union and the end of the Cold War. ACC focused on operational B-52H activities at just two bases: the 2nd and 5th Bomb Wings located at Barksdale AFB, Louisiana, and Minot AFB, North Dakota, respectively.

Furthermore, ACC decided to transfer a small element of the strategic bomber mission to the reserves. Air Force Reserve Command formed the 93rd Bomb Squadron on October 1, 1993, to operate eight B-52Hs, as part of the 917th Wing at Barksdale AFB,

which also flew the A-10A.

With retirement of all preceding models of the B-52 it was decided that the B-52H should receive the necessary modifications to the bomb bay to enable the carriage of a wide variety of conventional munitions. Furthermore, the introduction of many 'smart' weapons resulted in the B-52H having a host of weapons delivery-system updates. These included the installation of a global positioning system linked to the weapons delivery system.

Internally the bomb bay has been upgraded with heavy stores racks to accommodate conventional 2,000lb (900kg) bombs, as well as 500lb (230kg) and 1,000lb (460kg) 'dumb' munitions. Located beneath the wings between the fuselage and the

inboard engines is a large launch rail to house bulky weapons such as the Boeing AGM-84 Harpoon or Lockheed Martin AGM-142 Have Nap missile. More recently, several smart weapons have been added, including the Boeing AGM-86 conventional air-launched cruise missile (CALCM) and the Raytheon AGM-154 Joint Stand-Off Weapon (JSOW). Various enhancements to 'dumb' bombs, transforming them into smart munitions, include the Joint Direct-Attack Munitions (JDAM) kit and the Wind-Corrected Munitions Dispenser (WCMD) tail kit. The B-52 will also be able to use the Lockheed Martin AGM-158 Joint Air-to-Surface Missile (JASSM) when this becomes operational. Nuclear weapons include the Boeing ▶

Above: *If Flying Fortresses like the B-17G in the foreground had been expected to have as long a service life as the B-52, then the USAF would still be flying them for decades to come.* USAF

Above: *Wearing the classic Cold War SAC colour scheme, B-52H 60-0031 still serves America, flying with Air Force Reserve Command's 307th BW from Barksdale AFB, Louisiana.* Greg Spahr collection

AGM-86 Air-Launched Cruise Missile (ALCM), and the Raytheon AGM-129 Advanced Cruise Missile (ACM), as well as the B-61 and B-83 nuclear bombs.

To aid navigation at low level, the B-52H features the AN/ASQ-151 electro-optical viewing system (EVS), featuring the Raytheon AN/AAQ-6 forward-looking infrared (FLIR) in the starboard turret and Northrop Grumman AN/AVQ-22 low-light-level television camera (LLTV) in the port turret.

A highly effective offensive avionics system has been installed, which has been enhanced with an avionics mid-life improvement programme. To ensure compatibility with these new weapons, the USAF has awarded many contracts to the manufacturer, while other enhancements have been carried out by the Oklahoma City Air Logistics Center at Tinker AFB, Oklahoma, which is the Air Force Logistics Command facility responsible for all aspects of maintenance and sustainment for the type.

The void left by the retirement of the B-52G for potential combat operations in the Pacific region was filled by the B-52H, which deployed four examples from Barksdale AFB to Andersen AFB on a forward operating basis on September 1, 1996. Armed with 13 AGM-86C CALCMs, two aircraft flew a 34-hour combat sortie against prime targets in Iraq, such as communications facilities and power stations in Baghdad.

Some days earlier, the Saddam Hussein regime moved 40,000 troops into northern Iraq, threatening Kurdish nationals. The B-52Hs landed at Diego Garcia in the Indian Ocean on the return journey to refuel. The mission was known as Operation Desert Strike, and was flown under the auspices of Operation Northern Watch, the command for implementation of the air exclusion zone above northern Iraq. The sortie was the combat debut of the B-52H model, 35 years after the first example entered service. Whereas B-52Gs launched CALCMs from underwing rails at valuable targets during the opening stages of Operation Desert Storm, those launched during Operation Desert Strike were mounted in the weapons bay on Common Strategic Rotary Launchers (CSRL).

Later in the decade, ongoing aggression in the Balkans region, particularly Kosovo, following the break-up of the former Yugoslavia, resulted in the assembly of a large NATO body of combat forces during mid February 1999 under Operation Allied Force (NATO) and Noble Anvil (US).

Many of these forces were located in Italy for ease of operations across the Adriatic Sea. However, the B-52H contingent was flown to RAF Fairford, with seven 2nd BW aircraft arriving from Barksdale AFB on February 21, 1999 (and an eighth arriving the next day). B-52s attacked targets in Belgrade with CALCMs beginning on March 24, 1999. B-1Bs were added at the end of March. A total of 11 B-52Hs were at Fairford, primarily from the 2nd BW, but with a small number from the 5th BW, all operated under the umbrella of the 2nd Air Expeditionary Group.

Having exhausted precision objectives with their CALCMs, the B-52s switched to delivering conventional general purpose weapons against Serbian military targets.

A total of 184 combat missions were flown during the operation. The NATO offensive forced the forces of Slobodan Milosevic to withdraw from Kosovo and enabled combat operations to be suspended. The B-52s returned to their home bases at the end of June.

The B-52H was involved in combat for the third time during Operation Iraqi Freedom in 2003. Combat forces were assembled in Eastern Europe and the Middle East, but with a contingent of 14 B-52Hs operating from RAF Fairford. The B-52s began arriving on March 3, 2003 from the 5th BW at Minot AFB. Beginning on March 21, combat sorties were launched on lengthy round-trips from Fairford, with 100 AGM-86C and the new AGM-86D missiles being fired at lucrative targets. During April 2003 a B-52H was fitted with the Northrop Grumman AN/AAQ-28(V) Litening II laser targeting pod, which was used to strike targets in Northern Iraq.

While combat operations were taking place across Iraq, a second front was opened above Afghanistan. According to the US government, the Al Qaeda attacks on the United States using hijacked airliners on September 11, 2001, were planned and sponsored by terrorist organisations located in Afghanistan.

The US bolstered its already sizeable forces in the region by deploying B-52s to Diego Garcia. Unlike the strategic and tactical military targets across Iraq, Al Qaeda and Taliban terrorists were located in small groups that blended into the territory with ease.

SAC COMMAND'S B-52 UNIT STRUCTURE IN SOUTH EAST ASIA DURING THE VIETNAM WAR

- 8th Air Force moved from Westover AFB, Massachusetts to Andersen AFB, Guam on April 1, 1970; relocated to Barksdale AFB, Louisiana on January 1, 1975. Was the controlling element for SAC operations in South East Asia.
- 3rd Air Division activated at Andersen AFB, Guam on June 18, 1954, inactivated on 31 March 1970; replaced by 8th Air Force. Reactivated at Andersen AFB, Guam on January 1, 1975.
- Air Division, Provisional, 17 activated at U-Tapao RTAFB, Thailand on June 1, 1972 (attached to 8th AF); inactivated on January 1, 1975.
- Air Division, Provisional, 57 activated at Andersen AFB, Guam (attached on 8th AF); inactivated on November 15, 1973.
- Strategic Wing Provisional, 72 activated at Andersen AFB, Guam on 1 June 1972, and attached to Air Division, Provisional, 57; inactivated on November 15, 1973.
- Strategic Wing Provisional, 310 activated at U-Tapao RTAFB, Thailand on June 1, 1972, attached to Air Division Provisional, 17; inactivated on July 1, 1974.
- Consolidated Aircraft Maintenance Wing Provision, 303 activated at Andersen AFB, Guam on July 1, 1972, and attached Air Division, Provisional, 57; inactivated on November 15, 1973.
- Consolidated Aircraft Maintenance Wing Provision, 340 activated at U-Tapao RTAFB, Thailand on July 1, 1972, and attached to Air Division, Provisional, 17; inactivated on July 1, 1974.
- 43rd Strategic Wing activated at Andersen AFB, Guam on April 1, 1970 (assigned to 8th AF) and later attached to Air Division, Provisional, 57 while that unit was operational. Replaced 3960th Strategic Wing.
- 307th Strategic Wing activated at U-Tapao RTAFB, Thailand on April 1, 1970, assigned to 8th AF, and attached to Air Division Provisional 17.
- 376th Strategic Wing activated at Kadena AB, Okinawa on April 1, 1970. Replaced 4252nd Strategic Wing.
- 3960th Strategic Wing activated at Andersen AFB, Guam on April 1, 1955, assigned to 3rd Air Division. Changed to Air Base Wing and Combat Support Group. Inactivated on March 31, 1970, replaced by 43rd Strategic Wing.
- Bombardment Wing Provision 4133 activated at Andersen AFB, Guam on February 1, 1966. Transferred mission to 43rd Strategic Wing and inactivated on July 1, 1970.
- 4252nd Strategic Wing activated at Kadena AB, Okinawa on January 12, 1965, inactivated on April 1, 1970, replaced by 376th Strategic Wing.
- 4258th Strategic Wing activated at U-Tapao RTAFB, Thailand on June 2, 1966, redesignated to 307th Strategic Wing on April 1, 1970.

B-52H Weapons

NUCLEAR			18 MK 84(*) PRECISION
20 ALCM	51 CBU-71 (27# 18*)	8 Mk 55	18 JDAM (12*)
12 SRAM (*)	30 CBU 87 (6# 18*)	8 Mk 56	30 WCMD (16*)
12 ACM(*)	30 CBU 89 (6# 18*)	51 Mk 59	8 AGM-84 Harpoon
2 B-53 (#)	30 CBU 97 (6# 18*)	8 Mk 60 (CapTor)	20 AGM-86C CALCM
8 B-61 Mod11 (#)	51 M117	51 Mk. 62	8 AGM-142 Popeye(3*)
8 B-83 (#) CONVENTIONAL	18 Mk 20(*)	8 Mk. 64	18 AGM-154 JSOW (12*)
51 CBU-52 (27# 18*)	51 Mk 36	8 Mk 65	12 AGM-158 JASSSM(*)
51 CBU-58 (27# 18*)	8 Mk 41	51 MK 82	# = mounted internally; * = mounted externally
	12 Mk 52		

Operation Enduring Freedom sorties were flown from Diego Garcia on a regular basis. Tactics were developed which were specific to the theatre, although missions were more suited to fighter aircraft and unmanned aerial vehicles, rather than strategic bombers. This frequently involved B-52s loitering high above the battlefield to provide close air support to ground forces with precision guided weapons; some of these smart weapons having been slaved to targeting pods.

In late 2011 the Lockheed Martin AN/AAQ-33 Sniper advanced targeting pod (ATP) completed Phase II of trials to integrate it with the B-52.

Major Chris Chandler, Operations Flight Commander with the 49th Test and Evaluation Squadron at Barksdale AFB, Louisiana, said: "The picture quality was just unreal. In multi-target track, the track boxes stayed exactly where I placed them. The range from which I could identify targets was equally impressive."

In August 2011, the USAF awarded Lockheed Martin a Phase 3 Sniper ATP B-52 integration contract; Phase 3 will include full integration of the Sniper ATP on the B-52 with a new multi-function colour display and digital-integrated hand controller.

An alarming series of errors involving nuclear weapons led to changes in the control of the USAF's nuclear weapons. One incident involved six AGM-129 ALCMs armed with nuclear warheads being transported in error from Minot AFB to Barksdale AFB in August 2007. The warheads should have been removed before the flight, but were left in place. This prompted the USAF to create a new Command to oversee its nuclear weapons. B-2A and B-52H nuclear bombers of Air Combat Command, along with the Intercontinental Ballistic Missiles of Air Force Space Command were transferred to a new entity, Air Force Global Strike Command, formed at Barksdale AFB on August 7, 2009. AFGSC reorganised its B-52H assets, with two squadrons assigned to the 2nd BW instead of three, while the 5th BW increased from one squadron to two. Furthermore, the aircrew training role was transferred from the active duty to the reserves. The eight B-52s of the Air Force Reserve Command 917th Wing were transferred to the 307th Bomb Wing at Barksdale AFB when the latter was activated on January 8, 2011, increasing the compliment to 16 aircraft divided between two squadrons, both with a primary training role, but with a secondary combat mission.

The B-52H fleet has been established at 75; nine have been lost in accidents and 14 are in store with the 309th AMARG at Davis-Monthan AFB. Two others are used as instructional airframes and two are used for test-flying at Edwards AFB. One aircraft 61-0025, was painted in a civilian style colour scheme and modified with a purpose-built pylon to house aerospace test craft with NASA. However, a lack of funding for NASA research projects forced the B-52 to be withdrawn from use and flown to Sheppard AFB, Texas on May 9, 2008, for use as a maintenance trainer with the 82nd Training Wing. The requirement to support air launched vehicles has been transferred to the 412th Test Wing at Edwards AFB, California. The latest tests have involved the Boeing X-51 Waverider unmanned scramjet, designed for Mach 6 flight. The Waverider made its first flight was on May 26, 2010, when the craft was launched from B-52H 60-0050. ★

Cruise missiles, bunker busters, smart bombs, dumb bombs, laser-guided bombs, cluster bombs, naval mines, anti-shipping missiles, JDAM, JSOW or even nuclear weapons. Where do you want it dropped? USAF

Above: *One of the three North American X-15s, which at the time of writing still holds the record for being the fastest manned rocket-powered aircraft, is buzzed by its launch aircraft, NB-52A 52-0003, as it rests on Rogers Dry Lake Bed, California, in 1961.* NASA photo

B-52 Test Aircraft

Greg Spahr gives a brief rundown of the various test duties that have been performed by Buffs for more than half a century, work that is far from complete.

THROUGHOUT THE world, everybody knows the B-52 as a deadly bomber, but the icon has also been involved in many test programmes, some of which were aimed at improving the B-52 fleet, while others utilised the B-52 for its large size, stability, multi-engine configuration and performance characteristics, all of which made the aircraft a natural high-altitude-launch platform, drop vehicle, and jet engine test bed.

Proving and Improving the Stratofortress

The first 15 B-52 aircraft produced, including the XB-52, YB-52, the three B-52As, and the ten pre-production B-52Bs (52-0004 thru 52-0013), were all assigned

Above: *General Electric Company leased B-52E 57-0119 to test the CF6 and TF-39 engines flying from a facility at Edwards AFB in the 1960s and 1970s. The derelict hulk of the bomber still lingers on Rogers Dry Lake Bed.* USAF

immediate specific test duties to verify the characteristics and capabilities of the B-52. Notable among these were the MD-5 Fire Control System testing by B-52B 52-0009, the reconnaissance pod testing accomplished by 52-0010, and the IBM navigation system

testing performed by 52-0008.

After these initial representatives of the B-52, many more of the type were used in the continuing quest to constantly improve the aircraft.

B-52G 58-0182 tested Electronic Countermeasures Systems, and

B-52F 57-0038 trialled miscellaneous systems for the B-52G and H. Some B-52s were statically tested after their service lives had ended to assess the state of the airframe or to prove the functionality of new electronic equipment and to confirm its integration with existing systems. B-52Ds 55-0112 and 56-0616 were tested to destruction by being subjected to tremendous stresses and strains in special testing rigs at Boeing Wichita, and B-52G 59-2574, installed at the USAF's Stockbridge research facility after being damaged during landing in 1972 to determine the radar cross section of the aircraft and investigate ways to reduce it. In other tests, both the YB-52 and B-52A 52-0001 were flown with the shortened vertical fin used on the B-52G and H.

Frequently the trials involved launching or firing things: B-52D 56-0595 worked on the Quail decoy system; B-52G 58-0182 perfected launch techniques for early versions of the air launched cruise missile (ALCM) and B-52G 58-0204 was a test-bed for the fly-off between ALCM and Tomahawk missiles, as well as for the Phase VI ECM systems which were eventually fitted to B-52Gs and Hs. A number of B-52G and H aircraft participated in Skybolt missile testing, and other

Above: *NASA test-bed NB-52B 52-0008 flew most of its career with the administration as 'NASA 008', and was involved in launching scores of aerial test vehicles. It has been preserved at the Air Force Flight Test Center Museum at Edwards AFB, California, since October 2005.* NASA

B-52s tested Electro-Magnetic Pulse hardening on the amazing wooden 'Trestle' at Kirtland AFB, New Mexico.

Engine Testing

Some B-52s had one or all of their engines replaced in programmes to identify better engines for the Buff, or sometimes to test advanced engines for other aircraft. In 1956, B-52A, 52-0001 had its engines replaced with prototypes of what eventually became the J-57-P43 adapted by the B-52F. These differed from the standard J-57 in having no fixed stator blades in the intakes, a 'bullet' fairing added to cover the accessories, and oil cooler inlets added to the lower front of the engine cowlings.

B-52C, 53-0399, took those changes and added a bulge on the lower left side of each engine nacelle that contained the alternator, and a small teardrop-shaped bulge on the upper left for alternator accessories. The intake for the alternator was on the lower left engine cowling piece. This configuration became the trademark of the B-52F.

B-52E, 56-0632, had its engines replaced with J-57-P43 engines housed in the more aerodynamic nacelles eventually employed on the B-52G. The new nacelles eliminated the small bulge on the upper cowling while the alternator bulge on the lower cowling was reduced in size, and the air inlet for the alternator was moved forward so that the opening was on the front cowling rather than on the lower nacelle where it had been previously.

B-52G, 57-6471, had its engines temporarily replaced by TF-33 turbofans to verify the new powerplant's characteristics for the B-52H.

Three different B-52 aircraft have been used for testing prototypes of large jet engines.

In 1957, the XB-52 had both of its outboard engine pods replaced by new ones containing a single afterburning J-75 engine. These were tested until early 1959 at Wright-Patterson AFB.

In 1966, the General Electric Company (GE) was developing large engines for the USAF's upcoming heavy cargo plane, which became the Lockheed C-5 Galaxy. When GE's XTF-39 engine was ready for flight testing, the

Above: *Pratt & Whitney leased this B-52E 56-0636 to trial some of its engines, including the JT9D turbofan used on the Boeing 747. The Buff was scrapped at AMARC in February 1994.* Greg Spahr collection

B-52 was chosen. At this time, the B-52Es were being retired, so the logical course of action was for GE to lease one of these from the air force. The B-52 selected was 57-0119. The B-52E had its right inboard engine pod replaced by a single TF-39 engine. From June 1967 to August 1969, the B-52E carried the TF-39 aloft for a total of 255 hours. This jet later carried GE's CF-6-6 and CF-6-50 engines for a total of 171 hours between March 1970 and April 1972.

While GE was using the B-52 for the C-5's turbofans, Pratt & Whitney was developing engines for another aircraft, the Boeing 747. On December 7, 1967, the latter company leased B-52E 56-0636. This aircraft was configured in a similar way to 57-0119, with Pratt & Whitney's JT-9D engine replacing the inboard pair of J-57s on the starboard wing. It first flew in this configuration in July 1968, and over the next

several years this aircraft was used to test several types of JT-9D engines. This aircraft also trialled an advanced version of the JT-8D-200 engine proposed for McDonnell Douglas' YC-15, which never went into production.

Motherships

The B-52's most enduring testing legacy is an air-launch vehicle and air-drop test-bed. For decades, B-52 test aircraft have been carrying payloads to various altitudes and dropping or launching them, furthering the development of many aviation innovations, both military and civilian. The most famous B-52 motherships are the NB-52A (52-0003) and NB-52B (52-0008), which have been serving the USAF and NASA since 1969, launching manned aircraft such as the X-15, M2-F2, M2-F3, HL-10, X-24A and X-24B. These two aircraft have also launched or dropped many other test articles

such as the F-111 escape capsule, scale space shuttle boosters, Pegasus launch vehicles, scale F-15 spin test vehicle, Highly Manoeuvrable Aircraft Technology demonstrator, Firebee Drone for Aeroelastic Structures Testing, X-43 unpiloted Hypersonic Research Vehicle, and the X-38 scale experimental crew return vehicle. They have also tested the Space Shuttle drag-chute and pollution-reducing fuel additives in additional engines mounted on the fuselage.

Lesser-known B-52 mothership duties included B-1A escape capsule drop testing, which used B-52C 53-0399 and B-52G 58-0182, as well as drop tests of the US Army's Fairchild AN/USD-5 drone, which were conducted in 1960 by the 4925th Test Group (Atomic.)

Special Weapons Testing

B-52B 52-0004, B-52B 52-0013, B-52D 56-0591, B-52D 56-0620, B-52F 57-0168 and B-52F 57-0183 were utilised by Boeing, the 4925th Test Group and the Air Force Special Weapons Center in the testing of nuclear weapons and their effects. In the 1960s, these aircraft dropped live nuclear weapons, flew in the vicinity of nuclear tests to gather data, and dropped dummy nuclear devices.

Because of its size and robust construction it is an ideal platform for testing new engines. The Buff can fly quite happily on six of its eight engines and still lift a heavy load, so there is relatively little risk in removing one two-engine pod and replacing it with a single new engine. The powerplants for the revolutionary Jumbo Jets of the 1970s were all tested on Buffs.

Not a VSTOL Buff, but an unusual attitude nonetheless. This 'G' model was towed on to the so-called 'Kirtland Trestle' at Kirtland AFB, New Mexico, for electromagnetic pulse testing. The trestle is constructed entirely of wood and plastic so no metal parts affect test results. When viewed on the testing apparatus, the bomber appears to be suspended in the air, with no sign of the supporting trestle. Greg Spahr collection

Right: The cancellation of the Skybolt stand-off air-launched ballistic missile intended for use by both the B-52 and Britain's V-bomber force caused a serious political rift between the two nations. USAF
Below: Two Skybolts mounted on the wing of their B-52. USAF

Might have beens

Greg Spahr describes proposals for developments to the B-52 that didn't reach fruition.

HAVING BEEN in service for well over 50 years (and with perhaps as long to go!) it is not surprising that there have been a raft of proposals to improve the aircraft and its systems or to fit equipment to make the Buff suitable for different roles. While many have been adopted, others, mostly for cost reasons, have not. To the B-52's credit, the aircraft was never the reason why changes were not adopted.

Skybolt

The Douglas GAM-87 Skybolt was an air-launched ballistic missile with a solid-fuel rocket motor, designed for use on the B-52 and Avro Vulcan strategic bombers. The United States Air Force (USAF) conducted the Skybolt programme from 1959, and the UK joined in 1960. Several B-52G and B-52H aircraft took part in flight tests of the Skybolt. Although trials were progressing reasonably well, with successful flight tests finally

in December, 1962, Skybolt was cancelled by US President John F Kennedy – three days after the first successful test flight; Britain got the Polaris missile in compensation.

TACIT Rainbow

The Northrop TACIT Rainbow was a 1980s programme to produce an anti-radiation missile with a loiter capability. Designated AGM-136, the missile was able to fly a pre-programmed route over an area, and once a hostile radar emission was detected, fly to the radar site and destroy it. Unlike other anti-radiation missiles, the AGM-136 could resume loitering if the target radar stopped transmitting, so that it could engage another target when it became visible to the missile. The B-52 was to be one of the launch vehicles for the AGM-136, and Buffs served as test aircraft during the development of the weapon. It was cancelled in 1991 for cost reasons.

X-20

The Boeing X-20 Dyna-Soar ('Dynamic Soarer') was an aborted USAF programme to produce a reusable spaceplane that could perform various missions. Some versions of the X-20 were to be launched from a B-52 in a similar fashion to other manned B-52 payloads, such as the X-15 and the Lifting Bodies. The X-20 was similar in planform to the lifting bodies, and would have landed on retractable skids after skipping off the upper atmosphere to decelerate. B-52C 53-0399 was assigned to the programme, but the project was terminated in 1963 before any hardware had been completed, and the B-52C was assigned to other test duties, eventually performing air-drops of the B-1A escape capsule.

Electronically Agile Radar

Toward the end of the 1970s the USAF investigated improving the

B-52's radar systems. In 1979 the Westinghouse Electronically Agile Radar (EAR) was fitted to B-52G 59-2568. EAR is a phased array system with no moving antenna parts, containing instead a honeycomb matrix of phase-shifters. The testing was sponsored by the Air Force Avionics Laboratory. Although it was decided not to retrofit the B-52 fleet with this equipment, the EAR evolved into the AN/APQ-164 system and was subsequently employed in the B-1B aircraft.

EB-52

A 2002 USAF study indicated a need for an electronic attack architecture to provide comprehensive electronic countermeasures capabilities. As then envisioned, the B-52 would be central to the architecture, with the Boeing EA-18G Growler and Raytheon's miniature air-launched decoy-jammer (MALD-J) occupying lesser roles. This was cancelled in 2005 due to cost overruns. The

USAF again showed interest in the system in 2007, with Boeing and Northrop Grumman teaming up to provide the hardware, but again the USAF cancelled the programme within two years. The so-called EB-52 that would have resulted from these studies and proposals would have been fitted with advanced ECM equipment. It would possibly have utilised the currently empty crew station, formerly used by the tail-gunner, to house an additional electronic warfare officer.

Re-engine

As B-52 production continued throughout the late 1950s and early 1960s, the B-52 naturally took advantage of the latest jet engine advancements. The turbojet-powered models of the B-52 evolved with various versions of the J-57. Successive aircraft used the latest water or water-alcohol injection for advanced thrust, exotic engine materials such as titanium, reconfigured intakes and accessories and engine-mounted alternators. The final B-52H

model employed the most modern turbofan engines available at the time. It is no surprise that proposals to re-engine the B-52 with advanced powerplants arose once B-52 production was complete. The USAF has undertaken major engine replacement programmes for other jet aircraft such as the U-2 and KC-135. Some aircraft of the KC-135 series are on their third set of engines, after having their original J-57 engines replaced with TF-33 turbofans, only to have CFM-56 turbofans fitted years later. With the Buff likely to be in service for perhaps another half century, its probable the new engines will be fitted in the future, especially as the cost of fuel continues to rise.

A number of B-52 re-engining proposals have appeared over the years, but none have come to fruition: In 1975 the USAF Joint Bomber Study proposed re-engining the B-52 with four unspecified engines, to be designated B-52I.

In 1981 engine maker Pratt & Whitney proposed refitting the B-52G fleet with its PW2037

engine, then under development for the Boeing 757 airliner.

In 1987 Boeing proposed mounting either PW2037 or Rolls Royce 535E4 engines on the Stratofortress.

In 1996 Boeing made an unsolicited proposal to re-engine the B-52 with four Rolls Royce RB211 engines.

In 2003 Boeing was asked by the USAF to prepare studies including both four-engine and eight-engine configurations with advanced powerplants.

Glass Cockpit

Another Boeing proposal in the mid-1990s that was not accepted was conversion of the B-52 pilots' instrument panel to 'glass cockpit' configuration. This would have replaced the antiquated 'steam gauges' and monochrome radar displays with modern, computerised multi-function displays containing full-colour display screens.

Paint Schemes

Weapons systems, avionics,

and engines were not the only features tested on the B-52 that were not adapted by the fleet. A number of B-52 aircraft tested experimental camouflage schemes, which were never adapted.

In 1965, a trio of B-52 aircraft undertook trials of new camouflage schemes. Two aircraft were painted in different schemes, and the third was left in its natural metal and white for trial control purposes. One of these aircraft, B-52G 57-6480, was painted in a three-tone green scheme, with the gloss white belly of the typical B-52 left unaltered. Another B-52G was similarly painted, but the entire lower surface of the aircraft and the vertical fin were painted gloss black. The black-bellied camouflage was eventually applied to all B-52D aircraft, while the three-tone green and white scheme adorned many B-52C, B-52E, and B-52F aircraft, as well as all B-52Gs and B-52Hs, although the pattern was quite different from the initial test aircraft.

A final experimental scheme (not adapted by the fleet) was a wrap-around scheme applied to a single B-52G in the late 1960's, using the same three shades of green as the aforementioned schemes, with the pattern including all undersurfaces other than the bottom of the nose radome. Crews named this pattern 'Potato-Bug,' after a well-known American insect.

Above: *A number of modern, more fuel efficient powerplants have been proposed for the B-52 including the Rolls-Royce RB211, but the US Government Accountability Office decreed that the change would cost too much.* Boeing

SUBSCRIBE &SAVE

TO YOUR FAVOURITE AVIATION MAGAZINE

Over the years, **AIR INTERNATIONAL** has established an unrivalled reputation for authoritative reporting and coverage across the full spectrum of aviation subjects. With more pages than ever, all still dedicated to commercial and military aviation, we have more correspondents and top aviation writers from around the world, offering even more exciting news, features and stunning photography.

www.airinternational.com

As the UK's best selling military history title, **BRITAIN AT WAR** is dedicated in exploring every aspect of Britain's involvement in conflicts from the turn of the century through to modern day. From World War I to the Falklands, World War II to Iraq, readers are able to relive decisive moments in Britain's history through facinating insight combined with rare and previously unseen photography.

www.britain-at-war.com

As Britain's longest established monthly aviation journal, **AVIATION NEWS** is renowned for providing the best coverage on every branch of aviation - such as historic warbirds, military aircraft and airliners. The magazine is known throughout the world for its varied, easy-to-read features. Now with a fresh new look and the very best photography, plus all-new sections to help you get the most out of your hobby. *Aviation News* brings you the past, present and future of flight.

www.aviation-news.co.uk

FLYPAST is internationally regarded as *the* magazine for aviation history and heritage. *FlyPast* pioneered the reporting of 'living aviation history' and still leads the field today. Each issue is packed with news and features on warbird preservation and restoration, museums, and the airshow scene. Subjects regularly profiled include British and American aircraft type histories, as well as those of squadrons and units from World War One to the Cold War.

www.flypast.com

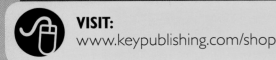

B-52 – the Ultimate Cold War Warrior

THE B-52 served in different key roles throughout the Cold War. When the bomber entered service it assumed a deterrent role, and was deployed in eleven wings, each consisting of three squadrons of 15 aircraft. This changed as international tensions started to rise and the

threat from Soviet ICBMs grew. The B-52s were dispersed and assigned to smaller strategic air wings to reduce the risk of their being destroyed on the ground in one strike. But top USAF officials considered even this as inadequate protection and proposed a number of solutions aimed

at getting the aircraft airborne as quickly as possible. There were several challenges, both from an engineering perspective and for personnel. One technical problem was the timing delay in having to start all eight engines independently; this was overcome by fitting cartridge-

From its initial design stage, the B-52 was intended to be the third component of the United States' triad of nuclear weapons delivery systems, complementing the USAF's and US Navy's intercontinental ballistic missiles (ICBMs) and submarine-launched ballistic missiles (SLBMs). Such was the three-pronged threat aimed at the Soviet Union during the dark days of the Cold War – a period lasting nearly 50 years – that, as **Derek Bower** tells us, the planet teetered on the edge of total annihilation

Below: *In this pre-1962 image crews scramble to their B-52E armed with Hound Dog stand-off missiles at a base 'somewhere in the United States'.* USAF

Bottom: *This 1958 shot of the ramp at Westover AFB Massachusetts, home at the time to the 346th and 348th Bombardment Squadrons, part of the 99th Bombardment Wing (Heavy), shows some significant machines. Nearest the camera are two 'B' models, and beyond them is one of the first 'D's, 55-0067, which is today preserved at the Pima Air Museum, Tucson, Arizona. After that is the first 'C' model to fly, 53-0400; she was eventually scrapped across the road from Pima at Davis-Monthan.* Key collection

starters to the engines, allowing all to be started simultaneously. Another timing challenge was that of crews on standby in squadron buildings and offices having to travel considerable distances across the airfield to their waiting aircraft. This was solved by moving them into accommodation close to their allocated bombers – reducing alert-to-take-off time to below the stipulated 15 minutes' readiness state.

Even these extra measures were deemed inadequate and further steps to ensure that the US could mount a secondary strike were taken. When it was first introduced into service, the fledgling Ballistic Missile Early

Warning System (BMEWS) could only give around four minutes' warning of incoming Soviet missiles. Consequently, senior USAF officers raised concerns that, even if a take-off time of less than 15 minutes could be achieved, holding the B-52s on any sort of ground readiness alert would present an easy target in a first-strike attack by the Soviets.

The SAC (Strategic Air Command) chief at the time, General Thomas S Power, thought the solution would be to have a number of B-52s airborne 24 hours a day, reducing the risk of losing all the bombers in coordinated multiple strikes. Having persuaded the USAF ▶

Above: *The American public gets the chance to inspect a B-52F and a Hound Dog thermonuclear stand-off missile at an air force open day in the 1960s.* Greg Spahr collection
Right: *Very early RB-52B, 52-8715, in all over natural metal and wearing the SAC band around the rear fuselage rather than the nose, as was the case later.* USAF
Top: *B-52E 56-0635 takes on fuel from short-tailed KC-135A 57-1467 that is also adorned with the SAC sash. Both aircraft ended up being scrapped at D-M.*

AMERICA'S RADAR EARLY WARNING SYSTEMS

After World War Two, and with the beginning of the Cold War, the US and Canada developed a layered radar-based early warning system against attack by Soviet aircraft. Along the Pacific and Atlantic seaboards the main defence was a picket line of radar-equipped ships augmented by aircraft such as the Lockheed WV-2 (later EC-121K) Warning Star. To cover the gap between the two coasts, three chains of radar stations were built. The most northerly was the DEW line (Distant Early Warning) which comprised a series of radar stations mostly within the Arctic Circle along the 69th parallel – from the Aleutian Islands, across the northern Alaskan mainland and northern and central Canada and as far east as Iceland. The intention was that the radar

stations would detect hostile aircraft approaching the US and Canada over the North Pole.

Two other lines of radars preceded the DEW line – the so-called Mid-Canada Line or McGill Fence which, as the name suggests, ran across the middle of Canada from coast to coast, was built to augment the first of the three systems (code-named the Pine Tree Line) which ran across the North American continent roughly following the 50th parallel. Such was the pace of development in radar and aircraft technology that these chains of radar stations rapidly became outdated, and within a short time only the DEW line would have been able to provide any useful warning.

In 1960 the Russians fielded their first ICBMs armed with

nuclear warheads. These crude missiles were not detectable by the DEW line so a means to track them was urgently sought. The chosen solution was called the Ballistic Missile Early Warning System (BMEWS) and comprised three radar stations located at Fylingdales in the UK, Clear Air Force Station, Alaska, and Thule Air Base, Greenland. The skyward-pointing radar dishes generated a blanket of cover over the North Pole and were designed to detect ICBMs launched towards North America from the USSR. The stations were linked via NORAD to SAC so that in the event of a pre-emptive missile strike by the Russians, the US could retaliate using nuclear weapons delivered by its fleet of bombers.

hierarchy of the soundness of his proposal, before he could order his bombers to begin flying continuously, he had the much harder task of 'selling' his idea – particularly the carriage of nuclear weapons – to the US Government and the American people. This he did on the grounds that, should the US suffer a first-strike attack destroying the B-52 fleet on the ground, at least a small number of aircraft would be airborne and able to provide a retaliatory strike. This so-called 'second strike' capability – ensuring that a Soviet attack would result in the devastation of the USSR – was a facet of US Secretary of Defense Robert McNamara's 'mutually assured destruction' (MAD) doctrine on which much of the arms race of the Cold War was predicated. Eventually, after intense campaigning by General Powers, President Eisenhower granted permission for the flights, subject to several conditions. These included gaining permission from the Canadian authorities for necessary over-flights of Canadian territory; no more than 12 aircraft airborne at a time; no flights directly towards the Soviet Union or the People's Republic of China; and no exercises carrying live nuclear bombs.

Chrome Dome, Head Start and other code-words

Once the missions were authorised, in keeping with US tradition for military operations and equipment, they were given code-names made up of two words. Some of these were officially released into the public domain while others

Above: *Britain, France and America had an independent nuclear strike capability in the 1960s and Buffs like this one were occasional visitors to the UK. B-52F 57-0039 of Castle AFB's 93rd BW is seen at RAF Marham in April 1967.* Bob Archer collection
Below: *The advent of another immensely important Boeing product, the KC-135 Stratotanker, greatly improved the efficiency, range and potency of SAC.* Rockwell Collins

airborne deterrent patrols were that, should communications with NORAD (North American Air Defense Command; responsible for monitoring information from BMEWS and passing orders to SAC) be lost, they should assume that the system had been destroyed in an attack and immediately launch their pre-briefed secondary strike on the Soviet Union. This clearly unacceptable situation was overcome in 1961 by operations like Hard Head, in which a B-52 orbited within visual range of the BMEWS at Thule, on the Danish territory of Greenland, 24 hours a day to determine whether a communications failure was a result of a nuclear strike or just a burnt-out fuse.

Head Start was chosen as the name for the first of a series of missions, flown for more than ten years, that involved nuclear-armed B-52s patrolling ▶

were kept secret and have come to light since, either through security breaches or by being taken off the 'classified' list. It can only be guessed if any are still classified. Some of the more well-known code-names for Cold War missions involving the B-52 include Chrome Dome, Hard Head, Giant Lance, Round Robin, Butterknife V and Head Start. These all related to a specific period of operations and were all allocated to a particular mission or series of missions. Whatever the code-word, they all had one thing in common: to put the Soviet Union on notice that if a response to a first strike from the Russians was necessary, then the USAF had the capability to provide it.

At the time the missions began, the communications chain between the BMEWS and SAC was not as good as it would eventually become and, especially in its early days, the failure rate was high. These reliability issues could lead to extremely dangerous situations; such a communications failure might mean that SAC commanders would have no way of knowing if it was merely a glitch in the system – or an indication that the BMEWS had been destroyed in the feared first strike. Terrifyingly, in those early days, standing orders to those aircraft engaged on

Above: *This line-up of B-52s at March AFB California, includes one aircraft in the so-called SIOP (Single Integrated Operational Plan) camouflage scheme; this suggests that the photo was taken after the start of the Vietnam War.* USAF
Below: *A pair of B-52Es in the mid-1960s. The jet nearest to the camera, 56-0703, bears the name 'The Untouchables'.* Greg Spahr collection

Above: *A B-52C returns to base from another Chrome Dome mission.* Greg Spahr collection

Above: *Caught on camera in a more peaceful era, B-52D 55-0061 became the 77th Buff to be lost when she was shot down during Linebacker II – at the time she would have been painted in the more familiar Vietnam-style colours.* Greg Spahr collection
Below: *Having recently been delivered, B-52D 55-0070 is seen seconds after touch-down as its drogue-chute starts to deploy.* Greg Spahr collection

Above: *With the rapid improvement of Soviet defences, especially SAMs, Stratofortress crews had to learn how to operate their huge bombers at very low-level – not something Buffs were designed for.* Key collection

DELIVERING THE PAYLOAD

The main nuclear weapon carried by the B-52 in the Cold War was the Mk 28 thermonuclear device; on an alert mission B-52s usually carried four of them. In production from 1958 through to 1966, the 8ft-long bomb was produced in at least 20 versions. It was designed to be delivered in a number ways, including free-fall and parachute-retarded, and could be fused to explode in the air or when in contact with the ground. Yields varied from 350 kilotons up to 1.45 megatons. At the beginning of the Cold War, planning assumed that bombers would fly over their targets at high speed and drop their bombs from altitude. A huge number of targets– more than 5,500 – were marked for destruction by nuclear weapons in the mid-1950s and the numbers only increased as time went on. Tactics changed in 1960 after the shooting-down of CIA pilot Francis Gary Powers near Moscow on May 1, whose U-2 had been flying very high – much higher that a B-52 could manage – but it was still shot down. Henceforth the B-52s were to go in very low in an attempt to evade detection by radar; and also to give Soviet air defences less time to bring their weapons to bear.

the skies near to Soviet territory, ready to provide the secondary-strike response to a nuclear attack. The series, which ran for three months from September 15 to December 15, 1958, involved B-52s from SAC's 45th Air Division maintaining a constant presence on a 'round robin' track, with the aid of air-to-air refuelling, from its base at Loring AFB, Maine, out to Greenland and back via Canadian airspace. The B-52s were required to monitor certain channels on their high-frequency single sideband (HF-SSB) radios for pre-programmed 'Foxtrot' messages – a stream of letters and figures, unintelligible to anyone without the corresponding code pad, prefixed by the words 'Skyking, Skyking, do not answer...' No answer was required because it might give away the bomber's position; it should be remem-

bered that this was in the early 1960s when keeping track of aircraft that wanted their position known was hard enough – it was much easier to hide then, and radio silence was a very

effective way of doing so. The message that no-one wanted to hear was one that included the phrase 'no test'; that would have been the signal for the bombers to fly their attack profile and

launch nuclear Armageddon.

Head Start was notable for another reason: the bombs used were of a new 'sealed-pit' type. These had their trigger mechanisms built-in, as

Above: *This early 'G' model, seen as her crew races towards her on yet another alert, carries a late-model Hound Dog missile camouflaged to match the jet. The last Hound Dog was retired in June 1975 and as we know, none was ever fired in anger – it was strictly a nuclear weapon.* USAF

opposed to earlier munitions which had required fuses to be physically inserted. Even though these new weapons had safety features to stop accidental nuclear detonation in the event of a crash, the US Atomic Energy Commissioner, John McCone, insisted that the Head Start trial mission be launched from Loring AFB, in the north-east coastal state of Maine, to minimise the risk of contamination through such a disaster. Even so, it was not until October 1958 that President Eisenhower authorised functioning weapons to be carried on Head Start. Reaction to the exercise was mixed, but it did demonstrate that the objective of keeping airborne alert could be achieved.

Another long-running programme was Operation Chrome Dome (from 1959 to 1968). Flying 24-hour missions – and carrying one bomb rack containing four live weapons with the other empty or loaded with dumb weapons – crews would operate on one of four sortie profiles. One involved flying the so-called northern

Above: *One of the later DEW line stations to be established, LIZ-2 was deactivated in 1994.* USAF
Below: *Period map showing the three early warning lines, Pinetree, Mid-Canada and the original and northernmost, DEW. The map indicates that those land-based stations were augmented by radar-equipped patrol aircraft, ships and permanent fixed-point sea-borne radars.* USAF

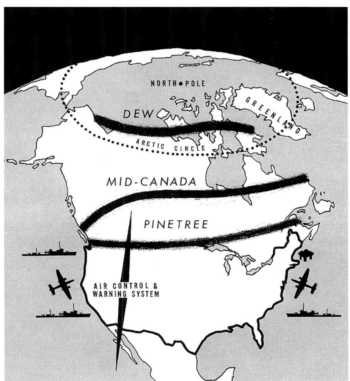

sector, which was effectively a large box-pattern flown around Canada. The second, western sector involved flying north to Alaska while the southern sector was flown from CONUS (the Continental United States) down over the Atlantic and along the Mediterranean. All three sorties profiles relied heavily on air-to-air refuelling tankers. A fourth, the 'monitor' sector, involved B-52s flying within visual range of the BMEWS site at Thule as described earlier.

Nuclear disaster

The dangers inherent in flying such mission profiles were obvious and unfortunately (but, perhaps, predictably given the number of sorties and miles flown in what today seem unsophisticated aircraft) a number of B-52s carrying live weapons were involved in crashes. Unsurprisingly, these attracted a lot of attention and caused extreme embarrassment to the US Government.

One of the most high-profile events became known as the Palomares incident. This oc-curred on January 17, 1966 and involved 68th Bomb Wing B-52G serial number 58-0256, call-sign 'Tea 16', which was flying from Seymour Johnson AFB, North Carolina, on a southern sector Chrome Dome mission. During an air-to-air refuelling bracket over the Mediterranean, the B-52 collided with the refuelling boom of its KC-135A tanker, serial 61-0273, resulting in a massive fuel leak. Shortly after this the tanker exploded, killing its four-man crew. The B-52 suffered massive structural failure and, after its left wing broke away from the fuselage, it crashed close to the village of Palomares on the southern coast of Spain. Four of its seven crew survived. As the wreckage fell to the ground four Mk 28R1 nuclear weapons separated from the aircraft; three fell near the main wreckage but the fourth went into the sea. Even though they did not detonate, a 490-acre (2km²) area was contaminated with plutonium from the bombs that hit the ground. Meanwhile, an enormous recovery effort was launched to find the fourth weapon. More than 20 US surface vessels and submersi- ▶

Above: *Early in their careers B-52Gs, like 58-0190 seen here, wore the nuclear strike white and silver grey colours. This aircraft caught fire at Kelly AFB, Texas in 1989 and was destroyed.* Greg Spahr collection
Below: *Newly delivered B-52G 57-6498 displayed next to its forerunner, a B-47.* Greg Spahr collection

00051

U.S. AIR FORCE

bles were used in the search and the bomb was located on April 2, 1967 at a depth of 2,900ft (880m). It was eventually recovered intact. Unsurprisingly, perhaps, this incident signalled the end of the southern sector mission.

Just two years later, on January 21, 1968, another nuclear-armed Buff engaged on a Chrome Dome flight crashed – with almost disastrous results. The 'Thule Incident', as it came to be known, occurred when, following an airborne fire, a 380th Strategic Aerospace Wing B-52G, serial number 58-0188, flying out of Plattsburgh AFB, New York, and flown by a crew from the 528th Bombardment Squadron, crashed just five miles from the USAF airfield in Thule on the western tip of Greenland, killing one of the crew members. The aircraft was carrying four B28FI (fused internally) one-megaton hydrogen bombs and rescue services were exposed to significant levels of radiation – conventional explosives, used to act as a catalyst for the nuclear chain reaction, had detonated and scattered fissionable material far and wide. Denmark had not been formally notified that US aircraft armed with nuclear weapons were using the base, and this added to the ensuing diplomatic maelstrom. By this time, the introduction of submarine-launched ICBMs had made the Chrome Dome mission far less important in terms of America's nuclear deterrent, but the US Air Force had successfully resisted efforts to have it terminated. Nevertheless, the number of daily B-52 missions flown had, in 1966, been reduced from 12 to four, one of which maintained the 'Hard Head' mission over Thule – and it was an aircraft performing this mission that crashed. Heat from the burning bomber's wreckage melted the ice on

Above: *B-52H 60-0051 flies today with the 93rd BS from Barksdale AFB. The refuelling receptacle above the cockpit of this Hound Dog-toting jet is open.* Key collection

Left: *Curtis Emerson LeMay, the father of SAC. Less reverentially he was known as 'Old Iron Pants' or 'Bombs Away LeMay', but his honours bear evidence of an illustrious career and include the Distinguished Service Cross, Army Distinguished Service Medal (three of those), the Silver Star, three Distinguished Flying Crosses, four Air Medals, Distinguished Flying Cross (UK), Légion d'honneur (France) and the Grand Cordon, Order of the Rising Sun, (Japan). His military career spanned 45 years, which sounds a long time, but is much shorter than the Buff's 59 years and counting!* USAF

CHROME DOME MISSIONS FIRST HALF OF 1967

Unit	Parent AF	Base	Daily Sorties	Route	Weapons
January 1 to February 14					
42nd BW	8th AF	Loring	1	Monitor	4 Mk28
70th BW	8th AF	Clinton-Sherman	1	West	2 Mk53
465th BW	8th AF	Robins	1	North	4 Mk28
450th BW	15th AF	Minot	1	Monitor	4 Mk28
15 February to March 31					
7th BW	2nd AF	Carswell	1	North	2 Mk53
410th BW	2nd AF	K I Sawyer	1	Monitor	4 Mk28
416th BW	8th AF	Griffiss	1	Monitor	4 Mk28
5th BW	15th AF	Travis	1	West	4 Mk28
April 1 to May 15					
96th SAW	2nd AF	Dyess	1	West	4 Mk28
319th BW	2nd AF	Grand Forks	1	Monitor	4 Mk28
449th BW	2nd AF	Kincheloe	1	Monitor	4 Mk28
17th BW	8th AF	Wright-Patterson	1	North	4 Mk28
May 16 to June 30					
2nd BW	2nd AF	Barksdale	1	North	4 Mk28
410th BW	2nd AF	K I Sawyer	1	Monitor	4 Mk28
380th SAW	8th AF	Plattsburgh	1	Monitor	4 Mk28
320th SAW	15th AF	Mather	1	West	4 Mk28

NORTHERN ROUTE: Aircraft on the Northern Route headed northeast out to Greenland before returning to base.
WESTERN ROUTE: Aircraft detailed to this patrol would go north to Alaska and then back to base.
MONITOR: A figure of eight flown in the vicinity of the BMEWS at Thule, Greenland.
SOUTHERN ROUTE: The bomber would pass through the Straits of Gibraltar before flying eastward across the Mediterranean before reversing coure and flying back the way from which it had come. This route was abandoned after the Palomares incident.

which it had crashed, and both the B-52 and the remains of the bombs plunged to the seabed. A massive operation to recover the weapons operated concurrently with an even larger US-Danish bid to clean up the site and repatriate all contaminated materials to the US. Despite those efforts, it seems certain that only three of the weapons were successfully recovered.

Many lessons were learned from the incident. It is possible that had the bomber crashed on Thule Air Base, and a nuclear blast had ensued, a full-scale attack on the Soviet Union would have been the result. Because of this and the Palomares incident, and another accident involving a B-52 carrying nuclear weapons near Seymour-Johnson AFB, the governments of Russia and the US established a protocol known as the 'Agreement on Measures to Reduce the Risk of Nuclear War' whereby the Washington-Moscow President-to-Premier hot-line would be used to advise of any nuclear incidents that might be misinterpreted. Another consequence was that US Secretary of Defense Robert McNamara immediately ordered the suspension of all Chrome Dome missions, and rules governing the carriage of nuclear weapons over foreign territories were rewritten.

This abrupt end saw all nuclear bombs removed from the B-52s within one day. The USAF was reluctant to terminate the airborne armed alert and replaced it with one whereby B-52s stood fully-armed on runway alert ready to be launched at very short notice. To prevent degradation in crew proficiency and readiness state the actual flight profiles of the armed bombers were still flown, but without the nuclear weapons.

Mad mission?

Giant Lance, another Cold War operation, is viewed by many as the most provocative, and potentially the most destructive, of all US B-52 missions. As the war in Vietnam dragged on, with mounting US losses provoking increasing opposition to the war among the American public, President Nixon and his national security adviser, Henry Kissinger, sought ways of bringing the war to a rapid end. They thought that by adopting a tactic evolved from an esoteric branch of mathematics called 'game theory', used to determine how people make choices, they might be able to convince Russia to persuade North Vietnam to end the war. At the time, many of even the most senior USAF officials were not fully, if at all, informed of the true nature of the plan which has since been dubbed the 'madman theory' by historians.

Giant Lance called for 18 nuclear-armed B-52s to be launched towards the Soviet Union with the intention of making the Soviets believe they were under attack. The aircraft duly departed on the morning of October 27, 1969 and headed for the USSR, where they continued to fly a race-track pattern outside Soviet airspace for 18 hours before returning to base. This continued for three days before Nixon ordered the missions to stop. The plan, which was coupled with intense diplomatic negotiations – included a meeting between Nixon and the Russian Ambassador to the US, during which the President used a strategy he had developed with national security adviser Henry Kissinger to try to convince the Communists that he was mad enough to risk nuclear war and it would be in their interests to do what he wanted. This obviously did not result in World War Three, nor did it persuade the Russians to intervene in Vietnam. But, according to several observers, it helped persuade the Soviets to

Above: *After the aborted Skybolt came the Short Range Attack Missile – up to 20 of these could be carried on each Buff, 12 on the wing pylons and eight internally.* USAF
Right: *This shiny 'H' model has a full load of four Skybolt missiles.* Key collection

negotiate with the US during the arms control discussions of the early 1970s.

The Cold War continued at various levels of intensity, most dangerously in 1983 when Able Archer 83, a NATO exercise in Europe designed to test new command, control and communications procedures, was misconstrued by Soviet military intelligence as camouflage for a build-up to a NATO invasion of the Warsaw Pact countries. The Soviets put their nuclear forces on a high state of alert and increased the state of readiness of air forces in Poland and East Germany. The end of the exercise led to a reduction in tension. ✪

Left: *Fifth BW B-52H 61-0023 inscribed TEAM MINOT at Barksdale AFB during a visit by a pair of Tu-95s and supporting An-124 on April 30, 1992. This scene would have been inconceivable just three years earlier!* Bob Archer
Below: *The cold war.* USAF

A working dog and its handler appear unmoved as yet another B-52D launches into the gathering gloom of the Pacific night. USAF

DURING AND immediately after the Southeast Asia War, the role of Boeing's B-52 Stratofortress was the subject of much debate. Anti-war activists singled out the heavy bombing of suspected, but often already vacated, Viet Cong and People's Army of North Vietnam (PAVN) jungle hideouts for particular criticism while others regarded the employment of the B-52s as wasteful and ineffective – a case of using a sledgehammer to crack a nut.

On the other hand, hard-pressed US Marines at Khe Sanh were eternally grateful that the four-month siege of their garrison by a PAVN force estimated as being three divisions-strong was ended by heavy B-52 bombing

Above: *B-52F 57-0144 just after going 'feet dry' en route to a target in South Viet-*

(800m) from their position – in Operation Niagara, a Seventh Air Force close air support campaign carried out between January and March 1968. POWs, whose freedom was regained after B-52 operations during Linebacker II that finally hastened the conclusion of peace negotiations, were also inclined to praise Strategic Air Command's (SAC) aircrews.

B-52s were involved from the outset when overt US military ac-

From Nuclear to Mudmover

Key Publishing's **Glenn Sands** looks at the role played by the B-52s of Strategic Air Command during the air war over Vietnam

Above: *A 750lb general purpose bomb, one of scores dropped from each B-52G, seen mounted inside the aircraft.* Paul Minert via Greg Spahr

with Operation Flaming Arrow on February 7, 1965. Four days later the Joint Chiefs of Staff (JCS) decided to up the ante with further 'gunboat diplomacy' by positioning a sample of SAC's 'big stick' at Andersen Air Force Base, Guam.

On February 9, 15 aircraft from the 20th Bomb Squadron, 2nd Bomb Wing, flew to Kadena AFB, Okinawa, Japan, and the 441st Bomb Squadron, 320th Bomb Wing dispatched another 15 to Andersen AFB. The Stratofortresses involved were B-52Fs – 28 of which, in 1964, had been modified to carry conventional bombs under the 'South Bay' modification programme.

The arrival of the B-52s in theatre did little to deter the Hanoi Government. At the time, US

policy ruled out the use of the B-52s for punitive strategic attacks on the then lightly defended North Vietnamese heartland. This was partly because of the likely hostile reaction from the USSR and China, but also took into consideration the US public's probable reaction to a military response that would have seemed grossly disproportionate: Vietnam was seen as little more than a sideshow for many American citizens and politicians. So Washington sought a more covert range of alternatives to stop the North Vietnamese.

Nevertheless, contingency plans were drawn up. In 1964 the JCS, together with Defense Secretary Robert McNamara, announced that their plan "embodied the

essence of American strategic bombing doctrine: air force planners designed it to destroy North Vietnam's ability to wage modern war" – after which it was assumed that "Hanoi would have to stop its aggression". The US plan was to hit 94 strategic targets in North Vietnam, the B-52F being

pencilled-in for those attacks. Ironically, seven years later, these same targets were still on the planners' list when Linebacker B-52 strikes commenced.

President Johnson was not prepared to give his military full rein, however. He maintained direct control of each raid and

Above: **B-52G 57-6484 receives attention on Guam in 1972.** Paul Minert via Greg Spahr
Below: **B-52F 57-0175 resplendent in its nuclear colour scheme and completed with SAC Star-Spangled Banner around the nose, is prepared for another mission from Guam in 1965.** David W Menard

> ## "WE COULD HAVE ENDED [THE WAR] IN ANY TEN-DAY PERIOD YOU WANTED TO, BUT THEY NEVER WOULD BOMB THE TARGET LIST WE HAD"

preferred a graduated increase of military force, hoping to avoid recriminations for using disproportionate force. Predictably this tactic found little favour amongst the military and General LeMay remarked: "We could have ended [the war] in any ten-day period you wanted to, but they never would bomb the target list we had."

The bombing of North Vietnam began in earnest on March 2, 1965 with the first Rolling Thunder strike. The task was handed to tactical fighter units to avoid the political consequences

of an overtly 'strategic' assault. But within weeks the distinction between 'strategic' and 'tactical' became blurred - single-seat fighters found themselves striking targets in the heart of North Vietnam; meanwhile, the 'strategic' B-52s took on a tactical role in support of US and South Vietnamese ground forces, their sorties unhindered by the monsoon conditions that grounded many fighter jets based closer to the fighting.

By bringing the B-52s' enormous firepower directly to the battlefield, the enemy's jungle

sanctuaries could be annihilated in a single raid, deterring any further raids by the North Vietnamese into the South; a very effective use of air power. General Westmoreland, commander of US forces in Vietnam between 1964 and 1968, declared: "Prisoners and defectors list the B-52 as the most feared of all weapons arrayed against them."

A New Dawn

The 3rd Air Division's B-52 attacks were codenamed Arc Light and all parties involved eventually agreed a list of potential targets. One of those selected was the dispersed base area in the Ben Cat special zone near Hanoi. This was the first use of tactics that were to become familiar to B-52 aircrews. A raid would split into formations of 30 B-52s and each formation would be further divided into ten 'cells' of three B-52s; each cell was designated a phonetically-distinct colour-name call-sign for the duration of the mission, eg TAN 01, 02 and 03. The call-signs were unique to individual aircraft for each particular mission. The B-52s were drawn from the 9th BS, 7th BW, which had replaced the 20th BS at Andersen, and the 441st BS. To aid navigation, the strike packages were guided to their targets by an MSQ-77 Combat Skyspot/Combat Proof radar beacon, which was flown to

Above: **Although Andersen's ramp seems crowded in this 1965 shot of the first B-52Fs to deploy to Guam, by 1972 the base was so congested that 30 jets had to be in the air at any one time simply to leave enough room for the rest to land, refuel, re-arm and take-off again.** USAF
Below: **Frantic activity around B-52F 57-0139 as armourers and other technicians work hard on Guam in 1965.** USAF

Left: *Although it probably wasn't high on the list of priorities, keeping up with the mission-tally markings must have used up a few cans of spray paint!* USAF
Below: *With each bomber carrying up to 120 individual bombs, simply keeping stocks of bombs on Guam was a mammoth logistical task. Another load arrives for a B-52F in 1965.* USAF Museum archives via Greg Spahr

Tan Son Nhut airport, Saigon, in June 1965.

Thirty B-52Fs left Guam's Andersen AFB on June 18 for the first Arc Light sortie, climbing to meet their KC-135A tankers near the Philippines. The leading cell (GREEN) arrived at the refuelling 'race-track' too early and began to circle to use up the time, but in doing so they turned back into the path of a following cell (BLUE). Two B-52s collided and fell into the ocean with only four of the 12 crewmen surviving. Another B-52F aborted with avionics failures and the remaining 27 bombers

scored mediocre results. The result of this first mission gave senior SAC generals and B-52 opponents in Washington much to think about. At an overall mission cost of $20 million, two of the enemy had been killed and 40 barrack-style buildings, a communication centre and a rice store destroyed. It was a disappointing start to B-52 combat operations, the first time the bomber had been used in anger.

Over the following days, SAC issued new procedures. The five refuelling air corridors were widened and separated from

each other by greater distances and altitudes. A complex system of timing triangles was also introduced to enable the aircraft to hold if they arrived too early, enabling them to turn back onto track to meet their tankers exactly on time. These changes to the routes enabled countless air-to-air refuellings to be conducted safely during the next seven years of Arc Light missions. During a normal 'contact' the B-52s would take on 89,000lb (40.369 tonnes) of fuel from the KC-135As, which required the pair of aircraft to remain in contact for about 17 minutes.

Often this was performed while flying into the sun, further complicating the demanding procedure for B-52 pilots who had to look up at the refuelling boom of the tanker while flying behind and slightly beneath it.

The next planned Arc Light raid in June was cancelled when intelligence showed the enemy had already vacated the target area. It was not until July that B-52Fs returned to combat when they flew five more Arc Lights, totalling 140 sorties. A further five raids (totalling 165 sorties) were flown during August. Despite the increase in the frequency of the raids, each had to be approved by the White House, and the lengthy chain of command resulted in considerable delays before authorisations were approved. It was clear from the outset that the B-52s would be incapable of being used as a 'quick reaction' response, or against mobile or changing targets.

By late August the White House had been taken out of the decision-loop for Arc Light missions. It now fell to the JCS to authorise strikes, although the process was still time-consuming and unwieldy. Tactics continued to be adjusted over the following months as USAF leaders struggled to find the best way to utilise the massive B-52 fleet. Smaller formations were tried, including single cells of three B-52Fs attacking multiple locations simultaneously. The ultimate goal was to fly missions in direct support of ground troops – in November this started to happen. ▶

Above: *The crew of this B-52F with its hastily applied black paint on its undersides, are happy to be back from yet another Arc Light mission over Vietnam.* USAF

B-52 profiles

Pete West's illustrations of Buffs across the years with badges of the units associated with the type today

Above: *The Grandaddy of them all, XB-52-BO Stratofortress 49-0230, took to the skies at the hands of Alvin M 'Tex' Johnston more than 60 years ago, on April 15, 1952.*

Above: *RB-52B 53-0369 wearing SAC's classic Cold War colour scheme of silver-grey painted top-sides and white anti-flash reflective paint underneath.*

Above: *MiG Killer! B-52D 55-0083, named 'Diamond Lil', downed a MiG-21 over Hanoi on December 14, 1972. Today she is preserved at the USAF Academy, Colorado.*

Squadron Badges

| 5th Bomb Wing (AFGSC) | 23rd Bomb Squadron | 69th Bomb Squadron | 2nd Bomb Wing (AFGSC) | 11th Bomb Squadron | 20th Bomb Squadron | 96th Bomb Squadron |

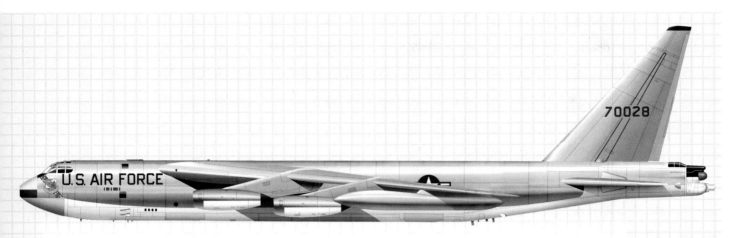

Above: *The larger fuel tanks on the wings, the redesigned gun system behind the tail and ECM aerials under the fuselage show 57-0028 to be a B-52E, one of only 100 of the variant produced.*

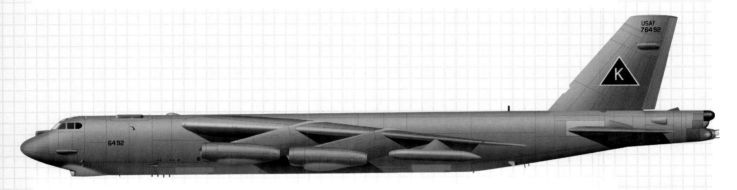

Above: *B-52G 57-6492 of the 379th BW flew 55 missions when based with the 1708th BW(P) at King Abdul Azziz IAP, Saudi Arabia during Operation Desert Storm in 1991.*

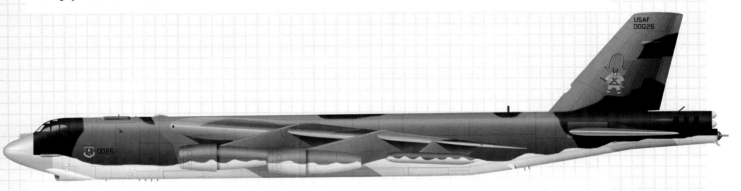

Above: *Newest of the type, although all of them are over 50 years old, is the B-52H, which is scheduled to remain in service for another 33 years. Example 60-0026 of the 319th BW is seen wearing the 'Yosemite Sam' tail-art she wore for the Giant Strike bombing competition, held at RAF Marham in 1981. She still serves the United States today, flying with the 5th BW from Minot AFB, North Dakota.*

307th Bomb Wing
(AFRC)

93rd Bomb Squadron
(FTU)

343rd Bomb
Squadron

53rd Wing (ACC)

49th Test & Evaluation
Squadron

412th Test Wing
(AFMC)

419th Flight Test
Squadron

B-52F 57-0144, to judge by the mission-marks painted on the nose already a veteran of several Vietnam raids, heads out on another Arc Light mission. USAF

Secret Raids in a Covert War

As SAC crews from across the US rotated into the combat theatre to fly B-52F sorties, their operational area was gradually expanded. No longer would targets be restricted to those in South Vietnam.

Intelligence obtained from special forces outfits operating along the Vietnamese and Laotian border made it clear the North was using the region for staging areas prior to launching attacks into the South. A series of counter-insurgency operations (titled variously Steel Tiger, Steel Cricket and Tiger Hound) was launched into Laos, aimed at denying the PAVN and Viet Cong (VC) the sanctuary unwittingly afforded by this neutral country.

Twenty-four B-52Fs laden with M117 high-explosive bombs and BLU-3 cluster bomb units participated in the first Laotian Arc Light – which was not notified to the Laotian Prime Minister, Souvanna Phouma. Thereafter, there were two categories of Laotian Arc Light: Category One targets were to be notified to the Laotians, and Category Two targets were not. Laotian Arc Lights continued throughout February and the following months in support of covert operations on the ground. But it was not until September 1966 that 'some' of these raids were acknowledged. Laotian B-52 strikes were disguised by diversionary raids by smaller numbers of B-52s in the same general area but on the Vietnamese side of the border. The reason for this was that attention drawn to the Laotian raids could be dismissed as misreporting of the target area, or as a result of a navigational error by the bombers attacking Vietnamese targets. This was how this shadowy war was kept secret from all but a few senior US officers.

By this stage of the war, B-52Fs had still not bombed North Vietnam, which remained the exclusive territory of the tactical jets – principally the Republic F-105 Thunderchief, which suffered very high attrition rates in Vietnam. The USAF was still using its tactical jets in a strategic role and vice-versa. But the decision had already been made to step up B-52 strikes across the whole of Vietnam, finally allowing the bombers to head north. It would be the B-52Ds that would now bear the brunt of the air war as the last of the B-52Fs had left the theatre by April 1966 after dropping more than 100,000 tons of bombs on enemy targets.

Along with the changes in aircraft came an organisational change at Andersen AFB. This saw a new provisional wing – the 4133rd Bomb Wing (Provisional) – established to control all B-52s deployed to the region. But for the foreseeable future the operational tactics established a year earlier would remain in place.

The B-52D would prove a far more suitable variant of the Stratofortress for the bombing sorties ahead. A four-phase electronic-countermeasures (ECM) improvement programme had been introduced across the fleet, along with an enhanced conventional bombing capability. Among the changes introduced to the B-52D fleet was the same wing pylon modification applied to the initial 28 'F' models that had received the 'South Bay' modification to increase their bomb-load, and 46 more that had undergone a similar programme codenamed 'Sun Bath' in order that they too could take part in

Above: *Gilding the Lily. B-52s look pretty mean without the addition of a shark's mouth. Clearly the crew of this 'D' model seen at Andersen AFB in 1972 didn't think so.* Paul Minert via Greg Spahr
Below: *Hardly any B-52Cs were painted in this colour scheme, known as SIOP, because the variant was being withdrawn from use before it was applied to the Buff fleet.* Paul Minert collection via Greg Spahr

Above: *A B-52D lands at U-Tapao with a KC-135A in the foreground.* USAF
Below: *B-52D 55-0115 high over Vietnam on November 22, 1967. It went on to be the 50th B-52 lost when it burnt out on the runway at Kadena on December 3, 1968.* USAF via Glenn Sands

the war in Vietnam. Many B-52Ds were also fitted with the so-called 'Big Belly' upgrade. These retained their ability to carry up to four free-fall nuclear weapons and they could also carry mines.

Shortly after the B-52Ds had taken over at Andersen, aircraft were sent north across the demilitarised zone (DMZ) into Route Pack 1, the southernmost part of North Vietnam to interdict supply routes along the Ho Chi Minh Trail. The first attack, known as Operation Rock Kick II, was made against Route 15 in the Mu Gia Pass on April 11, 1966. At the time it represented the largest single bombing attack since the Second World War, with the delivery of 600 tons of bombs. The mission involved 30 B-52Ds, each carrying 24 1,000lb (453kg) bombs internally with another 24 750lb (340kg) bombs under the wings. The package also involved a similar number of KC-135 tankers. It closed Route 15 for about 20 hours and cost $21 million. Another raid 15 days later left 32 craters in the road, although these were filled within a day. After this there was a five-month pause in attacks against North Vietnamese targets.

During April and May 1966, the B-52Ds also flew Arc Lights in support of Operation Birmingham – a major search and destroy operation in Tay Ninh province. During these raids, 14 enemy base camps were destroyed in 162 sorties. A total of 453 buildings, containing 1,267 tons of rice, were destroyed.

Over the following months a staggered series of raids was launched against North Vietnamese complexes along the Ho Chi Minh Trail and surrounding areas. Although the raids caused considerable damage in the short term, it needed to be verified by special forces teams before American troops could move into the areas, and the damaged infrastructure was quickly repaired within days, if not hours after the B-52s departed. US planners were reluctant to send the bombers back to the same targets again and again; they were afraid it would suggest their war policy was not achieving the desired results, lending credence to the increasing number of

people at home who were saying the war was simply unwinnable. Vietnam was the first war to be replayed nightly on the television screens of American voters and TV's influence on US public opinion cannot be overstated. But if Pentagon planners were not keen to up the ante in the air war, the North Vietnamese were.

Early in September 1966, on what was deemed to be another 'routine bombing mission', a B-52D from the 454th BW was unexpectedly engaged by two SA-2 Guideline SAMs. Luckily, the electronic warfare officer (EWO) aboard detected the Fan Song guidance radar and instructed the pilots to turn smartly towards the coast in the hope of increasing the chances that the crew would avoid capture when they baled out – as he assumed that would

be the inevitable consequence.

Fortunately the EWO managed to jam the two missiles, which exploded a mere 3,000ft (914m) from the bomber. Had they struck the aircraft, the loss of a B-52 to a SAM this early in the conflict would have provided the enemy with a significant propaganda coup. B-52 raids across the DMZ were quickly called-off for a short time, but in the following years the SA-2 Guideline was to take a terrible revenge on the previously untouchable Stratofortress fleets.

Another Arc Light

As the war progressed, B-52s were routinely called into action to provide close air support to surrounded American and South Vietnamese forces fighting in the South. Monsoon weather frequently grounded tactical aircraft or prevented them from attacking their targets, but the B-52s, bombing with the help of Combat Skyspot, could operate around the clock regardless of rain, mist or cloud. However, the steady increase in SAM sites along the DMZ meant every formation of B-52s was now shepherded by a Douglas EB-66C/E Destroyer electronic jamming aircraft.

The tempo of operations in the South increased to such a rate by mid-1968 and into early 1969 that a third B-52 operating base

Above: *SIOP-painted B-52Gs take off from Andersen AFB for another Linebacker II mission.* USAF

was established at Kadena on the island of Okinawa, operating under the auspices of the 4252nd SW. From here, the bombers could be over South Vietnam in six hours – a significantly shorter time than flying from Guam.

The addition of an extra base meant that more SAC crews were now thrown into the fray, helping to spread combat experience across all of SAC's wings. The addition of a SAC Contingency Aircrew Training (SCAT) School at Andersen AFB, where those flying B-52Es, Fs, Gs or Hs could be converted onto the D-model after just four sorties, resulted in many pilots seeking to leave the USAF and take jobs with the airlines – the punishing 'six months on, six months off' was taking its toll on the bomber crews. However, the duty would have seemed easy for the ground crews used to maintaining the early B-52s at the start of the Cold War when seven days a week, 18 hours a day, was the rule rather than the exception.

By the end of 1968, the bulk of the B-52s' work had been bombing targets in South Vietnam and Laos. The bombers had flown 35,680 sorties by November, dropping 886,490 tons of bombs.

Above: **Aerial view of U-Tapao in September 1972.** USAF via Glenn Sands

Only 2,380 of the sorties had been against North Vietnamese targets, which had been attacked in 304,000 tactical sorties, including aircraft such as F-105 Thunderchiefs and F-4 Phantom IIs. The B-52s had flown 5,217 Arc Lights in 1966 (including 650 over Laos and 280 over North Vietnam), 9,686 in 1967 and 20,658 during 1968. But these figures would soon pale into insignificance.

Bombing halt after bombing halt was mandated and then cancelled by senior White House officials, most of whom had no expertise when it came to running a bombing campaign, or indeed of how to fight a modern, technologically and logistically complex air war. The term 'Vietnamisation' (handing over responsibility for running the war to the South Vietnamese while the US gradually withdrew) became the buzzword for President Nixon's advisory staff and it seemed to many on the ground that it was more important to appease the growing US anti-war movement than to prosecute the war in order to end it as soon as possible. But SAC generals had long been pleading with the President and his advisers to lift what they saw as ludicrous bombing restrictions and to allow the B-52s to take 'their gloves off' and attack the heart of the North Vietnamese war machine around Hanoi.

Too much, but far too late

On March 30, 1972 the North Vietnamese launched the so-called Easter Offensive – an open invasion of the South. To no avail, President Nixon warned the

Above: **B-52Ds taxi out at U-Tapao on May 17, 1968 for another Arc Light mission.** USAF via Glenn Sands

Below: **A B-52D takes off on another bombing sortie over Vietnam in 1967.** Glenn Sands' collection

Throughout 1967 B-52 raids continued at a increasing rate and crews were rotated into theatre from stateside bases. There were a number of accidents, the most significant of which saw the loss of the 3rd Air Division's commanding officer, Major General William J Crumm, after his wingman in 56-0627 collided with his aircraft, 56-0595 as they started their bombing run on July 7. As yet more bombers arrived in theatre, the infrastructure had to be improved - the runway at Andersen AFB was short and getting airborne with a fully-laden B-52D was difficult. Guam was a long way from the target areas and the Royal Thai Navy airfield at U-Tapao already being used by SAC KC-135s, so became a second home for many B-52s. The distance from U-Tapao to Vietnam meant air-to-air refuelling was not normally required. Crews could work a 'normal' day, with less than eight hours between the pre-strike briefing and the post-mission debrief and mission lengths of no more than three hours.

The 15 U-Tapao-based B-52s came under the command of the 4258th SW and were initially restricted from operating against Laos, or even overflying the country.

But by December 6, 1967 these orders had been countermanded and strikes were permitted. By the end of 1968, the B-52s were reported to have dropped more bombs on Vietnam and Laos than the USAAF had dropped during the whole of the Second World War.

Above: *This is a 'Big-Belly' 'D' model. Twenty-eight bombs are pre-loaded into this structure, called a 'clip', which is then winched into the jet in its entirety.* Greg Spahr collection

Above right: *A 'clip' of 28 bombs prepared and ready to be loaded onto a 'Big Belly' B-52D.* USAF via Greg Spahr

North not to escalate the fighting while US forces were steadily being withdrawn from the theatre of operations, but the North continued its offensive. In accordance with Nixon's 'Vietnamisation' plan, SAC generals had been steadily withdrawing the B-52s from Kadena and Andersen while operations from U-Tapao, which by then hosted 42 B-52s, had continued. Nixon responded by bringing his huge war machine to bear upon the Hanoi Government for the first time. Large numbers of USAF tactical aircraft were deployed to the region as well as several US Navy Carrier Groups with their embarked air wings.

In a series of deployments known as Bullet Shot, B-52s returned to Andersen AFB in strength. By February 1972, U-Tapao had 50 B-52Ds on the pan in response to an increase in PAVN activity into the South. Bullet Shot deployments continued, and by May there were 140 B-52Ds at Andersen AFB, reinforced by 58 B-52Gs (in addition to a handful that had been standing on nuclear alert duty at the base throughout the war). The full B-52 force now deployed for use in Vietnam in 1972 was bigger than at any time during the war, representing over one-third of the active Stratofortress fleet. In terms of destructive potential, it was undoubtedly the most powerful air armada ever assembled in one place.

The huge number of aircraft at Andersen far exceeded the number of available parking spaces, a problem solved by ensuring that at least 30 aircraft were airborne at any one time. With missions lasting 12 hours, this system worked well and allowed

Above: *One advantage of the remoteness of the Buffs' bases from Vietnam is that there was little or no likelihood of attack - so bombs could be left out in the open before being loaded on to the jets.* Key collection

ground crews to continually cycle B-52s through the arming pits.

Under the codename Freedom Train, the restrictions of bombing North Vietnam were finally lifted on April 9, 1972. The USAF immediately began a steady interdiction campaign against the PAVN's supply lines and military infrastructure. The communist advance began to stall. The newly-arrived B-52s were quickly deployed, mounting the first cross-border attacks since the end of Rolling Thunder on October 31, 1968. For the first time in the war, the White House left target selection to the military commanders on the ground. Targets that had been 'off limits' to all US aircraft were now on the strike list. The new policy brought with it a change in name from Operation Freedom Train to Operation Linebacker. Continual B-52 strikes on the advancing North Vietnamese led President Nixon to announce on June 29 at the Paris Peace Talks that the South Vietnamese were on the offensive and driving back the PAVN. ▶

Above: *Work in progress. The sheer destructive power of the bomb-load of a single B-52 is amply illustrated in this shot taken above the jungles of Vietnam.* Key collection

B-52 operations continued throughout the summer of 1972, concentrating on the rail links between Vietnam and its principal source of weapons, China. The Linebacker missions, however, accounted for only 18% of the overall B-52 effort, which remained primarily focused on Arc Light sorties in the South and in neighbouring countries.

Even after the North Vietnamese offensive had been halted and PAVN units chased back across the border, daily Linebacker and Arc Light B-52 strikes continued unabated. Under such concerted pressure, the North Vietnamese negotiating teams in Paris adopted a more conciliatory tone in the peace talks.

By October, the sortie rate was reduced when it looked as though a breakthrough in the talks seemed imminent.

A Lost Opportunity

With the North Vietnamese under pressure, the US had the opportunity to enforce a peace settlement from a position of strength. But the move was not taken. Nixon and his National Security Advisor, Henry Kissinger, halted all air operations against Hanoi and the port of Haiphong, giving the North Vietnamese time to repair their bombed air defences and to reorganise and strengthen them. To the North Vietnamese Leader, Le Duc Tho, the US ceasefire looked like weakness and he decided to continue the war in the hope that further ground would be ceded by the US.

The US had not ended all bombing missions against Vietnam and a U-Tapao-based B-52D, 55-0110, was lost on November 22 during a raid on Vinh. It was the 13th B-52 lost in Southeast Asia in 100,000 sorties. Shortly after, the Nixon administration concluded that the peace negotiations were futile and that the US was being 'played'. When the North Vietnamese finally broke off negotiations on December 13, the 'hawks' in the US administration finally got their wish when the government resolved to mount an all-out air offensive against the North. This bombing campaign was to be known as Linebacker II.

Above: *750lb bombs loaded into a B-52D in 1967.* Glenn Sands' collection

THE FINAL BLOW

On December 14, 1972 President Nixon handed over control of the military conduct of the Vietnam War to the Chairman of the Joint Chiefs of Staff, Admiral Thomas Moore. His orders were simply to "win this war".

The first Linebacker II raid was launched on December 18. Opening his briefing, Col James R McCarthy, commander of the 43rd SW on Guam, said: "Gentlemen, your target for tonight is Hanoi." He later recounted that, for the rest of the briefing, "You could have heard a pin drop".

On this night, 129 bombers were dispatched from Andersen and U-Tapao. They included 54 B-52Gs alongside the B-52Ds. It took one hour and 45 minutes for the 87 B-52s to taxi and take off from Andersen – on average one aircraft launched every 72 seconds. The huge fleet joined up in the air with bombers from U-Tapao, the 129 aircraft forming into three waves. The targets for the bombers were the MiG fighter bases at Kep, Hoa Lac and Phuc Yen, the railway yards at Yen Vien, the vehicle repair and storage facility at Kinh No, the Hanoi railway repair yard and the radio station at Hanoi. During the attack, some 200 SAMs were launched at the bombers along with a pair of MiG-21s, which attempted to attack the bombers as they came off target.

Out of the three waves of bombers, two B-52Gs and a sole B-52D were shot down by SA-2 SAMs. Two further bombers were damaged and forced to divert to U-Tapao.

Day two (December 19) witnessed the launch of 93 B-52s in three waves. The first struck Kinh No and the second bombed the Hanoi Radio station again along with the Bac Giang shipping centre. The third wave bombed Yen Vien and a thermal power plant at Thai Nguyen. Over 180 SAMs were fired against the formation, but no bombers were hit.

During the following days, three-wave formations of B-52s struck high-priority targets throughout the North. But this was not without loss. The third wave of the formations proved to be the most vulnerable with three bombers being lost out of a formation of 21 on day three. It was the lightly-built B-52Gs, lacking the Phase V ECM upgrade, that proved the most vulnerable with three being downed in one raid. Over the next seven days, the Buffs' crews played a deadly game against the SAM sites, some calling for a change in tactics in

The ground crews worked round the clock in hot humid conditions. USAF

an effort to counter the rising losses. At first, the SAC generals declined. But following countless close-calls with B-52s limping home after sustaining damage from SA-2s, a change in routes and formations was granted.

On December 25, President Nixon called a 24-hour bombing halt to Linebacker II as a goodwill gesture. America closely watched the North Vietnamese reaction. The following day the campaign entered its final phase. Tactics were changed with the launch of a single near-simultaneous mass assault of 120 aircraft against 120 targets with a common bomb release time. The B-52Gs were sent against targets that avoided the heaviest concentrations of SAMs around Hanoi. Two B-52s went down during this raid. Both had flown in two-ship cells with the third having aborted, compromising the ECM jamming capability of the formation. Thereafter, such formations were prohibited and all cells were to maintain three aircraft.

By day ten of the campaign the effort focused on missile sites and SAM storage facilities. No

Above: *B-52G 57-6495 preparing to move off at a very crowded Andersen AFB, Guam in 1972. The jet remains stored at D-M to this day, one of 96; but in January 2012 it was announced that another 39 were to be scrapped under the terms of SALT agreement.* Paul Minert via Greg Spahr

bombers were lost and only 27* SAMs were fired. On December 29 (day 11) a similar pattern followed. B-52Ds and 'Gs attacked the Phuc Yen SAM support facility, the Tra Cam SAM storage area and the Lang Dang railway yards. No B-52s were shot down, but several were engaged and hit by fragments from exploding SA-2s.

As the last B-52G recovered to Andersen the following day, President Nixon announced a halt to the bombing campaign. Peace talks were to resume on January 8, with B-52 strikes restricted to targets in South Vietnam.

Linebacker II became popularly known as the 'Eleven Day War'.

B-52s had flown 729 sorties dropping over 15,000 tons of bombs. On the most intense day of the campaign – December 26 – 120 B-52s hit multiple targets in the space of 15 minutes. However, 15 Stratofortresses had been shot down, 24 had been hit by SAMs and nine had limped back to base having sustained various degrees of damage. The stalled peace talks resumed, as President Nixon had promised, on January 8, 1973. A week later he announced an end to all bombing of North Vietnam. A final agreement was reached 30 days later when Le Duc Tho and Henry Kissinger formally

signed the Paris Peace Accords on January 27, 1973.

History suggests that, if for no other reason than to save countless lives on both sides in the Vietnam War, the eleven days of intense B-52 strikes should have been carried out years earlier. The theory goes that it would have saved a generation from dying in the rice fields of Vietnam and would have saved the United States its reputation on the world stage. The reality at the time was that America was criticised from all sides (especially by China, Russia and an influential home-grown and, many believe, Communist-inspired peace movement) whenever it made any sign of using its military might to bring about a swift conclusion to hostilities. The fact remains that the tremendous financial cost of the war in Vietnam almost bankrupted the US, but as air force historian Dr Earl H Tilford wrote, Linebacker was "a watershed in aerial warfare…it was the first modern aerial campaign in which precision-guided munitions changed the way in which air power was used". To many, General LeMay's assertion a decade earlier that the B-52 could end the war in any given ten-day period was manifestly true.

Above: *A close-up of the nose of MiG-killer B-52D 56-0676, showing the red star recording its air-to-air victory on December 18, 1972.* Bob Archer

Below: *B-52D 56-0586, painted as 55-0100 is displayed near the flightline at Andersen AFB, Guam as a memorial to those who died flying Buffs during the Vietnam War.* USAF

70162

U.S. AIR FORCE

B-52s are often most closely associated with their nuclear role, but no B-52 has ever intentionally dropped an atomic bomb. However, the type has dropped many conventional bombs, most notably over Vietnam. **Dao Nhat Dinh** tells his story of what it was like to be on the receiving end

SURVIVING
ROLLING THUNDER AND LINEBACKER

Above: *The author's mother is seen here in 1969 when she returned from serving on Front B. During the war the Vietnamese designated Laos as Front C, Cambodia Front K and southern Vietnam as Front B. Also pictured are the author, his aunt Hoa and sister Uyen.*
Top: *This B-52F 57-0162, still in basic SAC nuclear-bomber colour scheme but with the underside painted black, had been upgraded to carry extra bombs on external pylons.* USAF photo

FOR THE population of Hanoi, and my family in particular, the summer of 1964 was the end of peacetime. At first the phrase 'American bombing' scared our parents so much that they sent me and my sister, with some other children of members of Hanoi's Central Theatre, to Lao Cai province, some 185 miles (300km) from Hanoi, to find a safe place – albeit in primitive living conditions. Of course, all we children wanted was to go back to Hanoi. Luckily, after a few months the fear of American bombers eased as people learned the Americans were confining their bombing to certain places, not every square metre of the country. More importantly, people got used to bombing. Our parents decided to bring us nearer, to a village some 12 miles (20km) to the north-east of Hanoi, in Hung Yen province. The Central Theatre established a camp there for all the theatre staff's children. Life in the camp was better than in Lao Cai – at least, the sanitation was better!

I was now of school age but the situation was very different from Hanoi, where the school was only a few steps from home. We had to go a long way, passing two or three villages to reach our school, a primitive building with bamboo fences dividing the classrooms, and earth walls. Many threats waited for us on the long journey: savage dogs, local children who saw us as a lucrative source of school stationery and rival kids from other camps. My mother gave the camp cook a tin of Chinese milk powder each time she visited us. The cook then prepared two glasses of milk for me and my sister to drink in a quiet place behind the camp. It was a luxury that we could not share with other children. Our parents also brought bread, another almost unimaginable luxury that could be used as currency as well as food.

First bombings
After a few months the air war touched our camp, with explosions and the roaring of jets, and I saw my first US warplanes flying in the Vietnamese sky. A bullet about the size of an adult's finger buried itself deep into the ground where we were playing. One day, an elder boy, who we knew as Brother Mai, brought two halves of a cluster bomblet (we called them 'bombies') into the

camp. One evening he carefully extracted the explosive from inside the small bomb, put some into a tin can and burned it; all the children stared at the fire.

We began to hear reports of heavy loss of life after the bombing of Lac Dao railway station and, as a result, it was decided that we should move to another camp in Ha Tay province. The theatre sent two trucks to take us and on the way we passed through the heavily bombed ruins of Gia Lam, targeted because of its railway yards and airfield. We broke our journey in the capital where we ate a lot and luxuriated in showering off the dirt after the long, hungry and dirty days in camp. I noticed that all the window panes were pasted with paper, cut into flower patterns, in an effort to prevent the glass splintering from the effects of bombs. The old water tank in the basement was turned into a bomb shelter big enough for all the people living in the house.

The SAC logo from 'ROSE 01' in the museum in Hanoi.

Top left: *Parts of an engine from B-52D 56-0608 'ROSE 01' shot down on December 27, 1972, are displayed at the Vietnamese Military History Museum in Hanoi. The English language text on the accompanying plaque gives the incorrect date for the loss as December 12, 1972.*
Top right: *A famous 'tourist' attraction in Hanoi is this lump of wreckage of 'ROSE 01' in Huu Tiep Lake near Hanoi Zoo, more commonly known as B-52 Lake. Two members of the crew were killed in the crash and the other four were taken prisoner.*
Right: *The author's father.*

After much too short a time, we moved on to Ha Tay where life became much more difficult. My mother carried a big bamboo tree, much bigger than herself, many miles to the teacher's house near the school. The bamboo was used to build the school and, thanks to my mother's efforts, I was able to be educated. Many children were not so lucky, never receiving any visits from friends or family. By now the war permeated every aspect of life – even the children's songs. One very popular air was set to the tune of the traditional American ballad 'Red River Valley', although our version told the story of an American F-4 pilot who flew his jet to the Red River, was shot down and taken to prison by a buffalo cart while his darling was missing him day and night. Not even food escaped its influence; we called a noodle soup without meat 'unpiloted' as opposed to 'piloted' soup with it.

Period of peace

In 1968 the bombing ended in the northern provinces. Like many children, the eight-year-old me could not wait for the theatre to send a vehicle, so we walked back to Hanoi. My mother's troupe of actors was sent to the south to ▶

"ON ONE MEMORABLE OCCASION I FOLLOWED A SAM'S SMOKE TRAIL, SAW THE SECOND STAGE IGNITE AND THEN SAW THE ORANGE CLOUD OF SMOKE AS IT EXPLODED NEAR ITS TARGET"

7-65

entertain those engaged in the fight against the Americans. It was an anxious time as I waited for her to come home, but finally the happy day arrived. She had a slight head injury, and malaria that persisted for ten years, but she also had souvenirs from the front and the Ho Chi Minh Trail, including a comb hand-made from aluminium from the fuselage of an American aircraft! The theatre team also brought home an American M15 auto-matic rifle and a Kalashnikov. A period of four years of relative peace for the residents of Hanoi now began. I often passed by the infamous 'Hanoi Hilton' prison, where many American prisoners of war were held. There was a loudspeaker in the small park at the back of the prison. One day as we walked, the popular patriotic song Quàng Bình quê ta oỉ was played on the speaker. A lot of people stopped their bicycles to listen. Those four years of peace passed quickly.

Wailing sirens once more

On April 16, 1972 my sister and I went to help our grandmother sell newspapers and afterwards, while she was cooking chicken with noodles for my birthday, we heard the almost forgotten sound of the air-raid warning: "Attention countrymen! Enemy aircraft are 30km (19 miles) from Hanoi," soon followed by wailing sirens. We children were ordered to hide under the stairs because the air-raid shelters had been neglected for so long and were unusable. The skies were soon filled with the roar of F-4 Phantoms and anti-aircraft fire. Children were evacuated to the countryside again and it was back to Ha Tay for me. My life was better than it was during [President Lyndon Baines] Johnson's war. We built A-shaped shelters out of bamboo and mud and watched US aircraft flying to Hanoi. We could identify

Above: *Mrs Quy burns incense for her son who was one of around 300 people killed in B-52 bombing of Kham Thien street on the night of December 26, 1972, on the 36th anniversary of the tragedy. Civilians were never intended to be the targets of the American bombing.*

smoke from anti-aircraft shells and SAM missiles, and the adults told us that a SAM exploding with orange smoke had hit its target. On one occasion we were terrified when we mistook a fighter's fuel tank, dropped right over our heads, for a bomb. At night we listened to the news on the BBC's World Service – and that is how we heard that our forces had captured Quang Tri, about Sino-US relations and the Paris peace-talks. We heard that Nixon's new 'laser bombs' were being used on our bridges, but the October 1972 daylight destruction of the French diplomatic mission

in which the chief envoy, M Pierre Susini, was killed convinced us that laser bombs did not improve US targeting very much. Having survived 'Rolling Thunder' during Johnson's time, we thought we had seen the worst the Ameri-cans could throw at us.

Now that I was older, I was allowed to spend more time in Hanoi. Because of the summer heat a dozen or more of us boys and girls slept on the roof of our building, rushing to a small staircase when we heard the siren. Sometimes we awoke in the middle of a raid to see lines of tracer fire from guns

> ## "WHEN AUNTIE THO BECAME LESS WORRIED I WAS ALLOWED OUT OF THE SHELTER TO PEE DURING A RAID AND SO IT WAS THAT I HAD MY LAST SIGHT OF A B-52 FALLING IN A HUGE FIREBALL"

Below: *The crew of a Vietnamese SAM battery poses for the camera. Vietnam-ese records show that around 300 SA-2s were launched during Linebacker II in December 1972. Supplies were rapidly running out and the crews assembling the missiles worked around the clock to keep up.* USAF photo

and artillery units on the top of the highest buildings in Hanoi. On one memorable occasion I followed a SAM's smoke trail, saw the second stage ignite and then saw the orange cloud of smoke as it exploded near its target. The enemy aircraft seemed to fall very slowly, burning more brightly as it fell. There was time to call out to the people sheltering from the raid, all of whom came out to cheer. After each air-raid there were clouds of chaff spread about the streets and caught in the trees and buildings. The electronic war had entered a new phase; we heard adults using terms like 'active radar jamming' and 'passive jamming'.

In October 1972 we heard on the radio about the failure of peace-talks in Paris. It seemed that peace was at hand and had slipped away. Everyone waited for the decisive battle; we repaired our shelters, stopped all trips to Hanoi and listened for the alarm signal given by a nearby military unit – a soldier using an iron rod to hit the casing of a defused and emptied American bomb. On the cold night of December 18, 1972 the bombing resumed with a vengeance. At first we thought that it was just another raid. Bombs exploded for half an hour with numerous jet engines roaring back and forth before the quiet returned. We left the supposed safety of our shelter but two missiles were launched, lighting up the sky, so we hurried back inside again and this time the explosions didn't stop. My aunt pushed me and my cousin, her son, into the furthest corner of the shelter, but even there strange flashes of vibrant light reached us. For the first time we spent all night in the shelter and even when we eventually left we could see explosions lighting up the sky from the direction of Hanoi.

Next morning we learned that it had been B-52s bombing and the strange light was a burning Stratofortress. Those B-52s flew so high that it took them a long time to fall to earth. The adults told us that they must carry a lot of fuel because they said they had never seen anything burning like that. My cousin and I went out in hope of finding a piece of debris, but only found a piece of shrapnel right on the top of our shelter. Two days later, dipping into the paddy mud, we found a piece like

a valve. We dug it out despite warnings from adults. After a few days the bombing eased and we had Christmas holidays. Uncle Chi visited us and took me on his Czech motorbike to Hanoi. First thing I saw was the great number of bomb craters along the road from Hoai Duc, Ha Tay province to Hanoi, especially around the antenna installation for the Voice of Vietnam radio station. In Hanoi, we learned about the bombing of Bach Mai hospital. My dad liked to stay on the roof of our house to watch SAMs targeting B-52s.

Linebacker II

The Johnson years taught us that Americans never bombed between Christmas and New Year. However, SAC let us down. On the evening of December 26, 1972 we heard the air-raid warning again. After the first wave of Phantoms, all of us recognised that B-52s were coming again. The target for the B-52s was Kham Thien Street, about one kilometre from my house. The nearest bomb was dropped in Thien Quang Lake, 500 metres north-west of my home. We heard continuous explosions and our shelter was shaken like a hammock. The horrible blasts continued so long that we thought all glass windows in the house were gone. As kids and old people stayed in the shelter, brave men stayed outside relaying the latest 'news' from the sky. Messages came clearly: 'Bombs, bombs, very close!... SAM!... B-52 burning!' In the early morning of December 27 my uncle rushed me back to Ha Tay. We passed Kham Thien Street and saw that the whole street was destroyed. People were still digging to rescue the trapped victims or just save their belongings. We zigzagged through the bomb craters towards Cau Giay, swept along in the stream of people who had learned that American pilots had no Christmas leave this year.

The bombing blitz continued for a few more nights with fewer and fewer sorties to Hanoi. From my escape village I often saw the anti-aircraft artillery and SAMs firing into the air. When Auntie Tho became less worried I was allowed out of the shelter to pee during a raid and so it was that I had my last sight of a B-52 falling in a huge fireball.

Above: *A SA-2 Guideline SAM in flight over Kep fighter base. The missile was called a 'flying telephone pole' by the Americans.* USAF Photo.

OPERATION
Desert Storm
1991

Tim Ripley and **Lt Gen E G 'Buck' Shuler Jr** tell the tale of the Buff's first major offensive operation since the end of the Vietnam War

Above: **B-52H 60-0009 'Cloud Nine' was one of several Buffs based in Saudi Arabia during Operation Desert Storm.** USAF
Below: **A B-52G belonging to the 1708th BW(P), takes off from King Abdul Aziz IAP, Jeddah, Saudi Arabia. Politically it was a bold move for the Saudis to allow the US to base bombers on their soil.** USAF

MINUTES AFTER Lockheed F-117A Nighthawk stealth aircraft had made the dramatic bombing attacks on strategic targets in downtown Baghdad on the morning of January 17, 1991, twelve B-52G Stratofortresses were powering across the desert at less than 100ft (30m) to rain destruction on the unsuspecting defenders of five Iraqi air bases.

At the same time, another seven B-52Gs were flying across the Saudi Arabian desert heading to launch points to unleash 39 Boeing AGM-86C conventional air-launched cruise missiles (CALCMs) at strategic targets deep in Iraq.

The prominent role of the aged B-52 'Buff' in the opening moves of Operation Desert Storm highlighted the importance of the bomber in the US-led offensive to drive out Iraqi forces occupying Kuwait. Over the next seven weeks, B-52Gs and crews from almost every unit in Strategic Air Command equipped with the bomber were committed to the war in the Middle East.

At its peak, 75 B-52s were allocated to the campaign, making this the biggest commitment of Buffs since Operation Linebacker II in 1973. Even though the Vietnam War had ended some 15 years earlier, perceptions about the participation of the B-52 in that controversial conflict shaped how the Buff would be used in the war against Iraqi dictator Saddam Hussein. The top US commander in the Middle East, General 'Stormin' Norman Schwarzkopf, had seen at first

hand the impact of B-52 'Arc Light' sorties against North Vietnamese army regiments, and how they created moonscapes of craters and demoralised survivors. Schwarzkopf wanted to use the B-52s to break the morale of the 500,000 Iraqi troops dug-in defending Kuwait. In equal measure, the Arab governments across the Middle East were afraid of the propaganda image created by the Hanoi communist regime that the B-52 was an indiscriminate 'baby killing' weapon. As a result, in the run up to the launching of Operation Desert Storm, the B-52 force had to be based outside the Middle East. Once war began, a B-52 wing operated from inside the

Above: *By the time this photo was taken at RAF Fairford on February 17, 1991, B-52G 58-0182 had already flown four Desert Storm missions. Although the bomber itself is now stored at D-M the panel with its 'What's up Doc?' nose-art has been removed and is displayed at the NMUSAF at Wright-Patterson AFB, Ohio.* Bob Archer

Kingdom of Saudi Arabia under conditions of great secrecy. The Egyptian government refused a US request to base B-52s at an air base near Cairo, resulting in the USAF having to set up bases in Spain and the UK from which to fly round-trips.

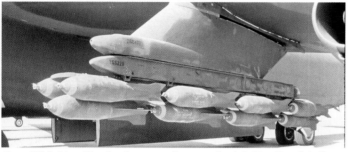

Above: *Old-fashioned iron bombs were used to carpet bomb Saddam Hussein's elite Republican Guard.* USAF

Provisional Bomb Wings

The build-up of the USAF strategic bomber force began soon after the Iraqi invasion of Kuwait on August 2, 1990. Within ten days a squadron of seven B-52Gs from the 43rd Bomb Wing had flown to the British Indian Ocean Territory (BIOT) of Diego Garcia to establish the 43rd Bomb Wing (Provisional) [BW(P)]. By August 16, some 20 fully armed B-52Gs were standing strip-alert on the tropical island ready to launch to pound any Iraqi troops that might be ordered to invade Saudi Arabia. Operation Desert Shield successfully deterred Saddam Hussein from further adventures

and by the end of the year, the US-led coalition was in the final stages of its preparations to launch an overwhelming offensive to remove Iraqi troops from Kuwait.

Central to coalition air commander Lt Gen Charles 'Chuck' A Horner's plan was the establishment of additional B-52 wings within striking range of Iraq. The Saudis agreed to open King Abdul Aziz International Airport near the Red Sea port of Jeddah to B-52s where the USAF set up the 1708th BW(P). The commander of 8th Air Force at the time, Lt Gen E G 'Buck' Shuler Jr, told us: "The Saudis would not permit B-52Gs at Jeddah New until 'H-hour' although we ▶

Above: *Three Buffs taxi out at RAF Fairford in March 1999 for a Desert Storm mission. The sharp-eyed observer will notice the three police vans in the background positioned to deter 'peace-protestors' from interfering with flight operations.* USAF

did have KC-135 tankers pre-positioned under the command of the Air Guard tanker wing from Forbes AFB, Kansas. We did persuade the Saudis to let us land one B-52G at Jeddah so we could check runway and taxiway clearances, etc. I was present for that event. The 379th Bomb Wing from Wurtsmith AFB, Michigan, was assigned to Jeddah with the bomb wing commander taking over command. What we did to facilitate matters was to fly some six B-52Gs from Wurtsmith out to Diego Garcia. The UK didn't place any restrictions on us. These aircraft flew a combat sortie on the first night [January 17, 1991] and recovered at Jeddah." Eventually some 16 B-52s were based at the Saudi airport.

After being denied the use of their air bases by the Egyptians, 22 B-52s were deployed to Morón de la Frontera airbase in southern Spain to form the 801st BW(P) in early January. Then the UK opened RAF Fairford in Gloucestershire to the 806th BW(P), and from February 8 it became the home of eight B-52Gs. This brought the strength of the strike force to nearly 70 B-52s – although, subsequently, many more aircraft were rotated through the forward-deployed bomb wings as aircraft had to return home for repair and overhaul during the period of the confrontation with Iraq (from August 1990 to April 1991). Additional aircraft were also on alert at Barksdale AFB in Louisiana to fly long-range strike missions against Iraq with CALCMs.

First day

The opening day of Operation Desert Storm saw the B-52Gs from Diego Garcia and Barksdale centre-stage in the plan to cripple Iraq's strategic air defences. They were intended to open the way for follow-on phases designed to inflict heavy damage on Iraqi ground forces in Kuwait and neighbouring regions of southern Iraq – the so-called Kuwait theatre of operations, or KTO. Schwarzkopf wanted the Iraqi army's combat power in the KTO to be degraded by 50% before he would send coalition ground forces into action. Several hundred coalition aircraft were launched in the early hours of January 17 against strategic targets across the length and breadth of Iraq. A dozen B-52Gs of the 4300th BW(P) were tasked with neutralising several Iraqi air bases in the desert south of the capital, Baghdad. The crews were highly trained in low-level tactics after spending years perfecting the skills needed to penetrate heavy Soviet air defences. This training paid dividends in the first days of Operation Desert Storm.

The first wave of B-52Gs penetrated Iraqi airspace undetected and were able to sew the Iraqi air bases at Tikrit, Mudaysis, Wadi al Khirr, Ghalayson and As

Above: *The bomb-load has received the seemingly traditional attentions of graffiti artists.* Bob Archer
Left: *Close-up of the nose-art on 'Old Crow Express'.* Bob Archer
Below: *B-52G 57-6492 'Old Crow Express' flew 55 missions from Jeddah, Saudi Arabia during Operation Desert Storm.* Bob Archer

Salman with scores of 1,000lb (454kg) bombs fitted with delayed-action fuses and hundreds of CBU-87 cluster bombs. The aim was to render the bases inoperable for several days. Iraqi Air Force personnel were forced to deal with munitions that exploded unpredictably over extended periods of time; and the cluster bomb sub-munitions took a heavy toll of Iraqi bomb disposal teams sent to defuse the bigger bombs. As the Buffs were exiting their target zones, Iraqi anti-aircraft artillery (AAA or triple-A) and surface-to-air missile (SAM) defences sprang into life, but none of the B-52s was hit.

While the Diego Garcia-based B-52 crews were experiencing the sights and sounds of war close-up, out across the Mediterranean, those of seven B-52Gs from the 596th Bomb Squadron at Barksdale, Louisiana, serial numbers 57-7475, 58-0177, 58-0183, 58-0185, 58-0238, 59-2564 and 59-2582, were making their final preparations for their AGM-86C strike. The mission was officially dubbed Senior Surprise by the USAF and, unsurprisingly perhaps, 'Secret Squirrel' by the aircraft crews. Their missiles were intended to strike eight power stations and telephone exchanges in mid-morning after the first wave of coalition strike aircraft had completed their attacks. Former Eighth Air Force commander Lt Gen 'Buck' Shuler said that 34 of the 39 CALCMs carried by the B-52s hit their intended targets; three could not be launched; another fell in the desert and was later recovered and destroyed; and one was

never located. The mission was kept secret by the USAF for over a year. At the time, the 14,000-mile (22,531km) 34.5-hour round trip was the longest bombing mission in history.

The Barksdale B-52s were not the only Buffs to set off for Iraq from the continental US that morning. Lt Gen Shuler explained that, while B-52s from the 379th Bomb Wing struck Iraq from Diego Garcia before recovering to Jeddah, nine more of the Wing's bombers back at their home base at Wurtsmith, Michigan, were loaded with iron bombs and flown in three 3-ship cells from the States to join in the attacks. "Only one of these cells was able to strike its targets," he said. "The other two ran into bad weather and, with fuel considerations, went directly to Jeddah. It's not widely known that two missions struck Iraq from the States. The bottom line was that, on the day after the war started, we had a full complement of B-52Gs at Jeddah commencing normal combat ops."

Kill boxes

After six days of low-level missions against air bases and other strategic targets, the B-52G force was switched to medium and high-level altitudes as the focus of the coalition campaign started to move to hitting the Iraqi army in the KTO. The target-set progressively moved to Iraqi troops in frontline trenches, artillery fire-bases, supply dumps, tactical SAM sites and vehicle parks. Schwarzkopf ordered his air commander, Lt General Charles 'Chuck' A ▶

Above: *Ordnancemen use an MJ-1 bomb loader to put Mark 117 750lb. bombs on a B-52 Stratofortress during Operation Desert Shield.* USAF
Below: *A special lift-truck is used to offer up a JDAM to the wing pylon of a B-52 at RAF Fairford during ODS.* USAF

Bomb truck. USAF

*Above: **Three KC-10A extenders taxi out together at King Abdul Aziz IAP, Jeddah, Saudi Arabia. Normal civilian operations carried on as usual while the Buffs and their tankers carried the war to Saddam Hussein.*** USAF

Below: ***A radar navigator adjusts the electronic optical viewing system of his B-52H in preparation for a bombing mission.*** USAF

Horner, to launch B-52 attacks on Iraqi frontline infantry divisions on a three-hourly basis to inflict maximum psychological impact on the under-equipped, under-fed and poorly-led conscripts. The idea was to deny them sleep and prevent them repairing bomb damage. It was hoped this would eventually lead to them deserting or surrendering to coalition troops rather than enduring this apparently never-ending bombardment. From mid-February some 40 to 50 B-52G strikes a day were taking place in the KTO. The psychological impact was increased by co-ordinating the strikes with BLU-82 'fuel explosive' bomb drops from USAF MC-130s combined with propaganda leaflet drops offering safe passage through coalition lines. By the third week of February, the B-52 offensive had done its work. Coalition tank columns rolled forward through the remains of the Iraqi army on February 24. Thousands of Iraqi troops surrendered to coalition

troops; many more had fled. Within four days Kuwait was free and the mission was over.

Round-up

Between January 17 and February 28, the USAF B-52G force flew some 1,741 sorties – nearly 25 sorties per aircraft on average. These missions were long, often in excess of ten hours for the

majority of the B-52s deployed as part of Operation Desert Storm. The bombers were not immune to loss or damage. Five B-52Gs suffered significant battle damage, but only one was lost (in a non-combat incident which killed three crew members - see the table at the end of this publication for details).

In a bizarre 'friendly fire'

incident, a B-52G was damaged on the first night of operations after being hit by shrapnel from an AGM-88 high-speed anti-radiation missile (HARM) fired from a USAF F-4G Wild Weasel assigned to escort a B-52 raid. The crew of the F-4 mistook the emissions from the B-52 for those from an Iraqi AAA site and launched the missile. Fortunately no-one suffered any injuries and the bomber recovered safely to Jeddah, Saudi Arabia. The bomber, 58-0248, was later nicknamed 'In HARM's way'.

The contribution to Desert Storm made by the B-52 was enormous. Stratofortresses dropped 72,389 individual bombs, including M177 750lb (340kg) general purpose bombs; 1,000lb (454kg) delayed action UK bombs; 500lb (230kg) general purpose bombs; and CBU-52/58/71/87/89 cluster bombs – altogether weighing some 27,000 tonnes. This total represented 40% of all bombs dropped by USAF aircraft and 30% of all coalition bombs; B-52s made up less than 10% the of total coalition combat aircraft strength. The physical destruction caused by these weapons was immense but US ground commanders said the psychological impact of the B-52s' presence in the skies over Kuwait was even more important.

*Above: **It's not all glamour in the air force! These lucky people have been tasked with scrubbing down their B-52 – all 159 feet of it. It took a dozen of them six hours to get the old Buff squeaky clean.*** USAF

DESERT STORM SECRETS

Lt Gen E G 'Buck' Shuler, former commander 8th Air Force reveals a little known aspect of the first night of Desert Storm

The commander of SAC's Eighth Air Force during Desert Storm, Lt Gen E G 'Buck' Shuler Jr, doesn't mince words when recalling what was required of seven of his B-52G fleet allocated to the start of the campaign and destined to fly what was then the longest bombing mission in history.

Shuler told us: "General Horner [the coalition's air chief] needed assets to punch the eyes and ears out of the Iraqi air defences and command and control system immediately at H-hour. He used the F-117s and the air-launched cruise missiles (ALCMs) to accomplish this aim of the air campaign. The trick for Eighth Air Force was to get the B-52Gs to the predetermined launch points over the Saudi Arabian desert so the ALCMs could fly out and explode over the assigned targets in the initial attack."

The story of how the Boeing AGM-86 ALCMs – which had been designed as nuclear weapons – came to carry conventional explosives in a curtain-raiser for Desert Storm was, as Buck Shuler explains, "a 'black world' programme that few people knew about because of international treaty concerns". So sensitive was their deployment that Operation Senior Surprise, as it was called, was dubbed 'Secret Squirrel' by the handful of 2nd Bomb Wing B-52G crews involved at their base at

Barksdale, Louisiana.

Senior Surprise was a masterpiece of hush-hush planning, involving a clandestine launch from Barksdale AFB, a 7,000-mile flight with air refuelling, launching of the ALCMs, a return 7,000-mile flight with more air refuelling and recovery at Barksdale – all without anyone knowing about or detecting the operation.

Buck Shuler recalls: "Not knowing when H-hour would be until the last moment, we had to configure the aircraft and place the aircrews on alert, which lasted a number of days before execution. I met with these young crew members a number of times. I recall that in one of the earlier meetings I had been concerned about the length of the mission and crew rest. I asked for a show of hands as to how many had flown a 24-hour mission in the B-52. No hands went up. In my day as a young B-52 pilot and aircraft commander, I had flown more than 20 airborne alert missions of some 24 hours' duration, known as Chrome Dome. I next asked how many had flown a 14-hour mission. Again, no hands went up. In my day a 14-hour training mission was common. I got together with Ron Marcotte, the wing commander, and we decided to put one extra pilot and one extra navigator on each aircraft for safety considerations. The aircrews were elated because it meant more guys would get to fly the mission, which they were eager to do!

"It was decided to send the mission off under strict radio silence procedures. What we did to facilitate this was to place members of the Eighth Air Force operations staff as trusted agents in each of the Air Traffic Control Centers at Fort Worth, Atlanta and Jacksonville. When the force launched during the hours of early morning darkness, they popped up on the ATCCs' radar. Our trusted agents told the controllers to route them at a predetermined altitude to a coast out point near Savannah, Georgia, and to keep all traffic away from them, adding: 'Oh, by the way, they will not be talking to you!'

"From coast out, the force went 'due regard' keeping a sharp look-out for other air traffic. We planned the route and altitudes so as not to interfere with international commercial air traffic. It got a little tricky at Gibraltar. The route was planned well north of Libya, so Gaddafi could not tip anybody off about the force's presence. If you know your geography, you know there's no way to get to the Saudi Arabian desert unless you overfly someone else's territory. The force was challenged but did not respond and pressed on.

"When I attended the final pre-

mission briefing, I was afforded the opportunity to make some comments of encouragement. During my career, having a keen interest in military history, I always used the opportunity to relate the exploits of airmen past. I did this when I was a wing commander, commenting before an operational readiness inspection flight etc. On this occasion I told these young troops that this mission may be the most important in our nation's history since we sent Doolittle to Tokyo. I was not attempting to be melodramatic; I just didn't want them to screw it up. It seemed to pump them up a bit.

"The mission commander was Lt Col John H 'Jay' Beard who had worked for me when I commanded the Third Air Division on Guam. An Air Force Academy graduate, I had great confidence in Jay and he didn't let us down. I met the crews on the ramp when they landed and, boy, were they tired puppies!"

Below: *Each Buff has a fuel capacity of 312,197lb (141,610kg) or more than 52,000 US gallons. And even that's not usually enough to get it to where it's going and back again!* USAF

The missions in support of Operation Desert Strike in 1996 saw the first use of the B-52H in combat. USAF

Operations Desert Strike 1996 & Desert Fox 1999

TENSIONS IN the Middle East continued through the 1990s as Iraqi leader Saddam Hussein remained defiant in the face of United Nations resolutions calling for the end of his country's attempts to build weapons of mass destruction. There were regular US air strikes against Iraqi targets to force compliance with those resolutions and to enforce the northern and southern no-fly zones.

Blooding the B-52H – Operation Desert Strike

USAF B-52Hs first became involved in these attacks in September 1996 when strikes using air and sea-launched cruise missiles were ordered against the Iraqi air defence infrastructure – including surface-to-air missile sites and command and control nodes in southern Iraq. Saddam had continued to persecute the Kurdish population in the north of Iraq and Marsh Arabs in the south in defiance of United Nations Security Council Resolution 688. In order to convince the Iraqi leader that the US-led coalition was serious about enforcing the resolution, the US National Command Authority decided to employ cruise missiles.

After 14 Tomahawk land attack missiles (TLAMs) were fired from US warships, it was the turn of two B-52Hs from the 96th Bomb Squadron, which had taken off from the US air base on the Pacific island of Guam. They flew across the Pacific and Indian Oceans, approaching Iraq via Kuwait, where Grumman F-14 Tomcats from the aircraft carrier USS *Carl Vinson* acted as their escort en route to their launch point – from which 13 AGM-86 conventional air-launched cruise missiles (CAL-CMs) were successfully fired in the early hours of September 4. This 33-hour mission, the first combat employment of the B-52H, did not beat the record set by the Senior Surprise CALCM mission, flown by B-52Gs, which opened Operation Desert Storm; but it did result in the crew of aircraft call-sign 'Duke 01' receiving the prestigious Mackay Trophy awarded by the National Aeronautics Association for "the most meritorious flight of 1996 by an air force person, persons or organisation".

Tension again came to a head in November 1997 when arms inspectors of the UN Special Commission claimed their work was being seriously hampered by the Iraqis: US President Bill Clinton ordered B-52Hs of the 2nd Bomb Wing to the RAF base on Diego Garcia, part of the British Indian Ocean Territory, for seven months.

In November 1998, the Iraqi leader refused to allow the return of the arms inspectors and the 12 B-52Hs, including seven from the 2nd Bomb Wing, were ordered back to Diego Garcia. On one occasion the bombers were airborne heading for Baghdad after the Iraqis refused to meet UN demands. Only 20 minutes before they were due to launch their CALCMs, Saddam Hussein backed down and the B-52Hs were ordered back to base.

Saddam Hussein's regime did not improve its cooperation with the UN inspectors and, barely a month later, they were withdrawn; the US and UK governments ordered Operation Desert Fox to begin on December 16. When it ended four days later, on the first day of Ramadan, both the B-52H force and, for the first time in combat, Rockwell B-1Bs had been in action – with the Buffs firing around 90 CALCMs at a variety of targets across southern and central Iraq. TIM RIPLEY

Above: *Armourers and other maintainers worked round the clock to keep the voracious appetite for munitions satisfied during the intense four days of Operation Desert Fox.* USAF

Operation Allied Force 1999

Above: **B-52H 60-0049 'LA' carrying a Rafael AGM-142 Have Nap missile at RAF Fairford on May 15, 1999.** Bob Archer

Tim Ripley tells us the tale of the next contribution to maintaining world peace, the NATO intervention in the Balkans at the end of the last century

EVEN AS the USAF's B-52 force was preparing for Operation Desert Fox in the final months of 1998, the Buff squadrons at Barksdale and Minot AFBs found themselves engaged in the latest crisis in the Balkans.

Conflict between Serbian Government troops and ethnic Albanian fighters in what was then the Yugoslav province of Kosovo had, over the previous 12 months, been steadily escalating. In the autumn of 1998 this prompted NATO to threaten air strikes in a bid to contain the situation.

Veteran US diplomatic troubleshooter Dick Holbrooke was dispatched to Belgrade to confront Serbian strongman Slobodan Milosevic. To give Holbrooke negotiating muscle, six B-52Hs of the 2nd Bomb Wing from Barksdale AFB, Louisiana, were flown to RAF Fairford in Gloucestershire, a little over an hour's drive from London.

The presence of the Buffs appeared to calm the situation; Milosevic agreed to back down and the B-52Hs returned home. By February 1999 the ethnic conflict was flaring again and B-52 crews were ordered to deploy to Fairford under Operation Noble Anvil. Eight aircraft, which arrived over February 21 and 22, were used to establish the 2nd Air Expeditionary Group (AEG) – a key part of NATO's response, Operation Allied Force, which was beginning to gain momentum. Aircraft and personnel for the operation were drawn from both the 2nd and 5th Bomb Wings, home-based respectively at Barksdale AFB and Minot AFB, North Dakota.

NATO attacked on March 24 – with the B-52Hs from Fairford at the forefront of efforts to neutralise the opposing air defence network and other strategic targets. Eight Stratofortresses, using the call-signs 'Havoc 11' to 'Havoc 18', launched on this first mission, armed with Boeing AGM-86C conventional air-launched cruise missiles (CALCMs). Two of the eight jets were 'air-spares' and returned to Fairford, but the other six continued to head for their missile launch 'boxes' over the Adriatic.

The targets for the raid were radar sites and communications nodes that were key components of the Serbian integrated air defence systems (IADS); their destruction opened the way for tactical fighters to penetrate contested airspace over the former Yugoslavia. Over the next two weeks, B-52H CALCM raids were launched on a daily basis from RAF Fairford against targets in Serbia and Kosovo. ▶

Above: **B-52H 60-0049 being loaded with 500lb bombs at RAF Fairford on May 15, 1999, before another mission to Kosovo.** Bob Archer
Left: **Nose art on the 2nd Air Expeditionary Group B-52H 60-0020 'The Mad Bolshevik' at RAF Fairford on June 15, 1999. Graffiti on the jet suggests that this aircraft took part in the 100th Operation Noble Anvil raid.** Bob Archer

Eventually some 60 to 70 CALCMs would be fired against targets, effectively exhausting the USAF's stock of the missile – so a crash programme had to be launched to begin converting nuclear-armed variants of the missile to carry conventional explosives.

NATO's initial air assault failed to force Milosevic to back down and, over the next few weeks, the alliance began to ramp-up its air power with additional aircraft being committed to the conflict. Eventually there would be eleven B-52Hs at any one time at RAF Fairford, along with six Rockwell B-1B Lancers and several Boeing KC-135R Stratotanker air-to-air refuelling aircraft. Aircraft were regularly rotated back to their home bases for maintenance during the three-month deployment.

After the initial cruise missile onslaught, the nature of the missions flown by the bombers changed. B-52Hs and B-1Bs flew strike missions, chiefly targeting

Above: Although Barksdale AFB provided the bulk of the Buffs assigned to Operation Noble Anvil, Minot AFB's 5th Bomber Wing supplied four jets including 60-0033 which wore the name 'Instrument of Destruction'. Bob Archer
Below: A B-52H, deployed to England as part of the 2nd Air Expeditionary Group supporting Operation Allied Force over Kosovo, lands at RAF Fairford with bombs still attached to its wing pylons. USAF

airfields and ammunition depots, during May 1999, using 'dumb' M117 750lb (350kg) and Mk 82 500lb (230kg) bombs. These targets were predominately in Kosovo and southern Serbia, where the air defences were deemed less capable.

To give the heavy bomber force committed to Operation Allied Force a precision strike capability, two aircraft – 60-0049 and 60-0062, equipped to fire the Israeli-made electro-optically guided Rafael AGM-142 Have

Nap missile – were dispatched to RAF Fairford. The USAF has not disclosed how many AGM-142 missiles were used, but they were reportedly not very effective because of poor weather and technical issues. One aircraft, 60-0062 'Cajun Fear', was seen wearing markings signifying it had launched at least one such weapon but it is believed that this was the extent of their use.

NATO's air assets were still struggling to inflict heavy damage on the targeted ground

forces in Kosovo largely because of the army's successful use of camouflage and concealment tactics to hide tanks and other heavy weapons.

For weeks, NATO commanders sent reconnaissance aircraft and unmanned aerial vehicles over Kosovo to try to find Serbian troops. It was hoped that a concentration of ground troops or tank columns could be found for the B-52Hs and B-1Bs to unleash their devastating fire power against. On a number of occasions in late May and early June, NATO commanders thought they had found suitable targets along the Albanian-Kosovo border where Serbian troops were locked in vicious fighting with Kosovo Liberation Army fighters. The targets were 'visited' by mixed forces of B-52Hs and B-1Bs, and NATO claimed heavy losses were inflicted. The last such attack occurred on June 9, on the eve of the ceasefire that resulted in the agreement that saw Serb forces leave Kosovo. By the end of June, the 2nd AEG at RAF Fairford was wound up and all the aircraft returned to their home bases. The B-52Hs had flown some 184 combat missions during Operation Allied Force, dropping around 6,600 individual munitions.

Mixed results

The way that NATO operations were carried out during the

Above: Not every Noble Anvil mission ended with bombs being released on target, which meant the aircraft were de-armed when they returned to base. USAF

Above: *An airman secures an Air Launch Cruise Missile during a maintenance inspection aboard a Stratofortress at RAF Fairford on March 25, 1999, during the early stages of Operation Allied Force.* USAF

Kosovo war drew criticism from many quarters – with the total reliance on airpower attracting particular disapproval. Even within the US military, there was less than total agreement that the tactics were appropriate; and a general consensus that they were less than totally successful. No definitive after-action review of the USAF's performance in the conflict, particularly a bomb-damage assessment, has ever been published.

Civilian and military visitors to Kosovo after the Serbian withdrawal reported that many infrastructure targets, such as radar stations and communication sites, had been hit with great precision. Visits to the sites of the B-52 attacks on Serbian forces failed to find more than a handful of wrecked vehicles and a few dead soldiers.

Perhaps the most important result of the war from a USAF point of view was that it added impetus to efforts to integrate the satellite-guided Boeing Joint Direct Attack Munition (JDAM) to the bomber to facilitate B-52H attacks in bad weather.

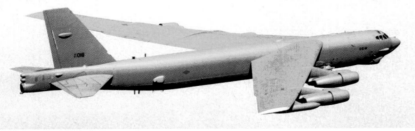

Above: *This Buff, caught on the way to Kosovo during Operation Noble Anvil, has apparently been rushed into service after maintenance without being fully painted. The aircraft appears to have received at least part of the Conventional Enhancement Modification (CEM) programme series of upgrades that have not been painted, which explains the uncamouflaged wing-tips and Miniature Receive Terminal (MRT) on the fuselage sides.* USAF
Below: *Minot AFB's 'Instrument of Destruction' leaves RAF Fairford for home on June 23, 1999 at the end of Operation Allied Force.* USAF

OPERATION NOBLE ANVIL, NATO OVER KOSOVO, FEBRUARY TO JUNE 1999

NO FEWER than 25 B-52Hs from both active-duty Bombardment Wings took part in the bombing of Kosovo in 1999.

Barksdale AFB's 2nd Bombardment Wing (BW) provided the following B-52Hs for Operation Noble Anvil (all aircraft carried the base's 'LA' tail-code):
The 11th Bombardment Squadron:
60-0011 '11th Bomb Sqn' (specially marked '11 BMS' on tail)
61-0011 (specially marked '11 BMS' on tail)
61-0016 'Freebird' and 'MIA/POW Remembered'
61-0031 'Ol' Smokey'
61-0039

The 20th Bombardment Squadron:
60-0020 'The Mad Bolshevik' (specially marked '20 BMS' on tail)
60-0043
60-0046
60-0049
60-0062 'Cajun Fear'
61-0002 'Eagles Wrath III' (specially marked '2nd OG' on tail)
61-0023

The 96th Bombardment Squadron:
60-0010 'Instigator'
60-0022
60-0037 'Wham Bam II' (this was confirmed as a 96th BS machine but did not carry the red fin-tip colour of that squadron or the 'LA' tail code)
60-0052
60-0059 (carried a badge '96 BS' on its nose and was specially marked '96 BMS' on tail)
61-0020
60-0014 and 60-0016 came from the Barksdale Wing, but did not carry unit markings or the 'LA' tail-code

Minot Air Force Base in North Dakota provided the following 5th Bombardment Wing machines:
60-0009 'Rolling thunder'
60-0033 'Instrument of Destruction'
60-0044
60-0051 'Appetite for Destruction'

All wore the red fin-tip of the 23rd B S, and Minot's 'MT' tail-code apart from one other Minot jet that bore no unit markings.

Operation Iraqi Freedom 2003

In 2003, the United States and its allies formed a coalition to oust President Saddam Hussein of Iraq after his repeated failure to permit United Nations inspectors to confirm or deny the existence of weapons of mass destruction in Iraq. Predictably, as **Tim Ripley** tells us, America's fleet of B-52 was at the forefront of military action against Iraq

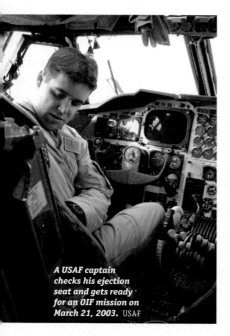

A USAF captain checks his ejection seat and gets ready for an OIF mission on March 21, 2003. USAF

US PRESIDENT George W Bush's determination to remove Iraqi President Saddam Hussein led to an escalation of tension in the Middle East during the final months of 2002. A build-up of forces in December was ordered to add weight to the President's threats to force Iraq to comply with United Nations resolutions requiring it to dismantle its alleged arsenal of weapons of mass destruction. Chief of US Central Command, General Tommy Franks, developed an ambitious plan to defeat Iraq's armed forces in less than a month of combat operations. This called for use of the 'shock and awe' doctrine. In this case it was characterized by an all-out precision air offensive against Iraq's air defences and strategic command systems in the heart of the Iraqi capital Baghdad, followed by a blitzkrieg-type advance on Baghdad by tank columns. Not surprisingly, the USAF's B-52H force was soon at the centre of Pentagon planning for Operation Iraqi Freedom. Fortuitously the USAF had maintained a small detachment of around half a dozen B-52Hs on Diego Garcia after the end of the major combat phase of the Afghanistan campaign in early 2002. During early 2003 the size of the detachment was increased by the addition of extra aircraft and crews from the 2nd

Above: *'Iron Butterfly' was one of the B-52Hs deployed to RAF Fairford in England to operate in support of OIF.* Bob Archer

Bomb Wing's two combat-ready squadrons, the 20th and 96th Bomb Squadrons. Preparations and training to get the crews of the 40th Air Expeditionary wing ready for a mass attack with AGM-86C Conventional Air Launched Cruise Missiles (CALCMs) began, and by the middle of March some 14 B-52H were positioned on Diego Garcia, ready to attack.

The remote location of the island meant these preparations could be undertaken away from prying eyes but the same could not be said for the establishment of the other B-52H forward deployed operations location at RAF Fairford in Gloucestershire. As soon as the first Buffs started arriving in the UK they were

greeted by anti-war protestors and a huge security operation had to be put in place to secure the air base's perimeter.

The 23rd Bomb Squadron of the 5th Bomb Wing from Minot AFB in North Dakota formed the core of what became the 457th Air Expeditionary Group. Eventually some 14 B-52Hs were deployed to the base, supported by 18 Boeing KC-135 Stratotankers from the Pennsylvania, Tennessee and Kansas Air National Guards based at RAF Mildenhall in Suffolk. Further tanker units were set up at Bourgas in Bulgaria, Souda Bay in Greece and RAF Akrotiri on Cyprus to support the RAF Fairford-based B-52s strikes into Northern Iraq.

Right: **On March 25, 2003 a radar navigator attached to the 23rd Expeditionary Bomb Squadron writes a message to Saddam Hussein on a JDAM prior to the first ever sortie by a B-52H armed with ALCMs and JDAMs.** USAF

Below: **'H' model 60-0023 assigned to the 457th Air Expeditionary Group takes off for its 100th OIF combat mission from RAF Fairford on April 11, 2003.** USAF

Shock and awe

General Franks was authorised to attack after Saddam Hussein was, in the third week of March 2003, judged by President Bush to have failed to comply with his demands for disarmament. Acting on intelligence that the Iraqi leader was attending a meeting on a farm south of Baghdad on March 19, Franks ordered a Lockheed F-117A Nighthawk strike to try to kill him. Fears of Iraqi missile strikes on Kuwait and so-called 'environmental terrorism' (such as the release of oil into the Northern Arabian Gulf) prompted Franks to order the ground offensive to commence on the evening of March 20, ahead of the now delayed 'shock and awe' air offensive. The following day it was the turn of the coalition air forces to strike. Hundreds of strike aircraft were in the air as US Navy and UK Royal Navy Tomahawk Land Attack Missiles (TLAMs) impacted around Baghdad. Almost simultaneously, the B-52Hs flown by 96th BS crews fired 153 Conventional Air Launched Cruise Missiles (CALCM) in the largest ever Buff-launched cruise missile attack. Dramatic television footage showed the TALMs and CALCM, as well as UK MBDA Storm Shadows fired by RAF Panavia Tornado GR4s, impacting around the Iraqi capital. Massive explosions rocked the city but as the dust settled the damage was clearly confined to military or command targets, and mercifully there were only a handful of civilian casualties.

Desert battles

Further south, US Army and Marine Corps armoured columns were racing north from Kuwait towards Baghdad. However, after a few days, near the city of Nasiriyah, they were held up by small bands of fighters loyal to the Iraqi leader. At the same time, US spearheads were starting to engage units of the elite Iraqi Republican Guard dug-in on the southern approaches to Baghdad. When southern Iraq and the Arabian Gulf region were enveloped in a huge sand storm that effectively grounded all fixed wing aircraft and helicopters US ground commanders begun to worry that their drive on Baghdad was stalled. This was the moment for the heavy bombers – the B-52Hs and the Rockwell B-1Bs – to step up to the plate. Guided by Northrop Grumman E-8 Joint STARS radar aircraft that could spot Iraqi tank columns and artillery positions at night or in storms, the heavy bombers started to work over the Republican Guard defensive lines with satellite guided Boeing Joint Direct Attack Munitions (JDAMs). This was a 21st Century version of Operation Desert Storm 'tank plinking' and in the space of just over a week the Iraqi defences were cracking open. During these raids B-52Hs also used the Wind Corrected Munition Dispenser for the first time to devastate Iraqi tank columns and artillery emplacements. On April 4, US tank columns had reach Baghdad international airport and begun a series of raids dubbed 'Thunder Rides' into the heart of the Iraqi capital.

Northern front

General Franks had hoped to land a US Army division in Turkey to open a northern front against the Iraqis but Ankara's parliament voted against direct participation in the US-led invasion. Instead, US special forces teams were now to be inserted into the Kurdish held 'safe haven' in Northern Iraq to tie down Saddam Hussein's troops. In a re-run of the Afghan campaign, US special forces forward air controllers began working with local Kurdish militias to identify Iraqi troop positions for precision air strikes.

RAF Fairford-based B-52Hs were to play an important role in this remarkable offensive, orbiting for extended periods over frontline positions waiting for forward air controllers to identify targets. JDAMs were then used to destroy the targets with pin-point precision. These missions frequently lasted over 14 hours and involved multiple air-to-air refuelling as the Buff crews waited on station for the special forces teams to find ▶

Below: **On April 11, 2003 – for the first time in combat history – this B-52H used a Litening advanced airborne targeting and navigation pod to target facilities at an airfield in northern Iraq. A crew of reservists from Barksdale AFB's, 93rd BS was joined by active duty airmen from Minot's 23rd BS and together they successfully dropped two laser-guided GBU-12s on a radar site and a command complex at the Al Sahra airfield.** USAF

above: *As usual, the bombers worked in close harmony with their 'tanker-puke' comrades without whom long-range missions are impossible.* USAF

them trade. The requirement for precision strikes meant that frequently the B-52Hs did not expend all their ordnance, and they often brought weapons back to base or jettisoned them over the sea near the UK before landing. This northern front campaign also saw the employment of a new capability for the B-52H. Since early 2002 the USAF had been working to integrate the Litening II advanced targeting pod onto the jet, to allow crews to better locate, identify, and verify assigned targets before delivering weapons. Litening II contains a high-resolution, forward-looking infrared sensor with a wide field-of-view search, coupled with a narrow field-of-view acquisition and targeting capability. The pod also contains a digital camera that is used to obtain target imagery in the visible portion of the electromagnetic spectrum, a laser designator for precise delivery of laser-guided munitions, and a laser rangefinder to determine exact target coordinates. Litening II gave B-52H crews the ability to pin-point their own targets for attack in the same way that fast jet pilots in aircraft fitted with the pod

could. Although the pod was still being tested for use on the big bomber, two B-52Hs crewed by reservists from Barksdale AFB's 93rd Bomb Squadron were flown to RAF Fairford in time to participate in the final phase of the Iraqi war. The specially modified and equipped aircraft used the Litening II to strike targets at an airfield in northern Iraq on April 11. A mixed crew of reservists from the 93rd BS and active-duty airmen flew the bomber from Fairford, dropping one laser-guided GBU-12 Paveway II munition on a radar complex and another on a command complex at the airfield.

With Baghdad in US hands and the Kurdish militia advancing south from near the Turkish border, the requirement for B-52H support dropped dramatically. Although aircraft were launched to fly combat air patrols from Diego Garcia and RAF Fairford on a daily basis, they were rarely called into action. The B-52H squadrons were already starting to head home before President Bush declared 'mission accomplished' on May Day 2003.

Round-up

The B-52 force contribution to the combat phase of Operation Iraqi Freedom in many ways built on its success during the opening months of the Afghan campaign. The type's long endurance and heavy bomb load meant they were

invaluable in the close air support role, orbiting over battlefields waiting to attack targets detected by US forward air controllers. The 20th BS alone dropped 212,000lbs (96,161kg) of JDAMs on Iraqi army targets during the drive on Baghdad. The 40th AEW and 457th AEG flew almost half of the 505 heavy bomber mission flown by the USAF during the campaign, with Diego Garcia-based units of the 2nd BW alone flying 150 combat missions. The 5th BW's B-52s flew more than 120 combat missions and logged more than 1,600 combat flying hours. Operation Iraqi Freedom showed that the B-52H now had awesome precision close air support capabilities.

Above: *Security was tight at RAF Fairford, one of the deployed locations for OIF, with police forces from around the country drafted in to assist the military police.* Bob Archer
Below: *Work goes on around the clock to keep the big bombers flying in support of OIF.* USAF

Operation Enduring Freedom 2001-2006

The other Southwest Asian country to occupy America's foreign policy makers in the early years of the 21st Century has been Afghanistan. **Tim Ripley** explains how the B-52 has been adapted to the changing demands of this challenging theatre of operations

I**N THE days after the September 11, 2001 Al Qaeda attacks** on New York and Washington DC, the Pentagon began mobilising its offensive forces to strike at Osama bin Laden's supposed sanctuary in Afghanistan.

The lack of air bases in countries neighbouring Afghanistan meant that the USAF quickly decided to commit its heavy bombers – Boeing B-52H Stratofortresses, Rockwell B-1B Lancers and Northrop Grumman B-2A Spirits – to Operation Enduring Freedom, as American involvement in Afghanistan was known. Although the bombers were designed at the height of the Cold War to deliver nuclear weapons into the heart of the Soviet Union, by 2001 they had been modified to utilise precision conventional weapons. The B-52H could carry 13 GBU-31 2,000lb (908kg) JDAMs (joint direct attack munitions) and 27 500lb (230kg) unguided Mk 82 'dumb' bombs. The decision to employ the heavy bombers in the Afghan campaign was influenced by their long range and endurance. No other aircraft in the US inventory in 2001 could reach Afghanistan and then stay on patrol for up to nine hours. When combined with the JDAMs, the USAF heavy bombers were transformed to precision close air-support aircraft.

Some of the most memorable images of the 2001 Afghan war were filmed by TV news crews covering the Battle of Mazar-e-Sharif. High above, the

When the Buff took wing for the first time it would have been inconceivable to have a female armourer but by the 1990s most trades were open to women. This weapons loader is preparing a JDAM during Operation Enduring Freedom. USAF

'NO OTHER AIRCRAFT IN THE US INVENTORY IN 2001 COULD REACH AFGHANISTAN AND THEN STAY ON PATROL FOR UP TO NINE HOURS'

distinctive outline of B-52Hs could be clearly seen, contrails flowing behind against the deep-blue winter sky. Minutes later the Taliban trenches below were engulfed by huge explosions as the bombers' payloads of satellite-guided bombs impacted in quick succession.

This was vivid evidence of the reach and precision of American airpower. While the handful of US special forces and Central Intelligence Agency (CIA) operatives on the ground were instrumental in identifying and mobilising opposition to the Taliban, this airpower was the essential weapon for delivering the killer blow.

Above: *The crew of this JDAM-toting B-52H shows the flag to its tanker as the aerial ballet of air-to-air refuelling plays out on the way to Iraq.* USAF

Island base

First to deploy to the British Indian Ocean Territory (BIOT) of Diego Garcia were the B-52H crews of the 2nd and 5th Bomb Wings, which joined together to form the 40th Expeditionary Air Wing on September 14, 2001. The next three weeks were spent building up supplies and preparing for their first strikes. By the morning of October 6, US President George W Bush had given up on the Taliban government in Kabul ever handing over the al-Qaeda chief – and he issued formal orders for the launching of Operation Enduring Freedom.

The operation was scheduled to kick-off during the evening of October 7 with several packages of strike aircraft and Raytheon Tomahawk land attack missiles (TALMs) hitting some 31 separate targets, involving 275 individual weapon aim-points around Afghanistan – including airfields, radar sites, SAM batteries, al-Qaeda and Taliban command buildings and al-Qaeda training camps. The strikes were spread across Afghanistan, from Tora Bora on the eastern border with Pakistan to Herat out in the west. A barrage of 50 TALMs from the USS *McFaul*, USS *John Paul Jones*, USS *O'Brien*, USS *Philippine Sea* and two US and two British nuclear submarines, HMS *Triumph* and

Trafalgar, opened the attack on radar and SA-3 SAM sites around Kabul as well as several barrack buildings. A few minutes behind the TALM strike was a package of Grumman F-14 Tomcats and McDonnell Douglas F/A-18C Hornets from the USS *Carl Vinson*. A Hornet fired a single AGM-84-ER stand-off land attack missile in a precision strike on the remains of the Afghan air defence network around Kabul. This was followed up with a laser-guided bomb attack by Tomcats, which also bombed a barrack complex.

The US Navy jets then turned south to provide top cover for a pair of US B-1Bs hitting Al Qaeda targets around Jalabadad with dozens of 2,000lb (908kg) JDAMs.

At the same time, ten B-52Hs were launching a wave of attacks on targets around the Tora Bora mountain range, which was believed to be home to several Al Qaeda bases. The USS Enterprise launched a follow-up strike on the Kabul air defences later in the night.

Trench battles

During late October 2001, the US began to refocus its airpower against Taliban front-lines around Kabul, as well as Mazar-e-Sharif and Kunduz in northern Afghanistan, where Taliban forces were battling poorly-equipped fighters of the Afghan Northern Alliance. US forward air controllers had been covertly inserted by helicopter to begin directing air strikes precisely onto Taliban positions. For the battles around Mazar-e-Sharif and Kunduz, formations, or 'cells', of three B-52s were ordered to circle above the Taliban front-lines, to wait for the order to attack. On several occasions these bombers unloaded all their weapons as a single stick

Above: *This image could have been taken more than a quarter of a century ago, but the date is October 2001 and these four B-52Hs are preparing to take off from Andersen AFB, Guam in support of Operation Enduring Freedom.* USAF
Below: *Refuelling the Buffs was a massive undertaking on its own involving regular air force units, such as the 6th AMW jet in the foreground, as well as ANG and AFRC assets.* USAF

Above: **A B-52 from the 28th Air Expeditionary Wing takes off from Diego Garcia for a combat mission in support of Operation Enduring Freedom on October 22, 2001. The Buffs shared the base with B-1 Lancers as well as tanker assets.** USAF

Above: **If the bombs aren't used on a mission they have to be removed from the aircraft – a task this airman is no doubt enjoying as he man-handles a M-117 750lb general purpose bomb atop a munitions trailer on Diego Garcia.** USAF

and turned the Taliban trench lines into moonscapes.

By the middle of November Kabul had fallen to the Northern Alliance and a month later the Taliban capital, Kandahar, had been entered by US troops. The B-52H crews of the 40th Expeditionary Air Wing were now attracting huge support from the American public for their role in the Afghan campaign after photographs were published in the media of their aircraft's patriotic nose art. The crews flew their missions from Diego Garcia in the Indian Ocean and their average time in the air was in excess of 15 hours. The bombers would fly north for three hours after taking off from the tropical island's huge runways. South of the Pakistani coast they would top-off their fuel tanks by air-to-air refuelling and then head into Afghanistan. In the first three weeks of the war, the bombers were used almost exclusively to strike fixed targets, but as the war continued they orbited over battlefields waiting for 'business' from the forward air controllers. At the height of the war in November 2001, one B-1B and up to five B-52Hs were on station over Afghanistan at any one time, ready to be deployed against targets.

There were only ten B-52Hs based on Diego Garcia during the first three months of the campaign, grouped into the 20th and 40th Expeditionary Bomb Squadrons. The crews lived in a huge tent-city erected alongside the tropical lagoons on Diego Garcia, and between missions enjoyed barbecues and went fishing. This contrasted starkly with their day-to-day business; during missions the crews could often hear the sound of machine-gun fire in the background as they spoke to troops on the ground in Afghanistan.

The use of the JDAM by the heavy bombers was a key battle-winning tactic because of its satellite guidance; but the weapon caused one of the most notorious 'friendly fire' incidents of the Afghan war. On December 5 on the outskirts of Kandahar, the future President of Afghanistan, Hamid Karzai, halted his convoy to receive a delegation of Taliban-supporting tribal elders who were considering defecting and handing over the city to Karzai. A team of US special forces had set up an observation post on a hill to monitor security during the talks and started to call in air strikes when Taliban fighters were spotted in nearby caves. During one of the strikes, a computer glitch resulted in the wrong co-ordinates being transmitted to a B-52H, which dropped a satellite-guided 2,000lb JDAM on the US troops and their Afghan allies. Two Americans and six Afghans

were killed. Karzai was slightly injured, along with dozens of other Afghans and US troops.

The cause of the incident was subsequently attributed to a forward air controller's GPS device being reset wrongly after a battery change when he transmitted his own position to a B-52H by mistake. The aircrew were cleared of any blame in the incident but it set in train projects to provide automated systems to reduce the chances of human error.

Success

The bulk of Operation Enduring Freedom's offensive air operations were carried out by US Navy and Marine Corps carrier-borne jets and USAF heavy bombers based on Diego Garcia.

Between October and December 2001, this broke down into 3,700 sorties by F/A-18, 1,200 by F-14s, 375 by B-52Hs, 320 by B-1Bs and six by B-2s. When statistics for the weight of bombs dropped are analysed, the B-52Hs and B-1Bs between them dropped 7,000

tons (6,350 tonnes) of munitions between October 2001 and March 2002 – or 75% of all weapons dropped by US aircraft.

For the B-52H crews, the opening phase of the Afghan campaign was a relatively straightforward affair. The Taliban air defence put up little organised resistance and the main challenge was finding valid targets to attack.

The effect on the ground of B-52H and B-1B strikes was profound: as well as the physical damage to enemy targets, the psychological effect on enemy and their local Afghan allies cannot be overestimated. US military commanders were so impressed by the combination of B-52Hs and special forces teams that, after the fall of the Taliban regime, a detachment of B-52Hs was maintained on Diego Garcia for more than four years, flying daily combat air patrols over Afghanistan to provide air support for small and isolated contingents of US and NATO special forces. ★

A fully-loaded B-52H awaits its crew on Diego Garcia during OEF. USAF

Stratofortress
Upgrades

Tom Kaminski outlines the efforts being made to keep the B-52 relevant and effective in today's modern battle-space

*Above: **Any upgrade that includes new engines might require extensive redesigning of the wings, which may be one reason that it hasn't been done – so far.*** USAF

ALTHOUGH THE Stratofortress is no longer considered capable of flying into heavily defended airspace, its ability to loiter for long periods makes it the ideal platform to deliver long-range precision-guided conventional weapons. Additionally, it remains capable of delivering both standoff and free-fall nuclear weapons, making it a vital part of the US nuclear deterrent. Under the terms of the current New Strategic Arms Reduction Treaty (New START) the US is permitted a maximum of 60 nuclear-capable bombers. By 2018, that fleet will include 16 B-2As and 44 B-52Hs – as a result, the remainder of the B-52H fleet will be converted to a conventional-only capability.

On average each B-52H has flown about 18,000 hours since entering service, but it's expected that the aircraft can continue to operate until they reach 28,600 hours or more. The USAF continues to modernise the aircraft and the latest series of upgrades will allow the venerable bomber to remain in service until at least 2040. Among modifications being planned or under consideration are new displays, datalinks, radar and weapons as well as structural upgrades.

Upgrades

Completed in 2009, the Avionics Midlife Improvement (AMI) upgraded the aircraft's ASQ-176 offensive avionics system (OAS), which controls navigation and weapons delivery. It replaced equipment that was rapidly approaching obsolescence, including the inertial navigation system, avionics control unit and data transfer system. New features included ring laser gyro inertial navigation units, upgraded processors and software as well as mission planning hardware and associated software. Flight testing of the AMI began in mid-December 2002 and was completed in early 2004. As well as providing the aircraft with upgraded capabilities, the modifications served as a building block for enhancements that have followed. Additionally, the bomber's ALR-46 digital warning receiver and ALQ-155 self-protection systems have also recently been

*Above: **Boeing's monopoly on tankers seems set to continue with a version of the Boeing 767 airliner, like this Italian example, set to replace the KC-135, which came into service with the USAF at about the same time as the Buff.*** Key collection

Left: *It seems inevitable that the dated technology of the 1970s will lead to the engines presently on the B-52 being replaced by modern turbofans. At least the mechanic will be able to stand up in those!* USAF
Left below: *Looking like it may be the control console of a submarine, the workstation for the navigator and radar navigator is in 'the hole' underneath the flight deck. The various displays and instruments have all been and will continue to be subject to upgrades.* Frank Noort
Below: *The control panel is dominated by the eight sets of 'steam gauges' for the Buff's engines, and most of the rest of the instruments are of a similar vintage. The two CRTs (not MFDs) are the screens for the EVS, the most modern looking thing in view.* USAF

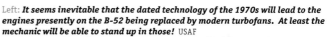

upgraded in order to be able to defeat emerging threats as they have been identified.

Development of the B-52 Combat Network Communications Technology (CONECT) programme began in March 2005, when Boeing received a four-year $216.7 million system design and development (SDD) contract. CONECT will provide the B-52H with new multi-functional colour displays (MFCD), computer architecture, multiple datalinks and enhanced voice communications capabilities. Incorporation of this equipment provides the aircraft with a network-centric operation (NCO) capability and gives the crew increased situational awareness, significantly enhancing their ability to conduct close air support (CAS) missions. Upgrades of the first aircraft began at Boeing's Wichita, Kansas, facility in October 2007 and the first B-52H upgraded with CONECT made its first test flight there on May 21, 2009. It was formally turned over to the 412th Test Wing at Edwards AFB, California, on August 5, 2009 for developmental testing and later carried out its first test flight there on January 17, 2010.

The integrated suite provides the B-52H with a machine-to-machine data transfer capability that supports mission re-tasking and weapons re-targeting for AGM-86C/D conventional air-launched cruise missiles (CALCMs) and AGM-158 joint air-to-surface standoff missile/JASSM-extended range (JASSM/JASSM-ER) J-series weapons. In addition, a new digital interphone system has been incorporated, designed to survive and function through the nuclear environment. Like the AMI, the CONECT is intended as the basis for other planned upgrades.

Flight testing of the CONECT systems required for initial production was completed at Edwards AFB in December 2011 and the programme recently finished its production readiness review. Boeing is currently awaiting a 'Milestone C' decision, expected in May 2012. The approval will allow CONECT to enter low-rate initial production (LRIP). The funding for eight LRIP 1 kits was included in Fiscal Year 2012 budgets, and they will modify six USAF and two AFRC aircraft. A second LRIP will include ten kits, and plans call for the incorporation of ▶

Above: *Starting with the B-52G, the Buff's profile was changed to accommodate various electronic systems. In 2011 this 69th BS machine has the now typical double blisters under the nose for the two components of the EVS, the ALQ-155 antenna in front of the cockpit window and cheek blisters for part of the ALQ-172 ECM. The tiny aerial above the technical data block is for the glide-slope indicator.* Jerry Gunner

Left: *Lockheed Martin's AAQ-33 Sniper Advanced Targeting Pod (seen here fitted to a Canadian Hornet) incorporates a third generation targeting FLIR, a laser tracker, a laser marker, a dual mode laser, and a CCD-TV providing superior image quality. It also has a 'non-traditional' intelligence, surveillance, and reconnaissance capability that can be integrated with the cyber battle-space.* Jerry Gunner
Below: *B-52s still have a sea-control mission and among its weapons is the Mk 60 CAPTOR (enCAPsulated TORpedo) mine.* Key collection

the CONECT modifications on an additional 67 aircraft up to 2017, with funding provided in 2015-2017. Kits will be installed by the Oklahoma City Air Logistics Center (OC-ALC) at Tinker AFB, Oklahoma – maintaining that organisation's long association with the Buff – during the aircraft's normal programmed depot maintenance (PDM) cycle. The USAF's schedule calls for equipping 15 USAF and five AFRC aircraft in 2015; 18 USAF and six AFRC aircraft in 2016; and 18 USAF and five AFRC aircraft in 2017.

In September 2009, Boeing received a $5.4 million contract to begin integrating a new satellite communication system on the B-52H. This extremely high frequency (EHF) apparatus will allow Stratofortress crews to exchange information through the so-called 'family of advanced beyond line-of-sight terminals' (FAB-T), enabling communication with ground, air and space platforms. A nuclear command and control network and communication system (NC2NCS) will integrate a secure, survivable two-way EHF SATCOM link that will allow transmission and acknowledgment of emergency action messages in accordance with Joint Chiefs' of Staff (JCS) nuclear protected information exchange requirements (IER). EHF will install an operator interface group, modem processor group and antenna group into the aircraft. A system requirements review (SRR) was recently completed but the programme to integrate the EHF with the B-52H as well as the B-2A is currently

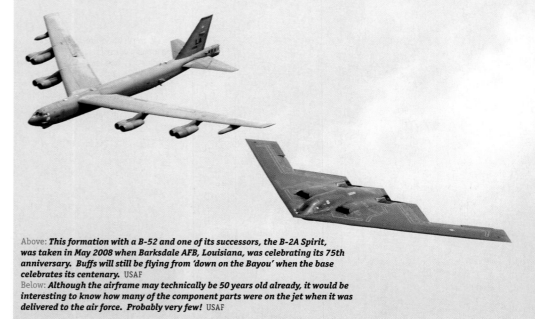

Above: *This formation with a B-52 and one of its successors, the B-2A Spirit, was taken in May 2008 when Barksdale AFB, Louisiana, was celebrating its 75th anniversary. Buffs will still be flying from 'down on the Bayou' when the base celebrates its centenary.* USAF

Below: *Although the airframe may technically be 50 years old already, it would be interesting to know how many of the component parts were on the jet when it was delivered to the air force. Probably very few!* USAF

on hold because of delays with the FAB-T, which is being developed by Boeing's Network and Tactical Systems group.

Between 2014 and 2016, the USAF plans to equip the fleet with modifications associated with the Mode 5/S identification friend or foe (IFF), which will allow the aircraft to operate safely in controlled airspace in the evolving air traffic environment. It's one of several communication navigation surveillance/air traffic management (CNS/ATM) capabilities under development for the B-52.

Targeting pods

The B-52H fleet was first equipped with electro-optical/infrared sensors in 1972. Located under the nose section in steerable chin turrets that form the ASQ-151 electro-optical viewing system (EVS), the sensors consist of the Raytheon

Above: *Another of the B-52s weapons is the CBU-105 Sensor Fuzed Weapon, a CBU-97 sub-munitions dispenser that has been fitted with a Wind Corrected Munitions Dispenser guidance tail kit, specially designed to attack enemy armour. The ten hockey-puck sized weapons in each sub-munition seek out targets using laser or infrared sensors.* Key collection

Below: *There is plenty of life in the old Buff yet, and the fleet has more than enough hours left on it to keep the B-52 flying to the middle of the century. It is not beyond the bounds of possibility that some jets will reach one hundred years of service.* USAF

AAQ-6 forward-looking infrared (FLIR) in a starboard turret and Northrop Grumman AVQ-22 low-light-level television camera (LLTV) in a port turret. Primarily used for low-level navigation, the images from the EVS are displayed on monochrome screens on the flight deck and the navigator station. Unlike newer electro-optical/infrared (EO/IR) systems, the EVS does not provide a targeting capability.

In the 1990s, led by the USAF's Weapons School and various test communities that develop tactics, techniques and procedures, B-52s practised the employment of laser-guided Paveway munitions using 'buddy lase' tactics. A targeting pod-equipped aircraft, such as an F-15E or F-16, would designate the target and the B-52H would deliver the weapons. The next logical step was to obtain an autonomous targeting pod capability for the B-52H.

The first evaluation of a targeting pod for the bomber occurred in 2003 when Northrop-Grumman AAQ-28 LITENING II pods were installed on two B-52H aircraft operated by the Air Force Reserve Command's 93rd Bomb Squadron at Barksdale AFB, Louisiana. Initial test flights took place in March 2003 and LITENING II was used operationally on April 11, 2003 during Operation Iraqi Freedom to deliver laser-guided GBU-12 Paveway II munitions against targets in northern Iraq. The squadron achieved full combat-ready status with the pod in July 2006. The success of this system caused the USAF to move forward with providing the entire fleet with a precision strike capability. Integration of

the Lockheed Martin AAQ-33 Sniper advanced targeting pod (ATP) began in September 2008 when Boeing received a $15 million contract to integrate the system. Operated from the navigator's station, the ATP gives the B-52H the capability to acquire real-time intelligence, surveillance and reconnaissance (ISR) with full-motion video, provide 'overwatch' presence and deliver precision-guided weapons in support of ground forces. In addition to providing aircrews with a critical long-range, positive target identification capability, the system's video downlink allows ISR information to be transmitted to forward-deployed forces. In August 2009, the USAF awarded Lockheed Martin a Phase 3 integration contract for the ATP: this provides for full integration of the pod by linking pod control, display and target

geo-location with the bomber's offensive avionics system via a new multi-function colour display and digital-integrated hand controller. The modifications will allow the B-52H to carry either the LITENING or Sniper pod.

Expanding arsenal

With a strike payload of more than 70,000lb (31,751kg), the B-52H is already capable of carrying the most diverse range of weapons of any combat aircraft in the USAF's inventory.

For the nuclear mission, the B-52H can carry up to 20 air-launched cruise missiles (ALCMs) comprising six under each wing on SUU-67/A pylons and eight in the bomb bay on the Common Strategic Rotary Launcher (CSRL). The B-52H is also equipped to carry and employ the very low observable ▶

Above: *The best replacement for a B-52 is... another B-52. There will always be work for the Buff at Edwards AFB. The silver machine nearer the camera served there for nearly 50 years, and the air force still has Buffs assigned to its 412th TW at the base.* Bob Archer collection

Current B-52H Fleet Locations

Location & Unit	CC	OT	DT	TF	BAI	AR	GI	Storage
Minot AFB, North Dakota								
5th Bomb Wing (AFGSC)							1	
23rd Bomb Squadron	11				2	1		
69th Bomb Squadron	11				2			
Barksdale AFB, Louisiana								
2nd Bomb Wing (AFGSC)							1	
11th Bomb Squadron (Borrows aircraft from 20th BS)								
20th Bomb Squadron	11				2	1		
96th Bomb Squadron	11				2			
307th Bomb Wing (AFRC)								
93rd Bomb Squadron (FTU)				16	2			
343rd Bomb Squadron (Borrows aircraft from 93rd BS)								
53rd Wing (ACC)								
49th Test & Evaluation Squadron		1			1			
Edwards AFB, California								
412th Test Wing (AFMC)								
419th Flight Test Squadron			2					
Sheppard AFB, Texas								
82nd Training Wing (AETC)							2	
Davis-Monthan AFB, Arizona								
309th Aerospace Maintenance & Regeneration Group (AFMC)								13
Total	44	1	2	16	11	2	4	13

Abbreviations. AR: Attrition Reserve, BAI: Backup Aircraft Inventory, CC: Combat Coded, DT: Developmental Testing, FTU: Formal Training Unit, GI: Ground Instruction, OT: Operational Testing, TF: Training Funded

AGM-129A Advanced Cruise Missile, but only on SUU-72/A wing pylons because the ACM is too large to fit the CSRL. However, the USAF recently withdrew the AGM-129A from service and is in the process of demilitarizing them. Both missiles employ the W80-1 nuclear warhead.

The CSRL is also capable of carrying up to eight B61-7 or B83 nuclear bombs. Although the launcher is physically capable of mixed bomb or bomb/ALCM loads, it is only operationally certified to carry one type of weapon at a time.

For conventional missions, the B-52H can employ a very wide range of conventional munitions using both internal and external carriage options. Using the internal CSRL and/or external cruise missile pylons, it can carry up to 20 AGM-86C/D Conventional Air-Launched Cruise Missiles (CALCM). Underwing conventional 'stub' pylons, equipped with the heavy stores adapter beam (HSAB), can carry up to nine weapons, each weighing more than 3,000lb (1,360kg) (the exact figure is classified). An alternative external weapons carriage option involves modified AGM-28 Hound Dog pylons, each with two multiple ejector racks (MER) that enable the aircraft to carry 12 weapons under each wing. However, the AGM-28 pylon/MER combination only supports ballistic or 'dumb' munitions in the 500lb (227kg) and 750lb (340kg) classes; these unguided weapons are being withdrawn from use.

The HSAB pylons support the widest range of conventional ordnance. With two pylons, the B-52H can carry 16 Wind-Corrected Munitions Dispensers (WCMD), 12 AGM-154 Joint Standoff Weapons (JSOW), 12 AGM-158 Joint Air-to-Surface Standoff Missiles (JASSM), or 12 Joint Direct Attack Munitions (JDAM). The pylons were also compatible with the AGM-84 Harpoon anti-shipping missile and the AGM-142 Have Nap missile, but those munitions are no longer in the USAF inventory.

Historically, internal conventional weapons carriage has been limited to free-fall ballistic or dumb weapons. For weapons such as the 500lb (227kg) class Mk 82 general purpose (GP)

bomb and 750lb (340kg) class M117 bombs, and similarly-sized naval mines, the bomb bay is fitted with three cluster racks, each with nine weapon stations thus enabling carriage of up to 27 weapons in the bay. For 2,000lb (907kg) class weapons, two four-station clip-in racks are used. Weapons in the latter class include the Mk 84 GP bomb, and naval mines including the Mk 60 CAPTOR (enCAPsulated TORpedo) and Mk 65 Quickstrike.

Whereas the WCMD was first deployed over Afghanistan in 2002, the JSOW entered service in 2003 and was deployed during Operation 'Iraqi Freedom'. The JDAM achieved limited initial operational capability in 1998 and the B-52H was the first aircraft to be equipped with the JASSM, which was cleared for operational use in October 2003. The steady shift away from ballistic 'dumb' ordnance toward employment of precision guided weapons has led to efforts to integrate a MIL-STD-1760 data bus capability to the internal weapons bay.

Modifications included in the B-52 Advanced Weapons Integration (AWI) and the 1760 internal weapons bay upgrade will expand the aircraft's conventional weapons carriage capability by modifying equipment and software. The USAF has designated 40 CSRLs as "excess" to nuclear requirements and will dedicate them to strictly conventional missions; as part of the project, they will be modified to carry a new integrated weapons interface unit (IWIU). Previously tested on a CSRL in 2005, the IWIU is already incorporated on the aircraft's external wing pylons and provides for the carriage and delivery of smart weapons. In a June 2005 test, a B-52H equipped with a prototype of the Boeing-designed IWIU released eight 2,000lb JDAMs from the aircraft's internal bomb bay at the Utah Test and Training Range. Once equipped with the IWIU, the launchers are no longer capable of deploying nuclear weapons and are referred to as common rotary launchers (CRL).

The aircraft's stores management and offensive avionics software will also be incrementally updated to allow for the installation and delivery of 2,000lb (907kg) GBU-31s, 500lb (227kg), GBU-38 JDAMs, 500lb (227kg) GBU-54 Laser JDAMs, AGM-158 JASSM and JASSM-extended range (JASSM-ER), ADM-160B miniature air-launched decoys (MALD) and ADM-160C MALD-jammers (MALD-J). Later upgrades will provide for carrying the family of WCMDs, laser-guided bombs (LGBs) and additional weapons such as the 2,000lb (907kg) GBU-56 laser JDAM – as well as mixed loads – on the CRL.

According to Lt Gen James Kowalski, commander of the USAF's Global Strike Command, "the B-52 delivers the widest variety of stand-off, direct-attack nuclear and conventional weapons in the air force". The CRL boosts the number of weapons the B-52H can carry from 12 to 20, an increase of 60%. Upgrades are planned for 70 aircraft in 2014, comprising 54 USAF and 16 AFRC aircraft; and six in 2015, comprising four USAF and two AFRC bombers. By 2015, 'Increment 1' of the upgrade programme should allow eight JDAMs, JSOWs or MALDs to be loaded on the CRL while 'Increment 2' will facilitate the various weapons to be carried simultaneously – allowing the aircraft to service more targets with greater flexibility. They might also be made capable of deploying the 250lb (113kg) small diameter bomb, further increasing the number of weapons available to

*Above: **Versatility ensures that the B-52 remains at the forefront of USAF planning. Its ability to loiter for a long time until cleared for a target makes it the perfect platform to act in support of infantry by delivering weapons to the battlefield on demand.** Key collection*

*Below: **Ready for wherever they have been needed, Buffs have been on call for half a century; air force planners are ensuring that they are kept up to date so that they can continue to serve for decades to come.** USAF*

mission planners. Integration of the MALD, MALD-J and JASSM-ER began in 2006 when Boeing received $150 million for the Smart Weapons Integration Next Generation (SWING) programme; demonstrations with the Laser JDAM took place in September 2008.

The air force plans to begin development of a long-range stand-off weapon in 2015. Intended as replacement for the AGM-86 ALCM, the LRSO will equip both the B-52H and B-2A. This stealthy weapon will enable the B-52 to carry out strikes deep

in enemy territory from stand-off ranges. It's part of the USAF's Long-Range Strike family of systems, which includes the new Long-Range Strike Bomber that will eventually replace the B-52. The air force hopes to acquire 80 to 100 new bombers at a cost of $550 million each to replace both the B-52H and B-1B, beginning in the 2020s.

Strategic Radar Replacement (SR2)

The USAF is also making plans to replace the B-52H's Northrop Grumman APQ-166 mechanical-

ly-scanned array (MSA) strategic radar. Last upgraded in 1985, it's become increasingly unserviceable and is nearing the end of its useful life. The air force intends its replacement to take advantage of advanced capabilities associated with modern non-developmental radars and wants to maximise commonality with other platforms.

Replacement by a system that delivers new and enhanced capabilities while performing all of the mission functions of the APQ-166 could result in the integration of a new active electronically-scanned array (AESA) system – however, budgetary restrictions might have an effect on such a plan. A request for information was issued to industry in November 2009 and risk-reduction work and trade studies will be completed in mid-2012. Boeing then expects to begin developing specific requirements and conducting source selection. The air force had planned to begin development in 2013 after an analysis of alternatives and competitive contract selection were completed; however, the current budget environment could also affect this plan. Nevertheless, the service hopes to begin installation of new systems on the bombers between 2016 and 2018. ▶

*Above: **One of Barksdale AFB's 307 Wing's Buffs, with a LITENING targeting pod visible under the wing.** Frank Noort*

Above: *Two bases are currently home to B-52s dedicated to wartime missions: Minot AFB, in North Dakota, and Louisiana's Barksdale AFB; the latter's busy ramp is shown here.* Frank Noort

Below: *Although this 307 Wing jet is more than 50 years old, it certainly doesn't look its age.* Frank Noort

Support

Boeing has provided engineering support for the B-52 since delivery of the first examples nearly 60 years ago and currently more than 360 employees support that work at the company's facility in Wichita, Kansas. In June 2009, Boeing received a USAF contract to provide continued engineering support for the B-52H fleet. As part of the Engineering Sustainment Program (ESP) contract, which could be worth as much as $750 million, Boeing will support the fleet with software updates, communications, avionics and electrical upgrades, structural analysis, rewiring and other tasks as directed by the USAF over ten years. Separately, in September 2010, Boeing was given a B-52 weapon system modernisation contract from the USAF that could be worth as much $11.8 billion over a period of eight years. This work will include production associated with numerous projects including CONECT, EHF, SR2 and others as they are developed.

Structurally, the B-52 fleet is considered to be in good shape and, as indicated above, the average aircraft has around 10,000 hours of service life left. The Oklahoma City Air Logistics Center's B-52 Sustainment Division (GKD) is responsible for the total life-cycle management of the fleet including development, modification, test, sustainment and support. The 76th Maintenance Wing's 76th Aircraft Maintenance Group is responsible for

carrying out programmed depot maintenance (PDM), repairs and modifications for the B-52H fleet. Its 565th Aircraft Maintenance Squadron (AMXS) conducts PDM on around 17 B-52Hs annually and each aircraft is rotated through the depot every four years. Air Force Materiel Command monitors and tracks the bombers by tail number and the service provided during PDM is virtually tailor-made for each individual airframe and based on numerous factors including its flight profiles. During PDM

the aircraft often receive minor modifications that improve the integrity of the structures, reduce corrosion and enhance safety and include minor service life extension efforts, replacing obsolete or removing inactivated systems, and carrying out weight reduction initiatives. Planned airframe modifications will replace the aircraft's anti-skid system, which is used to maintain safe braking during landings and taxiing. The new system, which will be fielded in 2014/2015, will correct support-

ability and obsolescence issues.

Continued modernisation will ensure that the B-52H's systems remain as capable as its airframe, which will serve the USAF for at least 28 years more.

An out of service date (OSD) in the 2040 to 2044 timeframe has often been mentioned when referring to the Stratofortress: however, Boeing engineers believe that the airframe is sound and that the estimate could be a conservative one. In fact, no major structural modifications are required until the first aircraft nears the 28,000 flight-hour milestone. At that point repairs and modifications, or replacement of upper wing surfaces, could add another eight to ten years to its service life – meaning the B-52H could conceivably still be in service when Boeing and the US Air Force celebrate the 100th anniversary of the YB-52's first flight! ✪

The author wishes to thank Mr Scot Oathout, Boeing B-52 Program Director, M Jim Kroening, Boeing B-52 Development Programs Manager, Ms Jennifer Hogan of Boeing Global Services and Support Communications and Lt Col Brian C Rogers (Ret) for their assistance with the preparation of this article.

Above: *The B-52H uses spoilers for yaw control, with no ailerons fitted. The massive 'barn door' flaps are fully deployed in this landing shot.* Frank Noort

Below: *The nearer of the two jets wears the marking of the USAF's training wing for the B-52, the 307th BW, while behind it is 8th Air Force's flagship, tail number 61-0008. Both units are based at Barksdale where this shot was taken.* Frank Noort

Your favourite magazine now on the iPhone, iPad and Android.
Download now.
Available from iTunes, Google Play and the App Store.

Available on the iPhone
App Store

App with FREE ISSUE
£2.49
IN APP ISSUES £3.99

Search: Airforces Monthly

Also available for download

Search:
Air International

Search:
Aviation News

App with FREE ISSUE
£2.49
IN APP ISSUES £3.99

NEW FREE Aviation Specials App **NEW**

Simply download to purchase digital versions of your favourite aviation specials in one handy place! Once you have the app, you will be able to download new, out of print or archive specials for less than the cover price!

Search: Aviation Specials

IN APP ISSUES £3.99

App with FREE ISSUE
£2.49
IN APP ISSUES £3.99

How it Works.

Simply download the AirForces Monthly app and receive the latest or a recent back issue (from December 2010 onwards) completely free. Once you have the app, you will be able to download new or other back issues for less than the newsstand price or, alternatively, subscribe to save even more!

Don't forget to register for your Pocketmags account. This will protect your purchase in the event of a damaged or lost device. It will also allow you to view your purchases on multiple platforms.

B-52 Database

Abbreviations
BS: Boeing serial number
USAFS: USAF serial number
OSD: Original & subsequent designation

BS: 16248 **USAFS:** 49-0230
OSD:: XB-52-BO
Used for development trials, including fitting of a shorter fin until flown to Wright-Patterson AFB, Ohio and scrapped.

BS: 16249 **USAFS:** 49-0231
OSD: YB-52-BO
Scrapped at Wright-Patterson AFB, Ohio. On display at USAF Museum 1957- 1960s.

BS: 16491 **USAFS:** 52-0001
OSD: B-52A-1-BO
Scrapped at Tinker AFB, Oklahoma in April 1961. Tinker was home to the Oklahoma City Air Material Area where major maintenance was carried out on B-52s and it is likely that some serious defect was discovered and it was cheaper to scrap it than effect repairs.

BS: 16492 **USAFS:** 52-0002
OSD: B-52A-1-BO > XB-52G
Used for development tests before being transferred to Chanute AFB in July 1959 for use as a GIA. Burnt in 1966 while being used to make a film for trainee fire-fighters.

BS: 16493 **USAFS:** 52-0003
OSD: B-52A-1-BO > NB-52A
First flight, Summer 1954 and then to US Air Force Flight Test Center, Edwards AFB, California. Modified to NB-52A to carry various experimental aircraft including North American X-15. Now at Pima Air & Space Museum, Tucson, Arizona; oldest B-52 to survive named 'The High and Mighty One'.

BS: 16494 **USAFS:** 52-0004
OSD: RB-52B-5-BO
To MASDC December 1, 1966 and scrapped.

BS: 16495 **USAFS:** 52-0005
OSD: RB-52B-5-BO > B-52B > GB-52B > B-52B
After being used for test flights for six months it was converted to B-52B standard and delivered to Castle AFB, California's 95th BW until it was flown to MASDC on February 10,1966 before leaving for the 3415th Maintenance and Supply Group at Lowry AFB, Aurora, Colorado, later the Lowry Technical Training Center, later that year for uses as a GB-52B GIA. It was put on display at Lowry AFB in April of 1984 and went to the co-located Wings Over the Rockies Air and Space Museum when Lowry AFB closed in 1994. Still preserved outside in 1960s grey and white colour scheme, on October 21, 2011 it was installed on a pedestal overlooking the 'Runway of Honor' exhibit.

BS: 16496 **USAFS:** 52-0006
OSD: RB-52B-5-BO
To MASDC May 2, 1966 and scrapped.

BS: 16497 **USAFS:** 52-0007
OSD: RB-52B-10-BO
To MASDC December 2, 1966. It was transferred to Holloman AFB, New Mexico, where it was tested to destruction.

BS: 16498 **USAFS:** 52-0008
OSD: RB-52B-10-BO > NB-52B
NASA test bed as 'NASA 008'. Preserved at

First of the line. XB-52 49-0230.
USAF

the Air Force Flight Test Center Museum (AFFTC), Edwards AFB, California since October 2005.

BS: 16499 **USAFS:** 52-0009
OSD: RB-52B-10-BO
The 34th B-52 to be lost and the last 'B' model, it crashed on February 5, 1964 near Tranquility, west of San Joaquin, Fresno, California after the crew of seven abandoned ship after a fire in the hydraulic system got out of control. The captain of the 93rd BW jet had set the controls to take the machine out to the open sea, a long way away, but it crashed on farmland. This was the RB-52B that was fitted with the MD-5 DFCS that incorporated a pair of M24A-1 20mm cannon as an alternative to the standard A-3A system employed on the other nine of the first ten RB-52Bs built.

BS: 16500 **USAFS:** 52-0010
OSD: RB-52B-10-BO
To MASDC February 15, 1966. Transferred to Holloman AFB, New Mexico, in May 1966 where it was tested to destruction.

BS: 16501 **USAFS:** 52-0011
OSD: RB-52B-10-BO
To MASDC August 6, 1966 and scrapped.

BS: 16502 **USAFS:** 52-0012
OSD: RB-52B-10-BO
To MASDC February 15, 1966. Returned to service but back to MASDC July 1, 1966 and scrapped.

BS: 16503 **USAFS:** 52-0013
OSD: RB-52B-10-BO
First B-52 to drop a nuclear weapon for which reason it was preserved at the National Atomic Museum, Kirtland AFB, Albuquerque, New Mexico. The museum has since been renamed the National Museum of Nuclear Science and History and moved off base but remains in Albuquerque.

BS: 16838 **USAFS:** 52-8710
OSD: RB-52B-15-BO
To MASDC September 30, 1965 and scrapped.

BS: 16839 **USAFS:** 52-8711
OSD: RB-52B-15-BO > B-52B > GB-52B > B-52B
First B-52 to be delivered to SAC on June 28, 1955 when it was handed over to the 93rd Bombardment (Heavy) Wing at Castle AFB, California. It was converted to B-52B standard before being transferred to the 22nd (Heavy) Bombardment Wing, March AFB, California in December 1963; finally it was transferred to the Strategic Aerospace Museum (since renamed the Strategic Air & Space Museum), Omaha, Nebraska on September 29, 1965 and dropped from the USAF inventory.

BS: 16840 **USAFS:** 52-8712
OSD: RB-52B-15-BO
To MASDC January 2, 1966 and scrapped.

BS: 16841 **USAFS:** 52-8713
OSD: RB-52B-15-BO
To MASDC March 2, 1966 and scrapped.

BS: 16842 **USAFS:** 52-8714
OSD: RB-52B-15-BO > GB-52B
First B-52B to be retired. Transferred to Chanute Technical Training Center, Chanute AFB, Illinois on March 8, 1965, where it was used as a GIA before eventually being scrapped there.

BS: 16843 **USAFS:** 52-8715
OSD: RB-52B-15-BO
To MASDC January 28, 1966; scrapped.

BS: 16844 **USAFS:** 52-8716
OSD: RB-52B-20-BO
The third B-52 to be lost it was flying with the training unit, the 93rd BW, on November 30, 1956. Two minutes and 44 seconds into what appeared to be a routine flight it crashed four miles north of Castle AFB, California and burnt out. Eye witnesses reported the aircraft was in flames before it hit the ground. Because this was a training flight there were ten souls onboard, all of whom lost their lives.

BS: 16845 53-0366
OSD: RB-52B-25-BO
To MASDC January 20, 1966; scrapped.

BS: 16846 53-0367
OSD: RB-52B-25-BO
To MASDC January 6, 1966; scrapped.

BS: 16847 53-0368
OSD: RB-52B-25-BO
To MASDC January 17, 1966; scrapped.

BS: 16848 53-0369
OSD: RB-52B-25-BO
To MASDC January 26, 1966; scrapped.

BS: 16849 53-0370
OSD: RB-52B-25-BO
To MASDC January 26, 1966; scrapped.

BS: 16850 53-0371
OSD: RB-52B-25-BO
The 15th B-52 to be lost. This 93rd BW aircraft was wrecked on the runway at Castle AFB, California on January 29, 1959 after take-off was aborted at high speed. The crew evacuated the jet safely.

BS: 16851 53-0372
OSD: RB-52B-25-BO
To MASDC February 18, 1967; scrapped.

BS: 16852 53-0373
OSD: B-52B-25-BO
To MASDC January 22, 1966; scrapped.

BS: 16853 **USAFS:** 53-0374
OSD: B-52B-25-BO
To MASDC January 8, 1966; scrapped.

BS: 16854 **USAFS:** 53-0375
OSD: B-52B-25-BO
To MASDC January 4, 1966; scrapped.

BS: 16855 **USAFS:** 53-0376
OSD: B-52B-25-BO
To MASDC January 14, 1966; scrapped.

BS: 16856 **USAFS:** 53-0377
OSD: RB-52B-30-BO > GRB-52B
To GIA Andersen AFB, Guam then scrapped.

BS: 16857 **USAFS:** 53-0378
OSD: RB-52B-30-BO
To MASDC June 29, 1966; scrapped.

BS: 16858 **USAFS:** 53-0379
OSD: RB-52B-30-BO
53-0379 was transferred to the Air Force Flight Test Center (AFFTC) in 1965, where it was used extensively for arrester barrier tests. It was deleted from the USAF

inventory in 1970 and is to this day stored, in a very dilapidated condition, at the south end of Rogers Dry Lake at Edwards AFB, California.

BS: 16859 **USAFS:** 53-0380
OSD: B-52B-30-BO

The 27th B-52 to be lost. On April 7, 1961 this 95th BW machine named 'Ciudad Juarez', flying from its base at Biggs AFB, Texas was shot down (inadvertently) by 188th Fighter Squadron New Mexico ANG F-100A 53-1662 with an AIM-9B Sidewinder air-to-air missile. The Super Sabre was conducting a practice intercept on the Buff with the intention of simulating a launch. Unfortunately the missile fired, struck the engine pylon on the B-52 causing the wing to break off. The jet crashed and three of the eight souls on board perished.

BS: 16860 **USAFS:** 53-0381
OSD: B-52B-30-BO

To MASDC May 12, 1965; scrapped.

BS: 16861 **USAFS:** 53-0382
OSD: B-52B-30-BO

The sixth B-52 to be lost. Another 93rd BW casualty, it was damaged beyond repair on landing at Castle AFB, California on November 6, 1957 after the landing gear lever latch failed during a touch and go landing, resulting in the gear retracting while the aircraft was still on runway.

BS: 16862 **USAFS:** 53-0383
OSD: B-52B-30-BO

To MASDC June 28, 1966; scrapped.

BS: 16863 **USAFS:** 53-0384
OSD: B-52B-30-BO

The first B-52 to be lost. One of the early aircraft delivered to Castle AFB, California for training with the 93rd BW, it broke up in flight on February 16, 1956 following an uncontrollable fire which started when the starboard forward alternator failed; it crashed near Tracey, Sacramento, California. Four of the crew of eight were killed, the remainder escaped.

BS: 16864 **USAFS:** 53-0385
OSD B-52B-30-BO

To MASDC February 4, 1966; scrapped.

BS: 16865 **USAFS:** 53-0386
OSD: B-52B-30-BO

To MASDC October 10, 1965; scrapped.

BS: 16866 **USAFS:** 53-0387
OSD: B-52B-30-BO

To MASDC June 29, 1966; scrapped.

BS: 16867 **USAFS:** 53-0388
OSD: B-52B-35-BO

To MASDC June 30, 1966; scrapped.

BS: 16868 **USAFS:** 53-0389
OSD: B-52B-35-BO

To MASDC February 8, 1966; scrapped.

BS: 16869 **USAFS:** 53-0390
OSD: B-52B-35-BO

The 23rd B-52 to be lost. The bomber crashed on January 19, 1961 while assigned to the 95th BW based at Biggs AFB, Texas after turbulence-induced structural failure at high level; another aircraft to be lost to this problem. Of the crew of eight, only the co-pilot survived after ejecting successfully.

BS: 16870 **USAFS:** 53-0391
OSD: B-52B-35-BO

To MASDC February 10, 1966; scrapped.

BS: 16871 **USAFS:** 53-0392
OSD: B-52B-35-BO

To MASDC June 28, 1966; scrapped.

BS: 16872 **USAFS:** 53-0393
OSD: B-52B-35-BO

The second B-52 to be lost and another one from the 93rd BW, it caught fire in flight

and lost a wing on September 17, 1956. It crashed near Highway 99, nine miles (14 km) south east of Madera, California. The pilot and co-pilot successfully ejected but the remaining five souls onboard were lost.

BS: 16873 **USAFS:** 53-0394
OSD: B-52B-35-BO

This aircraft was eventually flown to the US Air Force Museum, but was scrapped in the early 1990s; the nose section was preserved with the Walter Soplata collection, Newbury, Ohio. It flew with the 95th BW from Biggs AFB, Texas named 'City of El Paso' during the 1960s.

BS: 16874 **USAFS:** 53-0395
OSD: B-52B-35-BO

To MASDC June 25, 1966; scrapped.

BS: 16875 **USAFS:** 53-0396
OSD: B-52B-35-BO

To MASDC June 29, 1966; scrapped.

BS: 16876 **USAFS:** 53-0397
OSD: B-52B-35-BO

To MASDC June 25, 1966; scrapped.

BS: 16877 **USAFS:** 53-0398
OSD: B-52B-35-BO

To MASDC November 28, 1965; scrapped.

BS: 16878 **USAFS:** 53-0399
OSD: B-52C-40-BO

The first B-52C, although not the first to fly, it was retained for service and modification testing and assigned to the Aeronautical Systems Division at Wright-Patterson Air Force Base, Ohio. Redesignated as JB-52C or NB-52C depending on the specific project. To MASDC July 28, 1975 and was eventually broken up.

BS: 16879 **USAFS:** 53-0400
OSD: B-52C-40-BO

First B-52C to fly, on March 9, 1956, it was sent to MASDC September 28, 1971 where it was scrapped September 15, 1993.

BS: 16880 **USAFS:** 53-0401
OSD: B-52C-40-BO

To MASDC March 23, 1971 and scrapped in January 1994.

BS: 16881 **USAFS:** 53-0402
OSD: B-52C-40-BO

To MASDC September 29, 1971 and scrapped in October 1993.

BS: 16882 **USAFS:** 53-0403
OSD: B-52C-40-BO

To MASDC August 31, 1971 and scrapped December 1993.

BS: 16883 **USAFS:** 53-0404
OSD: B-52C-40-BO

To MASDC July 27, 1971 and scrapped in

September 1993.

BS: 16884 **USAFS:** 53-0405
OSD: B-52C-40-BO

To MASDC August 12, 1971 and scrapped in October 1993.

BS: 16885 **USAFS:** 53-0406
OSD: B-52C-40-BO

The 29th B-52 to be lost. Whilst engaged in a low-level training flight this 99th BW 'C' model broke up in flight on January 24, 1963 and crashed at Elephant Mountain, near Greenville, Maine. This aircraft was another of the 'high tailed' B-52s to suffer a structural failure at station 1655 in the fin due to buffeting stresses during turbulence, all with fatal results. The transition from high to low altitude bombing missions increased stress on the airframe. Only two of the nine crewmembers survived the crash. Almost exactly one year later, yet another aircraft was lost after failure in the same section of the tail. Modifications to modify the tail and remedy the fault began in earnest in 1964 and the vertical stabilizer was reinforced throughout the B-52 fleet. For more about the crash see *www. mewreckchasers.com/B52C.html*.

BS: 16886 **USAFS:** 53-0407
OSD: B-52C-40-BO

To MASDC August 5, 1971 and scrapped in January 1994.

BS: 16887 **USAFS:** 53-0408
OSD: B-52C-40-BO

To MASDC August 10, 1971 and scrapped in October 1993.

BS: 17159 **USAFS:** 54-2664
OSD: B-52C-45-BO

To MASDC August 26, 1971 and scrapped in January 1994.

BS: 17160 **USAFS:** 54-2665
OSD: B-52C-45-BO

To MASDC July 7, 1971 and scrapped December 1993.

BS: 17161 **USAFS:** 54-2666
OSD: B-52C-45-BO

The 61st B-52 to be lost, and the last 'C' model, crashed into Lake Michigan near Charlevoix, Michigan on January 7, 1971 during a practice bomb-run, exploding on impact. Only a small amount of wreckage, two life vests, and some spilled fuel of the 9th BW aircraft was found, in Little Traverse Bay. All nine souls onboard were lost.

BS: 17162 **USAFS:** 54-2667
OSD: B-52C-45-BO

The 47th B-52 to be lost. This 306th BW

jet crashed near Cape Kennedy, Florida on August 30, 1968 after it had been abandoned by its crew following electrical failure that resulted in fuel starvation.

BS: 17163 **USAFS:** 54-2668
OSD: B-52C-45-BO

To MASDC September 2, 1971 and scrapped December 1993.

BS: 17164 **USAFS:** 54-2669
OSD: B-52C-45-BO

To MASDC July 6, 1971 and scrapped in October 1993.

BS: 17165 **USAFS:** 54-2670
OSD: B-52C-45-BO

To MASDC September 23, 1971 and scrapped in September 1993.

BS: 17166 **USAFS:** 54-2671
OSD: B-52C-45-BO

To MASDC September 9, 1971 and scrapped in October 1993.

BS: 17167 **USAFS:** 54-2672
OSD: B-52C-45-BO

To MASDC August 24, 1971 and scrapped in October 1993.

BS: 17168 **USAFS:** 54-2673
OSD: B-52C-45-BO

To MASDC September 27, 1971 and scrapped December 1993.

BS: 17169 **USAFS:** 54-2674
OSD: B-52C-45-BO

To MASDC August 7, 1971 and scrapped in October 1993.

BS: 17170 **USAFS:** 54-2675
OSD: B-52C-45-BO

To MASDC July 22, 1971 and scrapped in October 1993.

BS: 17171 **USAFS:** 54-2676
OSD: B-52C-50-BO

The fifth B-52 to be lost and the first 'C' model on March 29, 1957. It had been retained by Boeing for tests and designated as a JB-52C and never delivered to the USAF. It crashed whilst on a test flight from the Boeing Plant at Wichita, Kansas. During negative 'G' conditions the constant speed drive failed leading to the complete loss of AC electrical power. Two of the four souls on board were lost; the pilot, Ross B Patrick, and the navigator, John W McCort.

BS: 17172 **USAFS:** 54-2677
OSD: B-52C-50-BO

To MASDC August 3, 1971 and scrapped in January 1994.

BS: 17173 **USAFS:** 54-2678
OSD: B-52C-50-BO

To MASDC August 19, 1971 and scrapped.

The first Buff to fly, YB-52 49-0231. USAF

BS: 17174   **USAFS:** 54-2679
OSD: B-52C-50-BO
To MASDC July 13, 1971 and scrapped in October 1993.

BS: 17175   **USAFS:** 54-2680
OSD: B-52C-50-BO
To MASDC July 8, 1971 and scrapped in October 1993.

BS: 17176   **USAFS:** 54-2681
OSD: B-52C-50-BO
To MASDC September 21, 1971 and scrapped in October 1993.

BS: 17177   **USAFS:** 54-2682
OSD: B-52C-50-BO
The 17th B-52 to be lost. The nose radome of this 99th BW machine failed in flight on August 10, 1959 and the crew ejected 20 miles east of New Hampton, NH.

BS: 17178   **USAFS:** 54-2683
OSD: B-52C-50-BO
To MASDC September 14, 1971 and scrapped in October 1993.

BS: 17179   **USAFS:** 54-2684
OSD: B-52C-50-BO
To MASDC September 16, 1971 and scrapped in October 1993.

BS: 17180   **USAFS:** 54-2685
OSD: B-52C-50-BO
To MASDC July 29, 1971 and scrapped in September 1993.

BS: 17181   **USAFS:** 54-2686
OSD: B-52C-50-BO
To MASDC September 7, 1971 and scrapped December 1993.

BS: 17182   **USAFS:** 54-2687
OSD: B-52C-50-BO
To MASDC July 20, 1971 and scrapped in October 1993.

BS: 17183   **USAFS:** 54-2688
OSD: B-52C-50-BO
To MASDC August 17, 1971 and scrapped in September 1993.

BS: 464001   **USAFS:** 55-0049
OSD: B-52D-1-BW
To MASDC October 4, 1978 and scrapped in September 1994.

BS: 464002   **USAFS:** 55-0050
OSD: B-52D-1-BW
The 78th B-52 to be lost. On Dec 22, 1972 this 43rd SW machine assigned to the 307th BW was using the callsign 'BLUE 01' when it was shot down by a SA-2 SAM over North Vietnam during Linebacker II, crashing near Bach Mai. All six crewmembers were KIA.

BS: 464003   **USAFS:** 55-0051
OSD: B-52D-1-BW
To MASDC November 15, 1978 and scrapped December 1994.

BS: 464004   **USAFS:** 55-0052
OSD: B-52D-5-BW
Landed back at U-Tapao with SAM damage November 22, 1972.; repaired and returned to service. To MASDC September 21, 1978 and scrapped in May 1992.

BS: 464005   **USAFS:** 55-0053
OSD: B-52D-5-BW
To MASDC August 22, 1978 and scrapped in September 1994.

BS: 464006   **USAFS:** 55-0054
OSD: B-52D-5-BW
To MASDC November 28, 1978 and scrapped December 1994.

BS: 464007   **USAFS:** 55-0055
OSD: B-52D-10-BW
To MASDC November 21, 1978 and scrapped December 1994.

BS: 464008   **USAFS:** 55-0056
OSD: B-52D-10-BW
The 83rd B-52 to be lost, this 307th SW, jet, call-sign 'RUBY 02', was hit by SA-2 SAM over Vinh, North Vietnam on January 3, 1973 and crashed into the South China Sea. The crew was rescued by helicopters from the USS *Saratoga*.

BS: 464009   **USAFS:** 55-0057
OSD: B-52D-10-BW
Preserved Historic Airpark, Maxwell AFB, Alabama, still wearing the markings of its last unit, Carswell AFB's 7th BW.

BS: 464010   **USAFS:** 55-0058
OSD: B-52D-10-BW
The 87th B-52 to be lost. 'BANDO 71' crashed near Guam on December 11, 1974 after instrument failure led to loss of control and structural failure.
Two of the crew of six survived. The bomber, which was assigned to the 43rd SW at the time of its loss, had already survived being struck by three SA-2 SAMs over Vietnam on the night of January 13/14, 1974 but on that occasion the crew managed to struggle back to U-Tapao, Thailand.

BS: 464011   **USAFS:** 55-0059
OSD: B-52D-10-BW
To MASDC May 3, 1982 and scrapped December 1994.

BS: 464012   **USAFS:** 55-0060
OSD: B-52D-10-BW
The 33rd B-52 to be lost. 484th BW 'D' model 'BUZZ 14' was on a ferry flight from Westover AFB, Massachusetts to Turner AFB, Georgia on January 13, 1964 having diverted there after a Chrome Dome mission, when it crashed near Cumberland, Maryland after turbulence caused the vertical stabilizer to break off at high altitude. Two Mk 53 nuclear weapons were recovered from the crash site, loaded on to flat-bed trucks marked explosives [!], covered with two tarpaulins and driven to the local airport where they were collected by a USAF C-124C Globemaster. Only two of the five crew survived although four of them ejected relatively safely; the unfortunate two succumbed to the winter cold before they could be rescued.

BS: 464013   **USAFS:** 55-0061
OSD: B-52D-15-BW
The 77th B-52 to be lost in action, 'SCARLET 01' was shot down on December 22, 1972 by a SA-2 SAM over North Vietnam during Linebacker II and crashed near Bach Mai. All six crewmembers of this 22nd BW jet that was assigned to the 307th SW were KIA.

BS: 464014   **USAFS:** 55-0062
OSD: B-52D-15-BW
Having been received into the SAC inventory in February 1957, 55-0062 went to Carswell AFB, Texas. It made its last flight to K I Sawyer AFB, Marquette, Michigan on September 15, 1983 and has been displayed there ever since. It has 14,984 flying hours on the clock.

BS: 464015   **USAFS:** 55-0063
OSD: B-52D-15-BW
With Pate Museum, Cresson, Texas but scrapped there in 1995.

BS: 464016   **USAFS:** 55-0064
OSD: B-52D-15-BW
To MASDC September 12, 1978 and scrapped in September 1994.

BS: 464017   **USAFS:** 55-0065
OSD: B-52D-20-BW
The 13th B-52 to be lost. This 42nd BW aircraft crashed between Inver Grove Heights and St Paul, Minnesota on September 16, 1958 following flight control failure which led to the tail section breaking off. Only one crewmember of the eight aboard survived.
Several members of a family living in a farm near the crash-site were injured. There is a plaque recalling the events on a granite monument at the site.

BS: 464018   **USAFS:** 55-0066
OSD: B-52D-20-BW
To MASDC October 20, 1982 and scrapped December 1994.

BS: 464019   **USAFS:** 55-0067
OSD: B-52D-20-BW
To MASDC May 11, 1982 and then towed across the road to be preserved at the Pima Air & Space Museum, Tucson, Arizona, still wearing (the very faded) marks of its last operator, the 7th Bombardment Wing from Carswell AFB, Texas and its name 'Lone Star Lady'.

BS: 17184   **USAFS:** 55-0068
OSD: B-52D-55-BO
Preserved USAF History and Traditions Museum, Lackland AFB, Texas.

BS: 17185   **USAFS:** 55-0069
OSD: B-52D-55-BO
To MASDC October 8, 1982 and scrapped December 1994.

BS: 17186   **USAFS:** 55-0070
OSD: B-52D-55-BO
To MASDC November 10, 1982 and scrapped December 1994.

BS: 17187   **USAFS:** 55-0071
OSD: B-52D-55-BO
To MASDC August 29, 1983 and from there to Mobile, Alabama and preserved at the USS *Alabama* (BB 60) Battleship Memorial Park Aircraft Collection It was damaged by Hurricane Katrina but is still present wearing its name 'Calamity Jane'.

BS: 17188   **USAFS:** 55-0072
OSD: B-52D-55-BO
To MASDC August 22, 1978 and scrapped in September 1994.

BS: 17189   **USAFS:** 55-0073
OSD: B-52D-55-BO
To MASDC October 18, 1982 and scrapped December 1994.

BS: 17190   **USAFS:** 55-0074
OSD: B-52D-55-BO
To MASDC April 29, 1982 and scrapped December 1994.

BS: 17191   **USAFS:** 55-0075
OSD: B-52D-55-BO
To MASDC October 14, 1982 and scrapped December 1994.

BS: 17192   **USAFS:** 55-0076
OSD: B-52D-55-BO
To MASDC June 23, 1977 and scrapped in September 1994.

BS: 17193   **USAFS:** 55-0077
OSD: B-52D-55-BO
To MASDC July 25, 1983 and scrapped.

BS: 17194   **USAFS:** 55-0078
OSD: B-52D-55-BO
The 93rd B-52 to be lost, and the last 'D' model, this 22nd BW jet crashed near La Junta, Colorado on October 30, 1981 during a low-level night mission, killing the eight crew members.

BS: 17195   **USAFS:** 55-0079
OSD: B-52D-55-BO
To MASDC October 12, 1982 and scrapped

BS: 17196   **USAFS:** 55-0080
OSD: B-52D-55-BO
To MASDC October 26, 1982 and scrapped December 1994

BS: 17197   **USAFS:** 55-0081
OSD: B-52D-55-BO
To MASDC August 15, 1978 and scrapped in September 1994

BS: 17198   **USAFS:** 55-0082
OSD: B-52D-55-BO
The fourth B-52 to be lost and the first 'D' model. This 42nd BW 70th BS crashed near Loring AFB, Maine on January 10, 1957 during a training flight. The Instructor Pilot (IP) had the co-pilot close his eyes while he put the aircraft in an unusual attitude and then instructed him to recover. The co-pilot misread the data from the flight instruments and took the wrong corrective action, which caused the aircraft to disintegrate. There were nine men aboard - the crew plus the IP, and two instructors. The co-pilot survived. It was his third time in a crash and his third time as the only survivor.

BS: 17199   **USAFS:** 55-0083
OSD: B-52D-55-BO
While flying in this aircraft, tail-gunner A1C Albert E More shot down a North Vietnamese MiG-21 on December 14, 1972 with the B-52's .50in radar-guided tail guns over North Vietnam during Linebacker II when serving with the 307th SW. Now preserved at the USAF Academy, Colorado.

BS: 17200   **USAFS:** 55-0084
OSD: B-52D-55-BO
To MASDC September 20, 1983 and scrapped in March 1995

BS: 17201   **USAFS:** 55-0085
OSD: B-52D-55-BO
Carswell AFB's 7th BW was one of the last units to fly the B-52D so it is no surprise that 55-0085 was delivered to what is now known as the Museum of Aviation at Robins AFB, Warner Robins, Georgia from that unit. It made its last flight on August 25, 1983.

BS: 17202   **USAFS:** 55-0086
OSD: B-52D-55-BO
To MASDC October 4, 1982 and scrapped in March 1995

BS: 17203   **USAFS:** 55-0087
OSD: B-52D-55-BO
To MASDC November 1, 1982 and scrapped there in March 1995.

BS: 17204 **USAFS:** 55-0088
OSD: B-52D-55-BO

To MASDC October 15, 1982 and scrapped December 1994.

BS: 17205 **USAFS:** 55-0089
OSD: B-52D-60-BO

The 59th B-52 to be lost, this 26th BW jet crashed at Ellsworth AFB, South Dakota during landing on April 3, 1970. All nine on board were saved despite the fact that the aircraft had crashed into a building containing 25,000 gallons of jet fuel.

BS: 17206 **USAFS:** 55-0090
OSD: B-52D-60-BO

To MASDC October 21, 1982 - no longer present.

BS: 17207 **USAFS:** 55-0091
OSD: B-52D-60-BO

To MASDC October 8, 1982 and scrapped in October 1993.

BS: 17208 **USAFS:** 55-0092
OSD: B-52D-60-BO

To MASDC July 25, 1983 and scrapped in March 1995.

BS: 17209 **USAFS:** 55-0093
OSD: B-52D-60-BO

The tenth B-52 to be lost. Eight of the crew of nine was killed when it flew into the ground in a farmer's field in bad weather on July 29, 1958, three miles south of Loring AFB, Maine where it was based with the 42nd BW 70th BS.

BS: 17210 **USAFS:** 55-0094
OSD: B-52D-60-BO

B-52D 55-0094 was delivered to Loring AFB, Maine for service with the 42nd BW on April 30, 1957. It was modified with the big belly fit and served in Southwest Asia. This aircraft is preserved with the Kansas Aviation Museum near, McConnell AFB, Kansas.

BS: 17211 **USAFS:** 55-0095
OSD: B-52D-60-BO

The nose section was saved when the bomber was scrapped and it was then preserved at the Chanute Aerospace Museum Foundation, Rantoul MAP, Illinois where it remains.

BS: 17212 **USAFS:** 55-0096
OSD: B-52D-60-BO

To MASDC November 8, 1978 and scrapped December 1994.

BS: 17213 **USAFS:** 55-0097
OSD: B-52D-60-BO

The 66th B-52 to be lost, it crash landed at U-Tapao AB, Thailand October 15, 1972 while flying with the 43rd SW and was eventually scrapped there in February 1973. Its tail was used in the repair of 56-0604.

BS: 17214 **USAFS:** 55-0098
OSD: B-52D-60-BO

BS: 17215 **USAFS:** 55-0099
OSD: B-52D-60-BO

Involved in an engine run accident at Andersen AFB, Guam and ripped open underneath the nose radome. Left out in the open as a decoy for Soviet satellite reconnaissance. Scrapped in Oct 1983 and moved to the fire training area.

BS: 17216 **USAFS:** 55-0100
OSD: B-52D-60-BO

55-0100 was heavily used in the Vietnam War. It flew its final combat mission on December 29, 1972 and was one of the three final B-52 aircraft to bomb North Vietnam as part of Operation Linebacker II. After the war, approval was obtained to retain the bomber at Andersen AFB, Guam as a memorial. The memorial was dedicated on February 12, 1974 and the jet remained on display at Andersen until severe corrosion was discovered. In 1984 it was replaced by 56-0586, painted as 55-0100 which was then taken to the west side of the airfield and slated for destruction under the Strategic Arms Limitation Agreement (SALT). It was dismantled between July 12 - 16, 1986 but was destroyed in a typhoon in 1987. Some small remains still survive and constitute another memorial with two plaques giving the machine's history.

BS: 17217 **USAFS:** 55-0101
OSD: B-52D-60-BO

To MASDC October 6, 1982 and scrapped December 1994.

BS: 17218 **USAFS:** 55-0102
OSD: B-52D-60-BO

The ninth B-52 to be lost. No one was hurt when this 42nd BW machine was destroyed on the ground when it caught fire on June 26, 1958 at Loring AFB, Maine. Such fires were not uncommon.

BS: 17219 **USAFS:** 55-0103
OSD: B-52D-60-BO

The 49th B-52 to be lost, on November 19, 1968. This 306th BW (machine, flown by a crew from the 99th BW's 346th BS but attached to the 4252nd SW, call-sign 'CREAM 02' was the fifth aircraft in a six-jet formation on a mission to bomb Vietnam from Kadena AB, Okinawa , Japan. The briefing called for the aircraft to takeoff at 60 second intervals. Take off was aborted on the takeoff run when it was decided that the aircraft had not gained enough speed to safely takeoff. Its load of 500lb bombs detonated and the aircraft was completely destroyed with only the undercarriage and engines identifiable as aircraft parts. Of the eight souls on board, all escaped before the bombs exploded but two subsequently died of burns. The crash was a catalyst to the movement to get Okinawa handed back to Japan; there was a series of serious disturbances and protests about the potential for an even larger disaster.

BS: 17220 **USAFS:** 55-0104
OSD: B-52D-60-BO

To MASDC May 27, 1982 and scrapped in March 1995.

BS: 17221 **USAFS:** 55-0105
OSD: B-52D-65-BO

To MASDC October 3, 1983. Transferred to Seoul, Korea and preserved at the War Memorial museum in the city.

BS: 17222 **USAFS:** 55-0106
OSD: B-52D-65-BO

To MASDC November 28, 1978 and scrapped in September 1994.

BS: 17223 **USAFS:** 55-0107
OSD: B-52D-65-BO

To MASDC October 13, 1982 and scrapped in October 1993.

BS: 17224 **USAFS:** 55-0108
OSD: B-52D-65-BO

The 35th B-52 to be lost. The 462nd SAW bomber had been engaged on a night low-level mission from Larson AFB, Washington on October 10, 1964 when it crashed 51 miles (80 km) southeast of Glasgow AFB, Montana killing the crew of seven.

BS: 17225 **USAFS:** 55-0109
OSD: B-52D-65-BO

To MASDC June 24, 1977 and scrapped in February 1994.

BS: 17226 **USAFS:** 55-0110
OSD: B-52D-65-BO

The 67th B-52 to be lost and the first to succumb to enemy action. Having taken off from U-Tapao in Thailand, this 307th SW B-52D call-sign 'OLIVE 02' was hit by a SA-2 SAM on November 22,1972 while attacking Vinh airfield in the south of North Vietnam during 'Linebacker I'. Crashed in Thailand after crew ejected safely .

BS: 17227 **USAFS:** 55-0111
OSD: B-52D-65-BO

To MASDC October 5, 1982 and scrapped in March 1995.

BS: 17228 **USAFS:** 55-0112
OSD: B-52D-65-BO

Tested to destruction by Boeing at Wichita, Kansas in 1973.

BS: 17229 **USAFS:** 55-0113
OSD: B-52D-65-BO

To MASDC May 4, 1983 and scrapped in October 1993.

BS: 17230 **USAFS:** 55-0114
OSD: B-52D-65-BO

The 21st B-52 to be lost. A 99th BW machine, it crashed December 9, 1960 on a flight from Westover AFB, Massachusetts. While descending to a low-level route the navigator ejected in the mistaken belief that the jet was in trouble. The pilot, unaware of what had happened, concluded that the aircraft was breaking up and ordered the rest of the crew to eject. One person, the gunner, was killed after ejecting. The pilot had established the aircraft in straight and level flight before giving the order for the remainder of the crew to eject and it flew round in circles before flying into the ground near Barr, Vermont, 70 miles (130 km) northeast of the bailout point.

BS: 17231 **USAFS:** 55-0115
OSD: B-52D-65-BO

The 50th B-52 to be lost. On December 3, 1968 when serving with the 306th BW but attached to the 4252nd SW it burnt out on the ground at Kadena AB, Okinawa, Japan.

BS: 17232 **USAFS:** 55-0116
OSD: B-52D-65-BO

The 84th B-52 to be lost, this 30th SW jet made emergency landing at DaNang AB, South Vietnam on January 13, 1973 after being hit by SA-2 SAMs. Because of the end of the Vietnam war on April 1, 1973 the machine was scrapped at DaNang on March 29, 1973 because there wasn't sufficient time to repair it.

BS: 17233 **USAFS:** 55-0117
OSD: B-52D-65-BO

To MASDC October 3, 1978 and scrapped April 1994.

BS: 464020 **USAFS:** 55-0673
OSD: B-52D-20-BW

To MASDC November 4, 1982 and scrapped.

BS: 464021 **USAFS:** 55-0674
OSD: B-52D-20-BW

To MASDC October 4, 1983 and scrapped.

BS: 464022 **USAFS:** 55-0675
OSD: B-52D-20-BW

To MASDC October 22, 1982 and scrapped.

BS: 464023 **USAFS:** 55-0676
OSD: B-52D-25-BW

The 54th B-52 to be lost while serving with 70th BW on July 19, 1969. The jet took off from U-Tapao AB, Thailand in heavy rain and immediately experienced engine problems. The crew tried to go-around, but the jet crashed just short of the runway; they had not had time to jettison the bomb load. Rescue HH-43B Huskie 59-1562, coming to fight the fire was destroyed when the bombs exploded; only one of three aboard survived. The crew of the BUFF had in fact already made good its excape.

BS: 464024 **USAFS:** 55-0677
OSD: B-52D-25-BW

Delivered to the Yankee Air Force Museum, Willow Run, Michigan on loan from USAF Museum October 26, 1983 direct from its last unit, the 7th BW at Carswell AFB, Texas. Still present in March 2012 but as a museum spokesman said, 'We're not sure

Roll-out of the first B-52D to be built at the Wichita plant. Key collection

for how long.' It is suffering from corrosion and being parked outside for three decades hasn't improved its condition.

BS: 464025   **USAFS:** 55-0678
OSD: B-52D-25-BW
To MASDC October 17, 1978 and scrapped.

BS: 464026   **USAFS:** 55-0679
OSD: B-52D-25-BW
Preserved March Field Air Museum,.

BS: 464027   **USAFS:** 55-0680
OSD: B-52D-25-BW
To MASDC September 14, 1978 and scrapped.

BS: 17263   **USAFS:** 56-0580
OSD: B-52D-70-BO
To MASDC October 19, 1982 and scrapped.

BS: 17264   **USAFS:** 56-0581
OSD: B-52D-70-BO
To MASDC August 17, 1978 and scrapped.

BS: 17265   **USAFS:** 56-0582
OSD: B-52D-70-BO
To MASDC September 19, 1978 where it was broken up. The nose was sent to the NMUSAF Wright-Patterson AFB, Ohio for display but it was scrapped in 1996.

BS: 17266   **USAFS:** 56-0583
OSD: B-52D-70-BO
To MASDC August 30, 1978 and scrapped.

BS: 17267   **USAFS:** 56-0584
OSD: B-52D-70-BO
The 80th B-52 to be lost. 'ASH 01' crashed on landing at U-Tapao AB, Thailand on December 26,1972 after being hit by SA-2 SAM over Kinh No, North Vietnam during Linebacker II. Four crewmembers of this 22nd BW machine were killed and only two survived.

BS: 17268   **USAFS:** 56-0585
OSD: B-52D-70-BO
Preserved Air Force Flight Test Center Museum, Edwards AFB, California.

BS: 17269   **USAFS:** 56-0586
OSD: B-52D-70-BO
This aircraft had been relegated to use as a GIA at Andersen AFB, Guam at the end of its operational career. A memorial to those who flew from Andersen while taking part in the Vietnam War, the 'Arc Light Memorial', featuring B-52D 55-0100 was dedicated on February 12, 1974, the date of the first anniversary of the return of prisoners war from north Vietnam to Clark AFB in the Philippines.
Because of corrosion and storm damage 55-0100 was scrapped and '586, painted to represent it, put in its place. It remains at the memorial park to this day.

BS: 17270   **USAFS:** 56-0587
OSD: B-52D-70-BO
To MASDC November 3, 1982 and scrapped December 1994.

BS: 17271   **USAFS:** 56-0588
OSD: B-52D-70-BO
To MASDC May 5, 1982 and scrapped in September 1994.

BS: 17272   **USAFS:** 56-0589
OSD: B-52D-70-BO > GB-52D
Severely damaged by SAM and landed at Da Nang. on a mission from U-Tapao on April 23, 1972. 20,000 man hours later the 400 holes in the airframe had been repaired and it returned to service on September 1, 1973. Sent to Sheppard AFB, Texas for use as a GIA but then renovated for display purposes at the Technical Training Center on the base.

BS: 17273   **USAFS:** 56-0590
OSD: B-52D-70-BO
To MASDC November 9, 1978 and scrapped.

B-52D 56-0595 was lost in an accident during the Vietnam war. USAF

BS: 17274   **USAFS:** 56-0591
OSD: B-52D-75-BO
The 16th B-52 to be lost. Named 'Tommy's Tigator', This aircraft was used to test hydrogen bomb blast effects during the Operation Hardtack tests at Eniwetok, Runit and Bikini. It crashed on June 23, 1959 during a test flight near Burns, Oregon after the horizontal stabiliser suffered turbulence-induced failure at low-level. The change in tactics bought about by improved Soviet defences meant that attack profiles had been changed from high to low-level penetration of enemy airspace and the airframe was not robust enough to withstand the stresses imposed on it flying at high speed below 500ft.

BS: 17275   **USAFS:** 56-0592
OSD: B-52D-75-BO
To MASDC December 7, 1978 and scrapped March 9, 1994; its nose was sent to Tinker AFB, Oklahoma on April 21, 2001 for use as a GIA in the CLSS Compound.

BS: 17276   **USAFS:** 56-0593
OSD: B-52D-75-BO
The 53rd B-52 to be lost, it was destroyed on May 10, 1969 when serving with the 509th BW, flying from Andersen AFB, Guam assigned to 4133 BW(P). It crashed into the Pacific after take-off from Andersen AFB, Guam using callsign 'GREEN 03'. All six souls on board were lost. This accident was perhaps doubly tragic because the aircraft and crew was acting as a spare for another aircraft that had aborted its mission minutes before the scheduled take off; they were not scheduled to be taking part in the mission.

BS: 17277   **USAFS:** 56-0594
OSD: B-52D-75-BO
The 91st B-52 to be lost, 22nd BW machine 'ARLEN 14' crashed on October 19, 1978 near Sunnymead, California after suffering multiple engine failure while attempting to land at March AFB in slight fog. Five of the crew of six were killed.

BS: 17278   **USAFS:** 56-0595
OSD: B-52D-75-BO
The 41st B-52 to be lost. On July 7, 1967 this 22nd BW, assigned to the 4133rd BW(P) and using the call-sign 'RED 02' collided with B-52D 56-0627, 'RED 01' over the South China Sea off the coast of Vietnam near Saigon while the aircraft were changing formation leader. When the collision occurred, RED 2 was passing under RED 01 to take the lead. RED 1's left wing dipped suddenly and severed the tail section of RED 02. One of the crew members, Captain

Toki Endo reported on *www.ejection-history.org.uk* 'General Crumm, our Division Commander, was on the 'plane that day as a third pilot. He went down with the 'plane. His wife and daughter were back on the base waiting on him so they could go back to the States. They were all packed; they had finished their two-year tour.' Of the six others onboard, three survived, two were confirmed as killed at the time and one other was reported missing in action.

BS: 17279   **USAFS:** 56-0596
OSD: B-52D-75-BO
To MASDC May 28, 1982 and scrapped in October 1993.

BS: 17280   **USAFS:** 56-0597
OSD: B-52D-75-BO
The seventh B-52 to be lost. A 92nd BW machine, so the first USAF aircraft lost that was not serving with the training Wing, the 93rd BW, it crashed on December 12, 1957 at the end of the runway at its base, Fairchild AFB, Washington. The stabilizer trim switch had been wired incorrectly so its function was reversed, so when the pilot thought he was trimming the aircraft to fly more nose down the nose tilted up more until the aircraft stalled and crashed. The tail section, housing the gunner, broke off in the crash and he was the only person to survive, relatively unscathed. The other eight souls on board perished.

BS: 17281   **USAFS:** 56-0598
OSD: B-52D-75-BO
To MASDC January 29, 1976 and scrapped in September 1994.

BS: 17282   **USAFS:** 56-0599
OSD: B-52D-75-BO
The 81st B-52 to be lost. 'ASH 02' crashed in Thailand on December 27, 1972 after being hit by a SA-2 SAM over Hanoi, North Vietnam during Linebacker II. It was a 7th BW aircraft assigned to the 307th SW at U-Tapao RTAFB; the crew came from the 28th BW. All six crewmembers ejected safely and were rescued by helicopter.

BS: 17283   **USAFS:** 56-0600
OSD: B-52D-75-BO
To MASDC November 8, 1982 and scrapped in March 1995.

BS: 17284   **USAFS:** 56-0601
OSD: B-52D-75-BO
The 43rd B-52 to be lost. This 22nd BW aircraft was assigned to the 4133rd BW(P) when it was hit over Vinh, North Vietnam on July 8, 1967. The aircraft used two call-signs on the fateful night, 'BROWN 02' when it was operating in its cell of three machines but

'CORNY 26' when it was on its own. When it suffered a complete hydraulic failure the pilot elected to divert to Da Nang AB, Vietnam for an emergency, flap-less landing. It landed about half-way down the 10,000 foot runway and, unable to stop, over-ran the end of the runway into a minefield. The mines detonated destroying the aircraft and killing the entire crew, who were from the 454th BW 736 BS, Columbus AFB, Mississippi, except for the tail gunner who was in the tail section that broke away from the rest of the jet.

BS: 17285   **USAFS:** 56-0602
OSD: B-52D-75-BO
To MASDC September 12, 1983 and scrapped in March 1995.

BS: 17286   **USAFS:** 56-0603
OSD: B-52D-75-BO > GB-52D
To MASDC September 12, 1978 but it was removed from storage and used as a GIA at Lowry AFB. It was dumped at Lowry AFB by October 1988 and it may be the source of the B-52 cockpit behind the bar of the B-52 Billiards Bar at 1920 Market Street, Denver.

BS: 17287   **USAFS:** 56-0604
OSD: B-52D-75-BO
Returned to U-Tapao on November 5, 1972 with more than 300 holes caused by SAMs. Repaired using vertical stabilizer from 55-0097. To MASDC September 27, 1978 and scrapped in March 1995.

BS: 17288   **USAFS:** 56-0605
OSD: B-52D-75-BO
The 82nd B-52 to be lost, on December 27, 1972, 'COBALT 01' was a 7th BW machine assigned to the 43rd SW. It was shot down over North Vietnam during Linebacker II and crashed near Trung Quan. Two crewmembers were KIA, and four ejected to become POWs. It is possible that this may be the second B-52 claimed as a MiG-21 air-to-air victory, corresponding to Vu Xuan Thieu of the 921st Sao Dao Fighter Regiment 'Red Star', based at Cam Thuy firing a K-13 (AA-2 *Atoll*) AAM from his MiG-21 . The MiG-21 was also destroyed by the resulting explosion and some sources claim that Vu Xuan Thieu deliberately rammed the Buff with his MiG.

BS: 17289   **USAFS:** 56-0606
OSD: B-52D-75-BO
To MASDC May 5, 1982 and scrapped in March 1995.

BS: 17290   **USAFS:** 56-0607
OSD: B-52D-75-BO
The 20th B-52 to be lost. This 92nd BW jet burned out on the runway at its base at

Fairchild AFB, Washington on April 1, 1960 following failure of the main wings. The crew managed to evacuate safely.

BS: 17291   **USAFS:** 56-0608
OSD: B-52D-75-BO

The 70th B-52 to be lost, this 99th BW B-52D, assigned to the 307th SW at U-Tapao and using call-sign 'ROSE 01' was shot down on December 18, 1972 by a SA-2 SAM during Linebacker II.
The aircraft landed in a lake in the Ba Dinh district, now named 'B-52 Lake'. Today bits of wreckage form a war memorial there and still more pieces are displayed in a museum. Of the crew of six, four bailed out and became PoWs and the other two were killed in the crash.

BS: 17292   **USAFS:** 56-0609
OSD: B-52D-75-BO

To MASDC November 27, 1978 and scrapped April 1994.

BS: 17293   **USAFS:** 56-0610
OSD: B-52D-75-BO

The eighth B-52 to be lost. Two of the eight crew and three on the ground were killed on February 11, 1958 when this 28th BW aircraft crashed short of the runway at Ellsworth AFB, South Dakota following fuel pump failure on final approach to land. Condensed water in the fuel had frozen in the fuel filters and stopped them working.

BS: 17294   **USAFS:** 56-0611
OSD: B-52D-80-BO

To MASDC August 24, 1978 and scrapped in September 1994.

BS: 17295   **USAFS:** 56-0612
OSD: B-52D-80-BO

Now preserved at the Castle Air Force Base Museum, Atwater, California, it last served with the 93rd BW at Castle and was retired from there in 1982.

BS: 17296   **USAFS:** 56-0613
OSD: B-52D-80-BO

To MASDC September 5, 1978 and scrapped in September 1994.

BS: 17297   **USAFS:** 56-0614
OSD: B-52D-80-BO

To MASDC September 12, 1983 and scrapped.

BS: 17298   **USAFS:** 56-0615
OSD: B-52D-80-BO

To MASDC October 5, 1978 and scrapped.

BS: 17299   **USAFS:** 56-0616
OSD: B-52D-80-BO

Tested to destruction by Boeing at Wichita, Kansas in 1971.

BS: 17300   **USAFS:** 56-0617
OSD: B-52D-80-BO

To MASDC September 20, 1983 and scrapped in March 1995.

BS: 17301   **USAFS:** 56-0618
OSD: B-52D-80-BO

To MASDC November 30, 1978 and scrapped in May 1995.

BS: 17302   **USAFS:** 56-0619
OSD: B-52D-80-BO

To MASDC August 24, 1978 and scrapped in September 1994.

BS: 17303   **USAFS:** 56-0620
OSD: B-52D-80-BO

To MASDC November 29, 1971; it had been assigned to permanent test duties with Air Force Systems Command and Air Force Special Weapons Center as a NB-52D and it was also used as a JB-52; as a result it was the only B-52D not to wear camouflage paint. It was also used for dropping nuclear weapons in tests in the Pacific. It was scrapped on October 25, 1993.

BS: 17304   **USAFS:** 56-0621
OSD: B-52D-80-BO

To MASDC October 1, 1982 and scrapped.

BS: 17305   **USAFS:** 56-0622
OSD: B-52D-80-BO

The 73rd B-52 to be lost, on December 20, 1972, was a 7th BW jet assigned to the 307th SW and based at U-Tapao RTAFB using the call-sign 'ORANGE 02'.
It was hit by a SA-2 SAM over North Vietnam during Linebacker II and finally crashed in Thailand. Four of the crew was KIA, and two others ejected to became POWs.

BS: 17306   **USAFS:** 56-0623
OSD: B-52D-80-BO

To MASDC November 29, 1978 and scrapped in September 1994.

BS: 17307   **USAFS:** 56-0624
OSD: B-52D-80-BO

To MASDC September 1, 1978 and scrapped in September 1994.

BS: 17308   **USAFS:** 56-0625
OSD: B-52D-80-BO

The 62nd B-52 to be lost. One engine failed and engine number seven caught fire and the fire spread to the starboard wing of this 306th BW jet, call-sign 'SIR 21', 20 minutes into a routine training flight from McCoy AFB, Florida, now Orlando IAP.
The crew attempted to return to the base, but the aircraft crashed just short of Runway 18R in a residential part of Orlando to the north of the airfield.
One person on the ground and the seven crew were killed.

BS: 17309   **USAFS:** 56-0626
OSD: B-52D-80-BO

To MASDC October 16, 1978 and scrapped December 1994.

BS: 17310   **USAFS:** 56-0627
OSD: B-52D-80-BO

The 42nd B-52 to be lost; it collided with B-52D 56-0595 'RED 02' over the South China Sea off the coast near Saigon while the aircraft were changing formation leader. The bomber was flying with the 452nd BW assigned to the 4133rd BW(P) at Andersen AFB, Guam.
Four of the crew survived but the other three were never found.

BS: 17311   **USAFS:** 56-0628
OSD: B-52D-80-BO

Used as ground instruction machine at Dyess AFB Texas before being scrapped in the early 1980s.

BS: 17312   **USAFS:** 56-0629
OSD: B-52D-80-BO

One of two Buffs preserved at the 8th Air Force Museum at Barksdale AFB, Louisiana, this B-52D arrived in 1983. It is displayed alongside the Buff's nemesis, an SA-2 SAM.

BS: 17313   **USAFS:** 56-0630
OSD: B-52D-80-BO

The 55th B-52 to be lost. This 70th BW jet assigned to 4133rd BW(P) at Andersen AFB, Guam, crashed into the Pacific on July 27, 1969 after the starboard wing came off as the aircraft was getting airborne for an Arc Light mission as 'BLUE 01'; there were no survivors.
The entire fleet of 'D' models was inspected after this incident to see if any of them were suffering from fatigue in the same area. Several needed urgent repairs.

BS: 17314   **USAFS:** 56-0631
OSD: B-52E-85-BO

To MASDC June 13, 1969 and scrapped in October 1993.

BS: 17315   **USAFS:** 56-0632
B-52E-85-BO > NB-52E

One of the most colourful of the Stratofortresses was the NB-52E Control Configured Vehicle (CCV), which had been operated by the Air Force Flight Dynamics Laboratory. It was retired to MASDC on June 26, 1974 and was scrapped there.

BS: 17316   **USAFS:** 56-0633
OSD: B-52E-85-BO

The 14th B-52 to be lost and the first 'E' model. This 11th BW jet crashed on December 10, 1958 killing all nine occupants when climbing away from Altus AFB, Oklahoma during a routine night-time training flight. A subsequent enquiry revealed that improper use of the stabilizer trim during an overshoot was the cause.

BS: 17317   **USAFS:** 56-0634
OSD: B-52E-85-BO

To MASDC December 8, 1969 and scrapped in October 1993.

BS: 17318   **USAFS:** 56-0635
OSD: B-52E-85-BO

To MASDC February 4, 1970 and scrapped in February 1994.

BS: 17319   **USAFS:** 56-0636
OSD: B-52E-85-BO

To MASDC July 30, 1981 and scrapped there in February 1994. It had been used to test the JT9D turbofan engine for the Boeing 747 programme.

BS: 17320   **USAFS:** 56-0637
OSD: B-52E-85-BO

GIA at Andersen AFB, Guam as GB-52E named 'The Gray Ghost' until May 21, 1976 when the base was hit by Typhoon Pamela and the bomber was flipped on to its back. Shortly thereafter it was relegated for use as a fire trainer at the base.

BS: 17321   **USAFS:** 56-0638
OSD: B-52E-85-BO

To MASDC March 13, 1970 and scrapped in January 1994.

92nd BW B-52D 56-0607 burned out at Fairchild AFB. USAF via Greg Spahr

BS: 17322   **USAFS:** 56-0639
OSD: B-52E-85-BO

To MASDC March 5, 1970 and scrapped.

BS: 17323   **USAFS:** 56-0640
OSD: B-52E-85-BO

To MASDC February 5, 1970 and scrapped in September 1994.

BS: 17324   **USAFS:** 56-0641
OSD: B-52E-85-BO

To MASDC May 26, 1969 and scrapped.

BS: 17325   **USAFS:** 56-0642
OSD: B-52E-85-BO

To MASDC May 12, 1969 and scrapped.

BS: 17326   **USAFS:** 56-0643
OSD: B-52E-85-BO

To MASDC June 26, 1969 and scrapped.

BS: 17327   **USAFS:** 56-0644
OSD: B-52E-85-BO

To MASDC January 23, 1970 and scrapped in September 1993.

BS: 17328   **USAFS:** 56-0645
OSD: B-52E-85-BO

To MASDC November 25, 1969 and scrapped in February 1994.

BS: 17329   **USAFS:** 56-0646
OSD: B-52E-85-BO

To MASDC November 19, 1969 and scrapped in September 1994.

BS: 17330   **USAFS:** 56-0647
OSD: B-52E-85-BO

To MASDC June 17, 1969 and scrapped in January 1994.

BS: 17331   **USAFS:** 56-0648
OSD: B-52E-85-BO

To MASDC March 12, 1970 and scrapped in January 1994.

BS: 17332   **USAFS:** 56-0649
OSD: B-52E-85-BO

To MASDC November 17, 1969 and scrapped in February 1994.

BS: 17333   **USAFS:** 56-0650
OSD: B-52E-90-BO

To MASDC January 21, 1970 and scrapped in January 1994.

BS: 17334   **USAFS:** 56-0651
OSD: B-52E-90-BO

To MASDC January 19, 1970 and scrapped in September 1994.

BS: 17335   **USAFS:** 56-0652
OSD: B-52E-90-BO

To MASDC January 12, 1970 and scrapped in January 1994.

BS: 17336   **USAFS:** 56-0653
OSD: B-52E-90-BO

To MASDC December 12, 1969 and scrapped in September 1994.

BS: 17337   **USAFS:** 56-0654
OSD: B-52E-90-BO

To MASDC June 6, 1969 and scrapped.

BS: 17338   **USAFS:** 56-0655
OSD: B-52E-90-BO

The 31st B-52 to be lost and the last 'E'. Destroyed by fire during maintenance at Walker AFB, NM on January 30, 1963.

BS: 17339   **USAFS:** 56-0656
OSD: B-52E-90-BO

To MASDC February 11, 1970 and scrapped in September 1994.

BS: 464028   **USAFS:** 56-0657
OSD: B-52D-30-BW

On display at the South Dakota Air and Space Museum, Ellsworth AFB since 1987.

BS: 464029   **USAFS:** 56-0658
OSD: B-52D-30-BW

To MASDC April 29, 1982 and scrapped in March 1995.

BS: 464030   **USAFS:** 56-0659
OSD: B-52D-30-BW

To MASDC May 25, 1982 and subsequently

56-0620 was the only B-52D not to wear camouflage paint. USAF

displayed at the Warrior Air Park at Davis-Monthan AFB, Arizona from June 1991 but it was scrapped in 2012.

BS: 464031   **USAFS:** 56-0660
OSD: B-52D-30-BW
To MASDC August 23, 1983 and scrapped in March 1995.

BS: 464032   **USAFS:** 56-0661
OSD: B-52D-30-BW
The eleventh B-52 to be lost. Two 92nd BW machines were lost on September 9, 1958. Both crashed 3 miles north east of Fairchild AFB, Washington after a midair collision at low-level between this jet, assigned to 327 BS call-sign 'OUTCOME 55', and B-52D 56-0681.
The pilot of the other jet was instructed to turn right after completing an overshoot from a GCA approach. The pilot of this machine was heard to radio the tower to tell the other machine to turn left instead but 12 seconds later they collided.
Of the 16 crew on the two jets, 13 were killed. The ECM was the only survivor from this one.

BS: 464033   **USAFS:** 56-0662
OSD: B-52D-30-BW
Scrapped and then blown up in April 1984 at Carswell AFB, Texas.

BS: 464034   **USAFS:** 56-0663
OSD: B-52D-30-BW
To MASDC May 25, 1982 and scrapped in March 1995.

BS: 464035   **USAFS:** 56-0664
OSD: B-52D-30-BW
To GIA at Andersen AFB. Scrapped some time after 1992.

BS: 464036   **USAFS:** 56-0665
OSD: B-52D-30-BW
Hit by SAM over North Vietnam April 9, 1972. Lost two engines, had fuel leaks and over 400 shrapnel punctures. Landed at Da Nang, repaired and returned to service and flew four further missions. After retirement from the 97th Bomb Wing at Blytheville AFB, Arkansas, it was flown to the National Museum of the United States Air Force (NMUSAF), at Wright-Patterson AFB, Dayton, Ohio where it remains.

BS: 464037   **USAFS:** 56-0666
OSD: B-52D-30-BW
To MASDC August 24, 1983 and scrapped in December 1994; its tail is displayed at the Mighty Eighth Air Force Heritage Museum, Savannah, Georgia.

BS: 464038   **USAFS:** 56-0667
OSD: B-52D-30-BW
To MASDC September 12, 1983 and scrapped in March 1995.

BS: 464039   **USAFS:** 56-0668
OSD: B-52D-30-BW
To MASDC November 2, 1982 and scrapped in October 1993.

BS: 464040   **USAFS:** 56-0669
OSD: B-52D-35-BW
The 76th B-52 to be lost, on December 21, 1972, this 306th BW B-52D assigned to the 43rd SW at Andersen AFB, Guam was using the call-sign 'STRAW 02' when it was hit by a SA-2 SAM after attacking the Gia Lam railway repair shops east of Hanoi during Linebacker II. Despite heavy damage, the crew attempted to divert to Thailand but shortly after it crossed into Laotian airspace, the aircraft became uncontrollable and was abandoned; all crewmembers except the radar navigator were rescued.

BS: 464041   **USAFS:** 56-0670
OSD: B-52D-35-BW
To MASDC May 3, 1982 and scrapped in March 1995.

BS: 464042   **USAFS:** 56-0671
OSD: B-52D-35-BW
To MASDC October 1, 1982 and scrapped in March 1995.

BS: 464043   **USAFS:** 56-0672
OSD: B-52D-35-BW
To MASDC May 3, 1983 and scrapped.

BS: 464044   **USAFS:** 56-0673
OSD: B-52D-35-BW
To MASDC September 14, 1978 and scrapped in September 1994.

BS: 464045   **USAFS:** 56-0674
OSD: B-52D-35-BW
The 79th B-52 to be lost, 'EBONY 02', was shot down over North Vietnam on December 26, 1972 during Linebacker II and crashed near Giap Nhi Rail Yard, Hanoi. Two of the crew were killed and four more became POWs. It is likely that this 96th BW aircraft, assigned to the 307th SW at U-Tapao RTAFB may, instead of having been brought down by an SA-2, actually be the B-52 claimed as having fallen to two K-13 (AA-2 *Atoll*) AAMs fired by a MiG-21 flown by Pham Tuan of 921st Sao Dao Fighter Regiment 'Red Star' based at Noi Bai.

BS: 464046   **USAFS:** 56-0675
OSD: B-52D-35-BW
To MASDC October 5, 1978 and scrapped April 1994.

BS: 464047   **USAFS:** 56-0676
OSD: B-52D-35-BW
On display at the Armed Forces and Aerospace Museum, Fairchild AFB, Washington, this B-52D, flying as 'BROWN 03' was credited with shooting down a MiG-21 over North Vietnam on December 12, 1972 during Linebacker II. SSgt Samuel O Turner (tail gunner) shot down the MiG with the bomber's 0.50in radar-guided tail guns.

BS: 464048   **USAFS:** 56-0677
OSD: B-52D-35-BW
The 65th B-52 to be lost. Five crewmen were killed on July 30, 1972 and one

survived when it was struck by lightning after take-off from U-Tapao on a combat mission. The strike knocked out most of the aircraft's instruments and started a fire in the port wing.

BS: 464049   **USAFS:** 56-0678
OSD: B-52D-35-BW
Landed back at U-Tapao on December 18, 1972 so severly damaged that it took 60,000 man-hours to repair. To MASDC October 12, 1978 and scrapped there in September 1994.

BS: 464050   **USAFS:** 56-0679
OSD: B-52D-35-BW
To MASDC October 11, 1982 and scrapped in September 1993.

BS: 464051   **USAFS:** 56-0680
OSD: B-52D-35-BW
Scrapped in April 1984 at Carswell AFB, Texas and the remains left in situ for several months in order that Soviet satellites could confirm its destruction under the Strategic Arms Limitation Treaty (SALT) agreement.

BS: 464052   **USAFS:** 56-0681
OSD: B-52D-40-BW
The twelfth B-52 to be lost. Two 92nd BW machines were lost on September 9, 1958. Both crashed 3 miles north east of Fairchild AFB, Washington after a midair collision at low-level between this jet, assigned to the 325th BS and using call-sign 'OUTCOME 54', and another B-52D 56-0661.
The control tower directed this aircraft to turn right after a GCA approach and the pilot of the other jet radioed for it to turn the other way. Twelve seconds later they collided.
Of the 16 crew on the two jets, 13 were killed. The tail-gunner and instructor pilot survived from OUTCOME 54.

BS: 464053   **USAFS:** 56-0682
OSD: B-52D-40-BW
To MASDC October 19, 1978 and scrapped in May 1992 but the nose was sent to NMUSAF at Wright-Patterson AFB, Ohio for display purposes.

BS: 464054   **USAFS:** 56-0683
OSD: B-52D-40-BW
This 'D' model has been preserved, since 1991, as a gate guard at the Arnold gate of the home of the USAF's B-2A Spirit fleet, Whiteman AFB, Missouri.

BS: 464055   **USAFS:** 56-0684
OSD: B-52D-40-BW
To MASDC May 5, 1983; scrapped October 25, 1993.

BS: 464056   **USAFS:** 56-0685
OSD: B-52D-40-BW
Dyess AFB, outside Abilene, Texas was once one of the main B-52 bases. This Vietnam veteran is preserved with other aircraft that have served at the base in the Linear Air Park just inside the main gate.

BS: 464057   **USAFS:** 56-0686
OSD: B-52D-40-BW
To MASDC August 22, 1983 and scrapped in March 1995.

BS: 464058   **USAFS:** 56-0687
OSD: B-52D-40-BW
On display at the B-52 Memorial Park outside Orlando IAP, Florida. In a former life the airport was McCoy AFB, home of the 306th BW. The jet made its last flight from its last base, Carswell AFB, Texas, where it had served with the 7th BW, on February 20, 1984.

BS: 464059   **USAFS:** 56-0688
OSD: B-52D-40-BW
Scrapped in April 1984 at Carswell AFB, Texas and the remains left in situ for several months in order that Soviet satellites could confirm their destruction under the Strategic Arms Limitation Treaty (SALT) agreement.

BS: 464060   **USAFS:** 56-0689
OSD: B-52D-40-BW
One of only two B-52s to be preserved outside the United States, this 'D' model dominates the American Air Museum at the Imperial War Museum, Duxford, England.

BS: 464061   **USAFS:** 56-0690
OSD: B-52D-40-BW
To MASDC October 28, 1982 and scrapped in October 1993.

BS: 464062   **USAFS:** 56-0691
OSD: B-52D-40-BW
To MASDC October 10, 1978 and scrapped in September 1993.

BS: 464063   **USAFS:** 56-0692
OSD: B-52D-40-BW
Used as a GIA at Tinker AFB, Oklahoma but scrapped some time after 2003.

BS: 464064   **USAFS:** 56-0693
OSD: B-52D-40-BW
To MASDC September 7, 1978 and scrapped in September 1994.

BS: 464065   **USAFS:** 56-0694
OSD: B-52D-40-BW
To MASDC August 22, 1983 and scrapped in March 1995.

BS: 464066   **USAFS:** 56-0695
OSD: B-52D-40-BW
It is appropriate that this bomber has been preserved at Tinker AFB, Oklahoma since being retired in 1984. Tinker has always been one of the USAF's main overhaul facilities and a great deal of the work to perfect the Buff as a weapons system was, and continues to be, done at the base.

BS: 464067   **USAFS:** 56-0696
OSD: B-52D-40-BW
The Jimmy Doolittle Air and Space Museum Foundation located at the Travis Air Force Base Heritage Center, also known as the Travis Air Museum is inside Travis AFB, California; it is one of the larger aircraft

museums in the State. From 1959 to 1968, the 5th Bombardment Wing flew B-52Gs from Travis Air Force Base. Today, the bomber that was delivered to the 28th BW at Ellsworth AFB, South Dakota on November 8, 1957 wears the name 'Twilight D'Light' that it acquired while serving with its last unit, the 7th BW. Having been retired from active service in March 1983, it arrived at Travis in August of that year.

BS: 464068   **USAFS:** 56-0697
OSD: B-52D-40-BW
To MASDC September 20, 1983 and scrapped in March 1995.

BS: 464069   **USAFS:** 56-0698
OSD: B-52D-40-BW
To MASDC November 9, 1982 and scrapped December 1994.

BS: 464070   **USAFS:** 56-0699
OSD: B-52E-45-BW
To MASDC May 22, 1969 and scrapped.

BS: 464071   **USAFS:** 56-0700
OSD: B-52E-45-BW
To MASDC June 5, 1969 and scrapped. It has been reported that the nose section of this aircraft was preserved at Chino and March Field Museum, California but those reports are erroneous, based on markings noted on the nose that were misinterpreted.

BS: 464072   **USAFS:** 56-0701
OSD: B-52E-45-BW
To MASDC May 27, 1969 and scrapped.

BS: 464073   **USAFS:** 56-0702
OSD: B-52E-45-BW
To MASDC June 10, 1969 and scrapped.

BS: 464074   **USAFS:** 56-0703
OSD: B-52E-45-BW
To MASDC May 15, 1969 and scrapped.

BS: 464075   **USAFS:** 56-0704
OSD: B-52E-45-BW
To MASDC February 12, 1970 and scrapped in February 1994.

BS: 464076   **USAFS:** 56-0705
OSD: B-52E-45-BW
To MASDC November 24, 1969 and scrapped in October 1994.

BS: 464077   **USAFS:** 56-0706
OSD: B-52E-45-BW
To MASDC January 9, 1970 and scrapped in September 1994.

BS: 464078   **USAFS:** 56-0707
OSD: B-52E-45-BW
To MASDC March 10, 1970 and scrapped in September 1993.

BS: 464079   **USAFS:** 56-0708
OSD: B-52E-45-BW
Used as GB-52E GIA at Chanute Technical Training Center then scrapped.

BS: 464080   **USAFS:** 56-0709
OSD: B-52E-45-BW
To MASDC June 4, 1969 and scrapped in October 1993.

BS: 464081   **USAFS:** 56-0710
OSD: B-52E-45-BW
To MASDC June 9, 1969 and scrapped.

BS: 464082   **USAFS:** 56-0711
OSD: B-52E-45-BW
To MASDC June 23, 1969 and scrapped in September 1994.

BS: 464083   **USAFS:** 56-0712
OSD: B-52E-45-BW
To MASDC May 15, 1969 and scrapped.

BS: 17408   **USAFS:** 57-0014
OSD: B-52E-90-BO
To MASDC January 20, 1967 and scrapped.

BS: 17409   **USAFS:** 57-0015
OSD: B-52E-90-BO
To MASDC November 13, 1969 and scrapped in September 1994.

BS: 17410   **USAFS:** 57-0016
OSD: B-52E-90-BO
To MASDC August 12, 1969 and scrapped in February 1994.

BS: 17411   **USAFS:** 57-0017
OSD: B-52E-90-BO
To MASDC March 4, 1970 and scrapped in September 1994.

BS: 17412   **USAFS:** 57-0018
OSD: B-52E-90-BO
The 30th B-52 to be lost. On January 30, 1963 on a flight from Walker FB, New Mexico, it crashed in snow-covered mountains in northern New Mexico after the aircraft broke up after encountering turbulence.
Two of the crew of six, the EWO and Gunner did not eject and were killed; the others ejected successfully.

BS: 17413   **USAFS:** 57-0019
OSD: B-52E-90-BO
Sent to Boeing-Wichita on December 1, 1965, where it was used for a teardown inspection to examine the airframe for fatigue and corrosion to assess the condition of the entire B-52 fleet. Long thought to have been scrapped, it may be the basis of the fuselage stored at Wichita to this day.

BS: 17414   **USAFS:** 57-0020
OSD: B-52E-90-BO
To MASDC January 28, 1970; scrapped in 1994.

BS: 17415   **USAFS:** 57-0021
OSD: B-52E-90-BO
To MASDC February 2, 1970 and scrapped in January 1994.

BS: 17416   **USAFS:** 57-0022
OSD: B-52E-90-BO
To MASDC June 20, 1969 and scrapped in February 1994.

BS: 17417   **USAFS:** 57-0023
OSD: B-52E-95-BO
To MASDC June 25, 1969 and scrapped in January 1994.

BS: 17418   **USAFS:** 57-0024
OSD: B-52E-95-BO
To MASDC November 18, 1969 and scrapped in October 1993.

BS: 17419   **USAFS:** 57-0025
OSD: B-52E-95-BO
To MASDC June 19, 1969 and scrapped in February 1994.

BS: 17420   **USAFS:** 57-0026
OSD: B-52E-95-BO
To MASDC June 26, 1969 and scrapped in September 1993.

BS: 17421   **USAFS:** 57-0027
OSD: B-52E-95-BO
To MASDC January 26, 1970 and scrapped in January 1994.

BS: 17422   **USAFS:** 57-0028
OSD: B-52E-95-BO
To MASDC June 28, 1967 and scrapped.

BS: 17423   **USAFS:** 57-0029
OSD: B-52E-95-BO
To MASDC January 17, 1967 and scrapped.

BS: 17424   **USAFS:** 57-0030
OSD: B-52F-100-BO
The first flight of the B-52F was on May 6, 1958, when this, the first of the Seattle-built 'F' models took off. To MASDC December 14, 1967 and subsequently scrapped.

BS: 17425   **USAFS:** 57-0031
OSD: B-52F-100-BO
To MASDC July 12, 1971 and scrapped in September 1994.

BS: 17426   **USAFS:** 57-0032
OSD: B-52F-100-BO
To MASDC November 17, 1978 and scrapped in January 1994.

BS: 17427   **USAFS:** 57-0033
OSD: B-52F-100-BO
To MASDC September 26, 1978 and scrapped in January 1994.

BS: 17428   **USAFS:** 57-0034
OSD: B-52F-100-BO
To MASDC September 5, 1978 and scrapped in March 1994.

BS: 17429   **USAFS:** 57-0035
OSD: B-52F-100-BO
To MASDC November 30, 1978 and scrapped in March 1994.

BS: 17430   **USAFS:** 57-0036
OSD: B-52F-100-BO
The 18th B-52 to be lost. While carrying out a night alert mission on October 15, 1959 from Columbus AFB, this 4228th SW bomber collided with KC-135A 57-1513 during refuelling. The B-52 crashed near Hardingsberg, Kentucky killing four of the eight crewmembers. Two nuclear weapons were recovered from the crash site, one of which was badly damaged by fire. All four aboard the KC-135 were killed when it crashed near Leitchfield, Kentucky.

BS: 17431   **USAFS:** 57-0037
OSD: B-52F-100-BO
To MASDC July 10, 1969 and scrapped in September 1994.

BS: 17432   **USAFS:** 57-0038
OSD: B-52F-105-BO
This aircraft was preserved for many years as the Oklahoma State Fairgrounds, Oklahoma City but in 2007 it was moved to the Joe Davies Heritage Airpark at Palmdale Plant 42, outside Palmdale, California for preservation there. A Hound Dog missile, as carried by the B-52, is also displayed here. This is the only complete B-52F model to be preserved.

BS: 17433   **USAFS:** 57-0039
OSD: B-52F-105-BO
To MASDC July 19, 1971 and scrapped in September 1994.

BS: 17434   **USAFS:** 57-0040
OSD: B-52F-105-BO
To MASDC July 10, 1968 and scrapped.

BS: 17435   **USAFS:** 57-0041
OSD: B-52F-105-BO
The 58th B-52 to be lost, and the last 'F' model, it was severely damaged in a landing accident at its home base of Castle AFB, Atwater, California on October 21, 1969. It was not repaired and scrapped, there were no fatalities.

BS: 17436   **USAFS:** 57-0042
OSD: B-52F-105-BO > GB-52F
At the end of its flying life this was redesignated as a GB-52F for use as a GIA at Chanute AFB. When Chanute closed the aircraft was scrapped but the front fuselage was moved to the Museum of Flying, Santa Monica, California and then to the Yanks Air Museum, Chino, California where it remains to this day. See image page 100.

BS: 17437   **USAFS:** 57-0043
OSD: B-52F-105-BO
The 32nd B-52 to be lost. While serving with the 454th BW the aircraft went into clouds shortly after take-off from Columbus AFB, Mississippi on December 23, 1963 and dived into the ground two minutes later, killing all nine souls aboard.

BS: 17438   **USAFS:** 57-0044
OSD: B-52F-105-BO
To MASDC January 28, 1967 and scrapped.

BS: 17439   **USAFS:** 57-0045
OSD: B-52F-105-BO
To MASDC September 28, 1978 and scrapped December 1994.

BS: 17440   **USAFS:** 57-0046
OSD: B-52F-105-BO
To MASDC July 25, 1969 and scrapped in September 1994.

BS: 17441   **USAFS:** 57-0047
OSD: B-52F-105-BO
The 36th B-52 to be lost and the first to be lost on operations. On June 18, 1965 During the first Arc Light mission it collided with 57-0179 over the Pacific while both aircraft were waiting to join up with KC-135As before carrying out pre-strike refuelling. The crew, temporarily assigned to Andersen AFB Guam, was from the 3960th SW 441st BS based at Mather AFB, Rancho Cordova, California. Five of the 12 people aboard the two jets ejected but one died of his injuries in the sea. The others are listed as Killed in Action (KIA) or Missing in Action (MIA).

BS: 17442   **USAFS:** 57-0048
OSD: B-52F-105-BO > GB-52F
To MASDC August 31, 1978. At the end of its flying career it was flown to MASDC on August 31, 1978 and from there to Lowry AFB, Colorado for use as a GIA on March 6, 1980. When the technical school closed the jet was scrapped and front fuselage went to J W Duff's yard at Denver Stapleton IAP, Colorado where it remains.

BS: 17443   **USAFS:** 57-0049
OSD: B-52F-105-BO
To MASDC July 8, 1968 and scrapped.

BS: 17444   **USAFS:** 57-0050
OSD: B-52F-105-BO
Scrapped at Andersen AFB, Guam in the 1970s.

BS: 17445   **USAFS:** 57-0051
OSD: B-52F-105-BO
To MASDC December 5, 1978 and scrapped in March 1997.

B-52E 56-0643, seemingly being prepared for display at an airshow at Wright-Patterson AFB, Ohio in the early 1960s. Greg Spahr collection

BS: 17446   **USAFS:** 57-0052
OSD: B-52F-105-BO
To MASDC September 7, 1978 and scrapped April 1994.

BS: 17447   **USAFS:** 57-0053
OSD: B-52F-110-BO
To MASDC June 27, 1969 and scrapped in February 1994.

BS: 17448   **USAFS:** 57-0054
OSD: B-52F-110-BO
To MASDC July 9, 1969 and scrapped in September 1994.

BS: 17449   **USAFS:** 57-0055
OSD: B-52F-110-BO
To MASDC September 13, 1971 and scrapped December 1994.

BS: 17450   **USAFS:** 57-0056
OSD: B-52F-110-BO
To MASDC April 7, 1971 and scrapped in September 1994.

BS: 17451   **USAFS:** 57-0057
OSD: B-52F-110-BO
To MASDC August 25, 1971 and scrapped December 1994.

BS: 17452   **USAFS:** 57-0058
OSD: B-52F-110-BO
To MASDC October 17, 1978 and scrapped in March 1994.

BS: 17453   **USAFS:** 57-0059
OSD: B-52F-110-BO
To MASDC August 11, 1971 and scrapped December 1994.

BS: 17454   **USAFS:** 57-0060
OSD: B-52F-110-BO
To MASDC July 26, 1971 and scrapped in January 1994

BS: 17455   **USAFS:** 57-0061
OSD: B-52F-110-BO
To MASDC July 21, 1971 and scrapped in September 1994.

BS: 17456   **USAFS:** 57-0062
OSD: B-52F-110-BO
To MASDC August 4, 1971 and scrapped December 1994.

BS: 17457   **USAFS:** 57-0063
OSD: B-52F-110-BO
To MASDC September 28, 1978 and scrapped December 1994.

BS: 17458   **USAFS:** 57-0064
OSD: B-52F-110-BO
To MASDC August 2, 1971 and scrapped December 1993.

BS: 17459   **USAFS:** 57-0065
OSD: B-52F-110-BO
To MASDC August 9, 1971 and scrapped in January 1994.

BS: 17460   **USAFS:** 57-0066
OSD: B-52F-110-BO
To MASDC June 11, 1969 and scrapped.

BS: 17461   **USAFS:** 57-0067
OSD: B-52F-110-BO
To MASDC July 7, 1969 and scrapped in September 1994.

BS: 17462   **USAFS:** 57-0068
OSD: B-52F-110-BO
To MASDC November 21, 1967 and scrapped.

BS: 17463   **USAFS:** 57-0069
OSD: B-52F-110-BO
To MASDC October 2, 1978 and scrapped in February 1994.

BS: 17464   **USAFS:** 57-0070
OSD: B-52F-110-BO
To MASDC January 31, 1967 and scrapped.

BS: 17465   **USAFS:** 57-0071
OSD: B-52F-110-BO > GB-52F
To the 82nd TRW at Sheppard AFB for use as a GIA and named 'City of Wichita Falls'; scrapped in the late 1990s. See image p102.

Vietnam vet and SAM-hit survivor, 'D' model 56-0665 is nowadays preserved at the NMUSAF, Wright-Patterson AFB, Ohio. USAF

BS: 17466   **USAFS:** 57-0072
OSD: B-52F-110-BO
To MASDC November 21, 1978 and scrapped in March 1994.

BS: 17467   **USAFS:** 57-0073
OSD: B-52F-110-BO
Never delivered and scrapped at Seattle.

BS: 464084   **USAFS:** 57-0095
OSD: B-52E-50-BW
First Wichita-built B-52F to fly on May 14, 1958; it was sent to MASDC November 14, 1969 and was scrapped in February 1994.

BS: 464085   **USAFS:** 57-0096
OSD: B-52E-50-BW
To MASDC January 29, 1970 and scrapped in February 1994.

BS: 464086   **USAFS:** 57-0097
OSD: B-52E-50-BW
To MASDC January 27, 1970 and scrapped in February 1994.

BS: 464087   **USAFS:** 57-0098
OSD: B-52E-50-BW
To MASDC January 22, 1970 and scrapped in January 1994.

BS: 464088   **USAFS:** 57-0099
OSD: B-52E-50-BW
To MASDC January 30, 1970 and scrapped in October 1993.

BS: 464089   **USAFS:** 57-0100
OSD: B-52E-50-BW
To MASDC January 7, 1970 and scrapped in February 1994.

BS: 464090   **USAFS:** 57-0101
OSD: B-52E-50-BW
To MASDC May 20, 1969. The bomber itself was scrapped at MASDC on May 29, 1981, but the nose was saved and by the 1990s was preserved at Gillespie Field, El Cajon, California. It then ended up at the Pacific Aviation Museum, Ford Island, Pearl Harbor, Hawaii where it currently resides.

BS: 464091   **USAFS:** 57-0102
OSD: B-52E-50-BW
To MASDC May 23, 1969 and scrapped.

BS: 464092   **USAFS:** 57-0103
OSD: B-52E-50-BW
To MASDC January 5, 1970 and scrapped in October 1993.

BS: 464093   **USAFS:** 57-0104
OSD: B-52E-50-BW
To MASDC June 12, 1969 and scrapped.

BS: 464094   **USAFS:** 57-0105
OSD: B-52E-50-BW
To MASDC March 9, 1970 and scrapped.

BS: 464095   **USAFS:** 57-0106
OSD: B-52E-50-BW
To MASDC March 11, 1970 and scrapped.

BS: 464096   **USAFS:** 57-0107
OSD: B-52E-50-BW
To MASDC June 16, 1969 and scrapped.

BS: 464097   **USAFS:** 57-0108
OSD: B-52E-50-BW
To MASDC February 10, 1970 and scrapped.

BS: 464098   **USAFS:** 57-0109
OSD: B-52E-50-BW
To MASDC May 19, 1969 and scrapped.

BS: 464099   **USAFS:** 57-0110
OSD: B-52E-55-BW
To MASDC May 21, 1969 and scrapped 1981.

BS: 464100   **USAFS:** 57-0111
OSD: B-52E-55-BW
To MASDC April 18, 1967; scrapped.

BS: 464101   **USAFS:** 57-0112
OSD: B-52E-55-BW
To MASDC February 9, 1970 and scrapped.

BS: 464102   **USAFS:** 57-0113
OSD: B-52E-55-BW
To MASDC January 18, 1967 and scrapped.

BS: 464103   **USAFS:** 57-0114
OSD: B-52E-55-BW
To MASDC, 1967 and scrapped.

BS: 464104   **USAFS:** 57-0115
OSD: B-52E-55-BW
To MASDC January 12, 1970 and scrapped.

BS: 464105   **USAFS:** 57-0116
OSD: B-52E-55-BW
To MASDC June 18, 1969 and scrapped.

BS: 464106   **USAFS:** 57-0117
OSD: B-52E-55-BW
To MASDC January 11, 1967 and scrapped.

BS: 464107   **USAFS:** 57-0118
OSD: B-52E-55-BW
To MASDC January 8, 1970 and scrapped.

BS: 464108   **USAFS:** 57-0119
OSD: B-52E-55-BW
Bailed to GE Flight Test in January 1966 and converted to NB-52E as engine testbed for TF39 and CF6. Put in long term storage in 1972. Decommissioned by GE in 1980 and towed to south end of Rogers Dry Lake bed on Edwards AFB. Still present but cut in to three pieces.

BS: 464109   **USAFS:** 57-0120
OSD: B-52E-55-BW
To MASDC August 14, 1969 and scrapped.

BS: 464110   **USAFS:** 57-0121
OSD: B-52E-55-BW
To MASDC January 6, 1970 and scrapped.

BS: 464111   **USAFS:** 57-0122
OSD: B-52E-55-BW
To MASDC May 28, 1969 and scrapped.

BS: 464112   **USAFS:** 57-0123
OSD: B-52E-55-BW
To MASDC March 2, 1970 and scrapped.

BS: 464113   **USAFS:** 57-0124
OSD: B-52E-55-BW
To MASDC June 11, 1969 and scrapped.

BS: 464114   **USAFS:** 57-0125
OSD: B-52E-55-BW
To MASDC May 29, 1969 and scrapped.

BS: 464115   **USAFS:** 57-0126
OSD: B-52E-55-BW
To MASDC February 6, 1970 and scrapped.

BS: 464116   **USAFS:** 57-0127
OSD: B-52E-55-BW
To MASDC June 24, 1969 and scrapped.

BS: 464117   **USAFS:** 57-0128
OSD: B-52E-55-BW
To MASDC January 12, 1970 and scrapped.

BS: 464118   **USAFS:** 57-0129
OSD: B-52E-55-BW
To MASDC March 3, 1970 and scrapped.

BS: 464119   **USAFS:** 57-0130
OSD: B-52E-55-BW
To MASDC February 3, 1970 and scrapped.

BS: 464120   **USAFS:** 57-0131
OSD: B-52E-60-BW
To MASDC March 6, 1970 and scrapped.

BS: 464121   **USAFS:** 57-0132
OSD: B-52E-60-BW
To MASDC Dec 10, 1969 and scrapped.

BS: 464122   **USAFS:** 57-0133
OSD: B-52E-60-BW
To MASDC May 13, 1969 and scrapped.

BS: 464123   **USAFS:** 57-0134
OSD: B-52E-60-BW
Scrapped at Tinker AFB in 1966. Tinker was home to the Oklahoma City Air Material Area, where major maintenance was carried out on B-52s - it is likely that a serious defect was discovered and it was scrapped.

BS: 464124   **USAFS:** 57-0135
OSD: B-52E-60-BW
To MASDC May 14, 1969 and scrapped.

BS: 464125   **USAFS:** 57-0136
OSD: B-52E-60-BW
To MASDC January 20, 1970 and scrapped.

BS: 464126   **USAFS:** 57-0137
OSD: B-52E-60-BW
To MASDC April 21, 1967 and scrapped.

BS: 464127   **USAFS:** 57-0138
OSD: B-52E-60-BW
To MASDC June 3, 1969 and scrapped.

BS: 464128   **USAFS:** 57-0139
OSD: B-52F-65-BW
To MASDC May 30, 1973 and scrapped 1994.

BS: 464129   **USAFS:** 57-0140
OSD: B-52F-65-BW
To MASDC September 21, 1978 and scrapped December 1994.

BS: 464130   **USAFS:** 57-0141
OSD: B-52F-65-BW
To MASDC January 4, 1967 and scrapped.

BS: 464131   **USAFS:** 57-0142
OSD: B-52F-65-BW
To MASDC October 10, 1978 then scrapped. Nose used as a GIA at Goodfellow AFB, TX.

BS: 464132   **USAFS:** 57-0143
OSD: B-52F-65-BW
To MASDC July 14, 1971 and scrapped in September 1994.

BS: 464133   **USAFS:** 57-0144
OSD: B-52F-65-BW
To MASDC November 2, 1967 and scrapped.

BS: 464134   **USAFS:** 57-0145
OSD: B-52F-65-BW
To MASDC October 11, 1978 and scrapped in March 1994.

BS: 464135   **USAFS:** 57-0146
OSD: B-52F-65-BW
To MASDC January 16, 1968 and scrapped.

BS: 464136   **USAFS:** 57-0147
OSD: B-52F-65-BW
To MASDC August 30, 1978 and scrapped in February 1994.

BS: 464137   **USAFS:** 57-0148
OSD: B-52F-65-BW
To MASDC August 15, 1978 and scrapped

April 1994.

BS: 464138   **USAFS:** 57-0149
OSD: B-52F-65-BW

The 52nd B-52 to be lost. On May 8, 1969 it crashed on the approach to Castle AFB, California and burned out. As part of his job in the Air Force, Reserve Brigadier General James Stewart, the movie star, flew on this aircraft as an observer on a combat mission from Guam when it was serving with the 320th BW in 1966. He ordered that no publicity be given to the event.

BS: 464139   **USAFS:** 57-0150
OSD: B-52F-65-BW

To MASDC August 17, 1978 and scrapped April 1994.

BS: 464140   **USAFS:** 57-0151
OSD: B-52F-65-BW

To MASDC September 8, 1971 and scrapped in May 1992.

BS: 464141   **USAFS:** 57-0152
OSD: B-52F-65-BW

To MASDC August 18, 1971 and scrapped in May 1992.

BS: 464142   **USAFS:** 57-0153
OSD: B-52F-65-BW

To MASDC September 22, 1971 and scrapped in January 1994.

BS: 464143   **USAFS:** 57-0154
OSD: B-52F-65-BW

To MASDC November 7, 1978 and scrapped in January 1994.

BS: 464144   **USAFS:** 57-0155
OSD: B-52F-70-BW

To MASDC July 11, 1969 and scrapped in September 1994.

BS: 464145   **USAFS:** 57-0156
OSD: B-52F-70-BW

To MASDC January 27, 1967 and scrapped.

BS: 464146   **USAFS:** 57-0157
OSD: B-52F-70-BW

To MASDC February 2, 1967 and scrapped.

BS: 464147   **USAFS:** 57-0158
OSD: B-52F-70-BW

To MASDC August 7, 1968 and scrapped.

BS: 464148   **USAFS:** 57-0159
OSD: B-52F-70-BW

To MASDC August 16, 1971 and scrapped.

BS: 464149   **USAFS:** 57-0160
OSD: B-52F-70-BW

To MASDC July 1, 1969 and scrapped in September 1994.

BS: 464150   **USAFS:** 57-0161
OSD: B-52F-70-BW

To MASDC September 24, 1971 and scrapped in September 1994.

BS: 464151   **USAFS:** 57-0162
OSD: B-52F-70-BW

To MASDC September 15, 1971 and scrapped December 1994.

BS: 464152   **USAFS:** 57-0163
OSD: B-52F-70-BW

To MASDC July 2, 1969 and scrapped 1993.

BS: 464153   **USAFS:** 57-0164
OSD: B-52F-70-BW

To MASDC April 18, 1967 and scrapped.

BS: 464154   **USAFS:** 57-0165
OSD: B-52F-70-BW

To MASDC September 21, 1978 and scrapped December 1994.

BS: 464155   **USAFS:** 57-0166
OSD: B-52F-70-BW

The 25th B-52 to be lost. Assigned to the 4134th SW at Mather AFB, California, it had been standing airborne nuclear alert and crashed near Yuba City, California on March 14, 1961 after cabin pressurisation failure forced the aircraft to descend below 10,000ft. This increased fuel consumption to such an extent that it ran out of fuel before it could meet up with a tanker; the crew of eight abandoned the aircraft, baling out between 7,000 and 4,000ft. Two nuclear weapons were later recovered.

BS: 464156   **USAFS:** 57-0167
OSD: B-52F-70-BW

To MASDC January 7, 1967 and scrapped.

BS: 464157   **USAFS:** 57-0168
OSD: B-52F-70-BW

To MASDC June 29, 1972 and scrapped in September 1994.

BS: 464158   **USAFS:** 57-0169
OSD: B-52F-70-BW

To MASDC October 20, 1978 and scrapped in February 1994.

BS: 464159   **USAFS:** 57-0170
OSD: B-52F-70-BW

To MASDC November 14, 1978 and scrapped in March 1994.

BS: 464160   **USAFS:** 57-0171
OSD: B-52F-70-BW

To MASDC December 7, 1978 and scrapped in May 1992.

BS: 464161   **USAFS:** 57-0172
OSD: B-52F-70-BW

The 57th B-52 to be lost, this 93rd BW 329th BS 'F' model crashed on October 9, 1969 about 1,000 feet beyond the end of the runway while doing touch-and-goes at Castle AFB, California. All six crewmembers were killed.

BS: 464162   **USAFS:** 57-0173
OSD: B-52F-70-BW

The 46th B-52 to be lost. This 7th BW machine, 'MEAL 88' crashed in the sea in the Gulf of Mexico on February 29, 1968 not far from Matagorda Island, Texas where it had successfully completed a low-level mission in the Matagorda low-level route. All eight aboard are assumed to have perished and the aircraft and its crew are still officially listed as missing.

BS: 464163   **USAFS:** 57-0174
OSD: B-52F-70-BW

To MASDC August 30, 1971 and scrapped in May 1992.

BS: 464164   **USAFS:** 57-0175
OSD: B-52F-70-BW

To MASDC July 14, 1969 and scrapped in September 1994.

BS: 464165   **USAFS:** 57-0176
OSD: B-52F-70-BW

To MASDC July 9, 1969 and scrapped in September 1994.

BS: 464166   **USAFS:** 57-0177
OSD: B-52F-70-BW

To MASDC September 1, 1971 and scrapped December 1992.

BS: 464167   **USAFS:** 57-0178
OSD: B-52F-70-BW

To MASDC July 28, 1971 and scrapped in September 1994.

BS: 464168   **USAFS:** 57-0179
OSD: B-52F-70-BW

The 37th B-52 to be lost and the second on operations. On June 18, 1965 during the first Arc Light mission it collided with 57-0047 over the Pacific while both were waiting to join up with KC-135As. The crew was from the 3960th SW, 441st BS based at Mather AFB, California, but temporarily assigned to Andersen AFB, Guam. Five of the 12 people aboard the two jets ejected but one died of his injuries in the sea. The others are listed as Killed in Action (KIA) or Missing in Action (MIA). In an attempt to rescue the survivors, Grumman HU-16B 51-5287 landed in heavy seas but was severely damaged and eventually sank. All were rescued by a Norwegian freighter.

BS: 464169   **USAFS:** 57-0180
OSD: B-52F-70-BW

To MASDC June 30, 1969 and scrapped in March 1994.

BS: 464170   **USAFS:** 57-0181
OSD: B-52F-70-BW

To MASDC June 29, 1967; transferred to Boeing Wichita for trials October 10, 1967 and destroyed in tests.

BS: 464171   **USAFS:** 57-0182
OSD: B-52F-70-BW

To MASDC September 20, 1971 and scrapped April 1994.

BS: 464172   **USAFS:** 57-0183
OSD: B-52F-70-BW

To MASDC June 27, 1972 and scrapped December 1994.

B-52Fs 57-0074 to 57-0094 and 57-0184 to 57-0228 were cancelled and not built.

BS: 464173   **USAFS:** 57-6468
OSD: B-52G-75-BW

Preserved as a gate guard at the STRATCOM gate of Offutt AFB, Omaha, Nebraska, still wearing the 'CA' tail code of the last unit to fly it, the 93rd BW at Castle AFB, California.

BS: 464174   **USAFS:** 57-6469
OSD: B-52G-75-BW > GB-52

To the 82nd TRW, Sheppard AF, Texas for use as a GIA but scrapped there in 1994.

BS: 464175   **USAFS:** 57-6470
OSD: B-52G-75-BW > JB-52G

To MASDC October 23, 1990 and scrapped.

BS: 464176   **USAFS:** 57-6471
OSD: B-52G-75-BW

To MASDC July 29, 1992; still present March 2012.

BS: 464177   **USAFS:** 57-6472
OSD: B-52G-75-BW

To MASDC July 8, 1992; still present March 2012.

BS: 464178   **USAFS:** 57-6473
OSD: B-52G-75-BW > JB-52G

To MASDC February 25, 1993; scrapped and the forward fuselage sent to McConnell AFB, Kansas in September 2007 where it is believed to remain. The rest of the aircraft was still present at MASDC in March 2012.

BS: 464179   **USAFS:** 57-6474
OSD: B-52G-75-BW

To MASDC February 25, 1993 and scrapped April 1996.

BS: 464180   **USAFS:** 57-6475
OSD: B-52G-75-BW

To MASDC October 15, 1991 and scrapped.

BS: 464181   **USAFS:** 57-6476
OSD: B-52G-80-BW

To MASDC August 20, 1991; still present March 2012.

BS: 464182   **USAFS:** 57-6477
OSD: B-52G-80-BW > JB-52G

To MASDC September 21, 1990; still present March 2012.

BS: 464183   **USAFS:** 57-6478
OSD: B-52G-80-BW

To MASDC July 27, 1989 and scrapped in March 1997.

BS: 464184   **USAFS:** 57-6479
OSD: B-52G-80-BW

The 98th B-52 to be lost. On October 16, 1984, the 92nd BW aircraft departed Fairchild AFB, Washington as 'SWOON 52' for a T-3 training mission. At 20:55, while flying in and out of snow showers, the B-52's right wing and number four engine pylon struck the north crest of Hunts Mesa on the Navajo Indian Reservation. Of the seven souls on board the aircraft, five ejected and survived, albeit with varying degrees of serious injury, and two others were sadly killed.

BS: 464185   **USAFS:** 57-6480
OSD: B-52G-80-BW

To MASDC May 8, 1992; still present March 2012.

BS: 464186   **USAFS:** 57-6481
OSD: B-52G-80-BW

The 72nd B-52 to be lost. On December 20, 1972, call-sign 'BRASS 02' a 42nd BW machine attached to the 72nd SW(P), was flying a Linebacker II mission to North Vietnam from Andersen Air Force Base, Guam. Shortly after releasing its bombs on Hanoi railroad yards, it was hit by two SA-2 SAMs and severely damaged. For the next 40 minutes, the pilot struggled with the aircraft as he headed towards Thailand, but it slowly lost height and at 10,000ft, with no hope of making a successful emergency landing at night, the six men onboard ejected near Nakhom Phanom Royal Thai Air Base; they all escaped with their lives. Items of the uniform and equipment belonging to the Electronic Warfare Officer of 'BRASS 02' are displayed in the Southeast Asia War Gallery at the NMUAF.

BS: 464187   **USAFS:** 57-6482
OSD: B-52G-80-BW

The 95th B-52 to be lost. During simulated Minimum Interval Take Off practice at

Mather AFB, California on December 23, 1982, the aircraft gained too much speed and threatened to collide with the B-52 it was following. The pilot pulled back on the throttles too much, causing the water injection to shut down the engines, and the ensuing loss of power caused the crash. All nine crew were killed.

SAC doctrine called for a minimum of nine seconds spacing between similar aircraft, but 30 second spacing between dissimilar aircraft. B-52Gs and Hs were not similar aircraft, they had different engines that needed to be managed differently but the flight-scheduling at Mather had not taken this into account with the result that the pilot of the B-52G was too close to the B-52H in front. He reduced power but the engines didn't respond quickly enough because of the design of the water-injection system and several engines flamed-out. Indirectly, the incident at Castle a month earlier was a cause of this accident because all the 'G' models from Castle had been moved to Mather, which was equipped with 'H' models while the runway at Castle was repaired.

BS: 464188   **USAFS:** 57-6483
OSD: B-52G-80-BW
To MASDC September 19, 1991 and scrapped April 1997 but the panel with its 'Ragin' Cajun' nose-art was removed and it is now displayed at the NMUSAF Wright Patterson AFB, Dayton, Ohio.

BS: 464189   **USAFS:** 57-6484
OSD: B-52G-80-BW
To MASDC July 7, 1989 and scrapped in March 1997.

BS: 464190   **USAFS:** 57-6485
OSD: B-52G-80-BW
To MASDC December 20, 1990; still present March 2012.

BS: 464191   **USAFS:** 57-6486
OSD: B-52G-85-BW
To MASDC August 15, 1991; still present March 2012.

BS: 464192   **USAFS:** 57-6487
OSD: B-52G-85-BW
To MASDC May 9, 1991 and scrapped.

BS: 464193   **USAFS:** 57-6488
OSD: B-52G-85-BW
To MASDC July 29, 1993; still present March 2012.

BS: 464194   **USAFS:** 57-6489
OSD: B-52G-85-BW
To MASDC March 20, 1990 and scrapped; but the panel with its 'Express Delivery' nose-art was removed and it is now displayed at the NMUSAF Wright Patterson AFB, Dayton, Ohio.

BS: 464195   **USAFS:** 57-6490
OSD: B-52G-85-BW.
To MASDC December 1, 1992; still present March 2012.

BS: 464196   **USAFS:** 57-6491
OSD: B-52G-85-BW
To MASDC August 9, 1990; still present March 2012.

BS: 464197   **USAFS:** 57-6492
OSD: B-52G-85-BW
To MASDC December 15, 1992; still present March 2012.

BS: 464198   **USAFS:** 57-6493
OSD: B-52G-85-BW
The 88th B-52 to be lost. When flying as 'EXALT 15' on September 3, 1975 from Seymour-Johnson AFB, North Carolina, the crew of this 68th BW jet noticed a fuel leak from the right outboard fuel tank and then

The forward fuselage of B-52F 57-0048 survives in a scrapyard outside Denver. USAF

experienced handling difficulties arising from the imbalance in the jet caused by the way the fuel was distributed around the aircraft.

Speed was reduced but in the space of five minutes the situation deteriorated to such an extent that the machine crashed after suffering major structural failure. The starboard wing broke between the third and fourth engine nacelles, and the broken piece of wing then broke off the horizontal stabilizer. The bomber rolled inverted and crashed near Aiken, South Carolina killing three of the seven people on board.

BS: 464199   **USAFS:** 57-6494
OSD: B-52G-85-BW
The 40th B-52 to be lost. The 72nd BW aircraft crashed into the Caribbean Sea on take off from Ramey AFB, Puerto Rico on July 5, 1967 after the co-pilot's life raft inflated causing the crew to lose control of the aircraft when the pilot was forced up against the control column. After this accident, knives were placed to hand on the flight-crew's ejection seats for the pilot and co-pilot to stab the life raft should there be a recurrence of the incident. Four of the seven souls on board were lost.

BS: 464200   **USAFS:** 57-6495
OSD: B-52G-85-BW
To MASDC August 26, 1992; still present March 2012.

BS: 464201   **USAFS:** 57-6496
OSD: B-52G-85-BW
The 71st B-52 to be lost. On December 20, 1972 this 456th BW jet attached to the 72nd SW(P), call-sign 'QUILT 03', was hit while attacking Hanoi; a SAM had already missed it by a matter of feet. Two of the crew of six were killed and the rest became PoWs.

BS: 464202   **USAFS:** 57-6497
OSD: B-52G-85-BW
To MASDC January 20, 1994 and scrapped April 1996.

BS: 464203   **USAFS:** 57-6498
OSD: B-52G-85-BW
To MASDC November 3, 1992 and scrapped but the panel with its 'Ace in the Hole' nose-art was removed and it is now displayed at the NMUSAF Wright Patterson AFB, Dayton, Ohio.

BS: 464204   **USAFS:** 57-6499
OSD: B-52G-85-BW
To MASDC August 7, 1990 and scrapped.

BS: 464205   **USAFS:** 57-6500
OSD: B-52G-90-BW
To MASDC May 11, 1989; still present March 2012.

BS: 464206   **USAFS:** 57-6501
OSD: B-52G-90-BW
To MASDC October 3, 1991 and scrapped.

BS: 464207   **USAFS:** 57-6502
OSD: B-52G-90-BW
To MASDC February 15, 1990 and scrapped in March 1997.

BS: 464208   **USAFS:** 57-6503
OSD: B-52G-90-BW
To MASDC August 19, 1992; still present March 2012.

BS: 464209   **USAFS:** 57-6504
OSD: B-52G-90-BW
To MASDC July 2, 1991 and scrapped in January 2001 but the panel with its 'Snake Eyes' nose-art was removed and it is now displayed at the NMUSAF Wright Patterson AFB, Dayton, Ohio.

BS: 464210   **USAFS:** 57-6505
OSD: B-52G-90-BW
To MASDC August 27, 1990 and scrapped in January 2001.

BS: 464211   **USAFS:** 57-6506
OSD: B-52G-90-BW
To MASDC March 8, 1990 and scrapped in March 1997.

BS: 464212   **USAFS:** 57-6507
OSD: B-52G-90-BW
The 96th B-52 to be lost. Five maintenance crew were trapped inside and killed and eight more injured when, owing to an overheated fuel pump, this 319th BW jet caught fire on January 27, 1983 on the ramp at Grand Forks AFB, North Dakota. The Stratofortress was undergoing routine fuel-cell maintenance after flying a training mission the previous night. Tech Sgt John T Fears was awarded the Airman's Medal for his bravery in towing another fully-laden B-52, 57-6479 away from the conflagration with no thought to his own safety.

BS: 464213   **USAFS:** 57-6508
OSD: B-52G-90-BW
To MASDC July 22, 1992; still present March 2012.

BS: 464214   **USAFS:** 57-6509
OSD: B-52G-90-BW
This is the second of two Buffs preserved at the 8th Air Force Museum at Barksdale AFB, Louisiana, this B-52G arrived in 1993.

BS: 464215   **USAFS:** 57-6510
OSD: B-52G-90-BW
To MASDC October 11, 1990; still present March 2012.

BS: 464216   **USAFS:** 57-6511
OSD: B-52G-90-BW
To MASDC October 6, 1992; still present March 2012.

BS: 464217   **USAFS:** 57-6512
OSD: B-52G-90-BW
To MASDC April 25, 1991; still present March 2012.

BS: 464218   **USAFS:** 57-6513
OSD: B-52G-90-BW
To MASDC August 7, 1989 and scrapped.

BS: 464219   **USAFS:** 57-6514
OSD: B-52G-90-BW
To MASDC October 18, 1990; still present March 2012.

BS: 464220   **USAFS:** 57-6515
OSD: B-52G-90-BW
To MASDC September 30, 1992; still present March 2012.

BS: 464221   **USAFS:** 57-6516
OSD: B-52G-90-BW
To MASDC October 8, 1991; still present March 2012.

BS: 464222   **USAFS:** 57-6517
OSD: B-52G-90-BW
To MASDC July 13, 1990 and scrapped.

BS: 464223   **USAFS:** 57-6518
OSD: B-52G-90-BW
To MASDC April 23, 1991 and scrapped in January 2001.

BS: 464224   **USAFS:** 57-6519
OSD: B-52G-90-BW
To MASDC December 11, 1990; still present March 2012.

BS: 464225   **USAFS:** 57-6520
OSD: B-52G-90-BW
To MASDC January 27, 1994; still present March 2012.

BS: 464226   **USAFS:** 58-0158
OSD: B-52G-95-BW
This was displayed at Fairchild AFB but had been broken up by August 2003. The nose has been preserved for the base museum.

BS: 464227   **USAFS:** 58-0159
OSD: B-52G-95-BW > JB-52G
To MASDC October 10, 1991; still present March 2012.

BS: 464228   **USAFS:** 58-0160
OSD: B-52G-95-BW
To MASDC November 19, 1992; still present.

BS: 464229   **USAFS:** 58-0161
OSD: B-52G-95-BW

The 97th B-52 to be lost, on April 11, 1983 when 'LURE 75' and 'LURE 76', two 19th BW B-52Gs were flying from Robins AFB, Georgia to take part in a Red Flag exercise. At 1220L while flying at about 320 knots, 'LURE 75' impacted the south face of 7,050 foot (2,148m) Square Top Mountain near St George, Utah, a little more than 200ft (66m) from the summit.
None of the crew of seven survived the impact.

BS: 464230   **USAFS:** 58-0162
OSD: B-52G-95-BW

To MASDC April 16, 1991 ; scrapped April 9, 1996.

BS: 464231   **USAFS:** 58-0163
OSD: B-52G-95-BW

To MASDC April 14, 1994 ; still present March 2012.

BS: 464232   **USAFS:** 58-0164
OSD: B-52G-95-BW

To MASDC November 5, 1992. The nose and a wing section are in use at the Boeing Avionic Antenna Laboratory, St Charles County Airport, Missouri; the rest of the airframe was still present at MASDC in March 2012.

BS: 464233   **USAFS:** 58-0165
OSD: B-52G-95-BW

To MASDC August 10, 1992; still present March 2012.

BS: 464234   **USAFS:** 58-0166
OSD: B-52G-95-BW

To MASDC December 21, 1992; still present March 2012.

BS: 464235   **USAFS:** 58-0167
OSD: B-52G-95-BW

To MASDC May 28, 1991; still present March 2012.

BS: 464236   **USAFS:** 58-0168
OSD: B-52G-95-BW

To MASDC October 22, 1991 and scrapped.

BS: 464237   **USAFS:** 58-0169
OSD: B-52G-95-BW

The 75th B-52 to be lost, call-sign 'TAN 03', a 97th BW 340th BS machine assigned to the 72nd SW(P), crashed on December 21, 1972 at Kinh No, North Vietnam after being hit by a SA-2.
Only the gunner survived to be taken prisoner; the remainder of the crew of six perished in the crash.

BS: 464238   **USAFS:** 58-0170
OSD: B-52G-95-BW

To MASDC November 10, 1992 and scrapped in March 1998.

BS: 464239   **USAFS:** 58-0171
OSD: B-52G-95-BW

To MASDC August 16, 1990; still present March 2012.

BS: 464240   **USAFS:** 58-0172
OSD: B-52G-95-BW

To MASDC June 30, 1989 and scrapped.

BS: 464241   **USAFS:** 58-0173
OSD: B-52G-95-BW

To MASDC August 5, 1992 and scrapped by September 1995 but the panel with its 'Lets Make a Deal' [sic] nose-art was removed and it is now displayed at the NMUSAF Wright Patterson AFB, Dayton, Ohio.

BS: 464242   **USAFS:** 58-0174
OSD: B-52G-95-BW

The 85th B-52 to be lost. After a routine take off roll at Beale AFB on February 8, 1974 the 456th BW, 744th BS Buff experience multiple engine failure, flipped over and burned out.
The mission was a training flight and there were no weapons aboard. Seven of the eight souls on board were killed in the crash and the only survivor was an instructor pilot who had just boarded the jet that had been engaged in circuit training for two hours; he suffered severe burns.

BS: 464243   **USAFS:** 58-0175
OSD: B-52G-95-BW

To MASDC October 16, 1991; still present March 2012.

BS: 464244   **USAFS:** 58-0176
OSD: B-52G-95-BW

To MASDC November 17, 1992 and scrapped in October 1998.

BS: 464245   **USAFS:** 58-0177
OSD: B-52G-95-BW

To MASDC September 5, 1991 - no longer present.

BS: 464246   **USAFS:** 58-0178
OSD: B-52G-95-BW

To MASDC December 18, 1990 and Still present in March 2012. This jet is lucky to have survived so long. In March 1983 it was severely damaged at March AFB, California, during refuelling. Valves, known as vent caps, designed to allow air to escape from the fuel tank as fuel is pumped in were accidentally left closed with the result that the port wing was almost severed from the airframe.
The jet was repaired by taking a wing from 59-2574 that was being used for radar tests at Stockbridge Research Facility, Oneida, New York and grafting that on to the bomber. It was given the name 'Phoenix II' and went on to serve for a further decade and a half.

BS: 464247   **USAFS:** 58-0179
OSD: B-52G-95-BW

To MASDC December 10, 1992; still present March 2012.

BS: 464248   **USAFS:** 58-0180
OSD: B-52G-95-BW

The 19th B-52 to be lost. It was destroyed while assigned to the 72nd BW on Feb 1, 1960 at Ramey AFB, Puerto Rico during a practice approach to land.
This, the first B-52G to be lost, crashed killing all seven crewmembers because the wrong trim setting had been used.

BS: 464249   **USAFS:** 58-0181
OSD: B-52G-95-BW

To MASDC September 23, 1992 and scrapped.

BS: 464250   **USAFS:** 58-0182
OSD: B-52G-95-BW > JB-52G

To MASDC June 10, 1992; still present March 2012 but the panel with its What's Up Doc?' nose-art has been removed and it is now displayed at the NMUSAF Wright Patterson AFB, Dayton, Ohio.

BS: 464251   **USAFS:** 58-0183
OSD: B-52G-95-BW

To MASDC July 9, 1991. Having been selected for preservation at the adjacent Pima Air & Space Museum it was dragged across the road in September 1991. It is still painted in the markings of its last user, the 2nd BW which now flies the 'H' model from Barksdale AFB, Louisiana.

BS: 464252   **USAFS:** 58-0184
OSD: B-52G-95-BW

To MASDC September 26, 1991; still present March 2012.

BS: 464253   **USAFS:** 58-0185
OSD: B-52G-95-BW

This Gulf War veteran is preserved at the Air Force Armament Museum, outside Eglin AFB, Florida still wearing the 'El Lobo II' nose-art it was wearing on the night of January 16, 1991 when it took part in the Secret Squirrel mission on the first night of the Gulf War as 'DOOM 37'.

BS: 464254   **USAFS:** 58-0186
OSD: B-52G-95-BW

To MASDC March 29, 1990 and scrapped in March 1997.

BS: 464255   **USAFS:** 58-0187
OSD: B-52G-95-BW

The 24th B-52 to be lost. Crashed on approach to Seymour-Johnson AFB on January 24, 1961 when making an emergency landing following a fuel leak from wing tanks at high altitude followed by an explosion during a 'Coverall' airborne alert mission. The starboard wing of the 4241st SW machine failed when flaps were selected for landing. Two nuclear weapons were on board; one had its landing cushioned by its parachute but the other broke apart on impact with the ground. There was no radiation leak reported but the second bomb was never completely recovered because it landed in a bog. Three of the eight people aboard were killed.

BS: 464256   **USAFS:** 58-0188
OSD: B-52G-100-BW

The 45th B-52 to be lost. Whilst on a 'Chrome Dome' global alert flight from Plattsburgh AFB, New York on January 21, 1968, 380th SAW B-52G 'HOBO 28' crashed near Thule Air Base in Greenland following an in-flight cabin fire. The aircraft was flown by a crew from the 528th BS and was carrying four B28 hydrogen bombs

when it crashed into an ice covered bay at the western tip of Greenland. One of the crew members died in the initial crash but many of the rescue service personnel were exposed to radiation.
Chrome Dome missions were immediately halted following this, one of the world's worst military nuclear accidents.

BS: 464257   **USAFS:** 58-0189
OSD: B-52G-100-BW

To MASDC February 1, 1990 and scrapped.

BS: 464258   **USAFS:** 58-0190
OSD: B-52G-100-BW

The 101st B-52 to be lost, this machine was destroyed by fire on July 24, 1989 during depot maintenance at Kelly AFB.

BS: 464259   **USAFS:** 58-0191
OSD: B-52G-100-BW

This Wichita built B-52G was Delivered to the USAF on October 16, 1959 and was assigned to the 72nd Bombardment Wing (Heavy) at Ramey AFB, Puerto Rico.
It arrived at Hill AFB, Utah for preservation with the Hill Aerospace Museum on July 11, 1991 having been ferried from its last user, the 93rd BW at Castle AFB, California.

BS: 464260   **USAFS:** 58-0192
OSD: B-52G-100-BW

To MASDC February 10, 1994; still present March 2012.

BS: 464261   **USAFS:** 58-0193
OSD: B-52G-100-BW

To MASDC December 8, 1992; still present March 2012.

BS: 464262   **USAFS:** 58-0194
OSD: B-52G-100-BW

To MASDC October 24, 1991; still present March 2012.

BS: 464263   **USAFS:** 58-0195
OSD: B-52G-100-BW

To MASDC November 18, 1993; still present March 2012.

BS: 464264   **USAFS:** 58-0196
OSD: B-52G-100-BW

The 28th B-52 to be lost. 'POGO 22' was one of six 4241st SW B-52Gs from Seymour Johnson AFB simulating an attack on Pittsburgh, Pennsylvania on October 15, 1961 as part of an air defence exercise. The aircraft is assumed to have flown into the sea of the coast of Newfoundland with the loss of all aboard.
No wreckage or survivors were ever found.

BS: 464265   **USAFS:** 58-0197
OSD: B-52G-100-BW

To MASDC November 16, 1993; still present March 2012.

BS: 464266   **USAFS:** 58-0198
OSD: B-52G-100-BW

The 74th B-52 to be lost, 'OLIVE 01', a B-52G of the 92nd BW 325th BS assigned to 72nd SW(P), was struck by a SA-2 SAM whilst attacking Kinh No, Vietnam on December 20, 1972, during Linebacker II; there were only three survivors.

BS: 464267   **USAFS:** 58-0199
OSD: B-52G-100-BW

To MASDC June 4, 1991; still present March 2012 but the panel with its 'Specter' nose-art has been removed and it is now displayed at the NMUSAF Wright Patterson AFB, Dayton, Ohio.

BS: 464268   **USAFS:** 58-0200
OSD: B-52G-100-BW > GB-52

To GB-52G 82nd TRW, Sheppard AF, Texas for use as a GIA but was scrapped in 2010.

BS: 464269   **USAFS:** 58-0201
OSD: B-52G-100-BW

The 68th B-52 to be lost. Perhaps doubly

tragic, on December 18, 1972 this crew was flying a 2nd BW 72nd SW(P) jet after the end of their tour because their replacement crew was delayed by bad weather in the US. 'CHARCOAL 01' was hit by two SA-2s over the Yen Vien railway yards and was the first Buff to be lost on Linebacker II.
Four of the crew of seven were killed.

BS: 464270   **USAFS:** 58-0202
OSD: B-52G-100-BW
To MASDC March 10, 1994; still present March 2012.

BS: 464271   **USAFS:** 58-0203
OSD: B-52G-100-BW
To MASDC March 3, 1994; still present March 2012.

BS: 464272   **USAFS:** 58-0204
OSD: B-52G-100-BW
To MASDC September 24, 1991; still present March 2012.

BS: 464273   **USAFS:** 58-0205
OSD: B-52G-100-BW
To MASDC November 15, 1990 and scrapped.

BS: 464274   **USAFS:** 58-0206
OSD: B-52G-100-BW
To MASDC February 1, 1994; still present March 2012.

BS: 464275   **USAFS:** 58-0207
OSD: B-52G-100-BW
To MASDC July 25, 1991 - no longer present.

BS: 464276   **USAFS:** 58-0208
OSD: B-52G-100-BW
The 60th B-52 to be lost, this 42nd BW machine burned out on the ramp at Loring AFB, Maine on July 20, 1970.

BS: 464277   **USAFS:** 58-0209
OSD: B-52G-100-BW
The 92nd B-52 to be lost, a 19th BW machine, burned out on the ramp at Robins AFB, Georgia on August 19, 1990.

BS: 464278   **USAFS:** 58-0210
OSD: B-52G-100-BW
To MASDC March 10, 1993; still present March 2012.

BS: 464279   **USAFS:** 58-0211
OSD: B-52G-100-BW
To MASDC September 2, 1992; still present March 2012.

BS: 464280   **USAFS:** 58-0212
OSD: B-52G-105-BW
To MASDC February 8, 1994; still present March 2012.

BS: 464281   **USAFS:** 58-0213
OSD: B-52G-105-BW
To MASDC November 23, 1993; still present March 2012.

BS: 464282   **USAFS:** 58-0214
OSD: B-52G-105-BW

BS: 464283   **USAFS:** 58-0215
OSD: B-52G-105-BW
The 56th B-52 to be lost. This 42nd BW machine was destroyed on April 9, 1969 when, because of a problem with the water-injection system, it crashed after all four engines on the right wing flamed out during takeoff from Loring AFB, Maine. All seven on board died. The jet had needed attention from the maintenance crew before take off and the Constant Speed Drive on engine seven had been changed twice.

BS: 464284   **USAFS:** 58-0216
OSD: B-52G-105-BW
To MASDC March 8, 1994; still present March 2012.

BS: 464285   **USAFS:** 58-0217
OSD: B-52G-105-BW
To MASDC November 15, 1991; still present March 2012.

Seen here on roll-out, the first B-52G, 57-6468 is marked as 'America's First Missile Platform Bomber'. Key collection

BS: 464286   **USAFS:** 58-0218
OSD: B-52G-105-BW
To MASDC January 18, 1994; still present March 2012.

BS: 464287   **USAFS:** 58-0219
OSD: B-52G-105-BW
The 99th B-52 to be lost, this 93rd BW machine over-ran the runway at Castle AFB, California on February 11, 1988 after an aborted takeoff.

BS: 464288   **USAFS:** 58-0220
OSD: B-52G-105-BW
To MASDC May 5, 1990 and scrapped April 1997.

BS: 464289   **USAFS:** 58-0221
OSD: B-52G-105-BW
To MASDC October 21, 1993; still present March 2012.

BS: 464290   **USAFS:** 58-0222
OSD: B-52G-105-BW
To MASDC August 12, 1992; still present March 2012.

BS: 464291   **USAFS:** 58-0223
OSD: B-52G-105-BW
To MASDC July 31, 1990 - no longer present.

BS: 464292   **USAFS:** 58-0224
OSD: B-52G-105-BW
To MASDC February 12, 1990; still present March 2012.

BS: 464293   **USAFS:** 58-0225
OSD: B-52G-105-BW
On May 9,1991, B-52G 58-0225 'Mohawk Valley' piloted by Col Mike Loughran, landed at Griffiss AFB, New York for the last time to be preserved. 'Mohawk Valley' was its name when it was delivered to Griffiss on January 12, 1960 by Major Bill Penzier and his crew. When the base closed in 1993, the American Legion took custody of the bomber and today it is still displayed at the Griffiss Business and Technology Park alongside an Air Launched Cruise Missile.

BS: 464294   **USAFS:** 58-0226
OSD: B-52G-105-BW
To MASDC October 19, 1993; still present March 2012.

BS: 464295   **USAFS:** 58-0227
OSD: B-52G-105-BW
To MASDC July 15, 1992; still present March 2012

BS: 464296   **USAFS:** 58-0228
OSD: B-52G-105-BW
The 39th B-52 to be lost. During a flight from Barksdale AFB, Louisiana on November 18, 1966 this 2nd BW flew into the ground near Stone Lake, Wisconsin 72 miles south of Duluth, Minnesota with the loss of all nine souls on board.

BS: 464297   **USAFS:** 58-0229
OSD: B-52G-105-BW
To MASDC November 12, 1992; still present March 2012.

BS: 464298   **USAFS:** 58-0230
OSD: B-52G-105-BW
To MASDC May 6, 1993; still present March 2012.

BS: 464299   **USAFS:** 58-0231
OSD: B-52G-105-BW
To MASDC December 3, 1992; still present March 2012.

BS: 464300   **USAFS:** 58-0232
OSD: B-52G-105-BW
To MASDC April 3, 1990. The aircraft was scrapped but the nose was sent to Randolph AFB, Texas, for use as an ejection seat trainer. It has since been preserved at the Hangar 25 Air Museum at Big Spring, TX.

BS: 464301   **USAFS:** 58-0233
OSD: B-52G-110-BW
To MASDC February 17, 1994; still present March 2012.

BS: 464302   **USAFS:** 58-0234
OSD: B-52G-110-BW
An examination of the airframe discovered cracks that led to the aircraft being declared unfit to fly; it was scrapped at Andersen AFB, Guam in December 1993.

BS: 464303   **USAFS:** 58-0235
OSD: B-52G-110-BW
To MASDC March 29, 1994; still present March 2012.

BS: 464304   **USAFS:** 58-0236
OSD: B-52G-110-BW
To MASDC October 13, 1992 and scrapped in March 1998.

BS: 464305   **USAFS:** 58-0237
OSD: B-52G-110-BW
To MASDC October 29, 1991; still present March 2012.

BS: 464306   **USAFS:** 58-0238
OSD: B-52G-110-BW
To MASDC August 22, 1991; still present March 2012.

BS: 464307   **USAFS:** 58-0239
OSD: B-52G-110-BW
To MASDC September 9, 1992; still present March 2012.

BS: 464308   **USAFS:** 58-0240
OSD: B-52G-110-BW
To MASDC May 3, 1994; still present March 2012.

BS: 464309   **USAFS:** 58-0241
OSD: B-52G-110-BW
To MASDC May 2, 1991; still present March 2012.

BS: 464310   **USAFS:** 58-0242
OSD: B-52G-110-BW
To MASDC February 22, 1994; still present March 2012.

BS: 464311   **USAFS:** 58-0243
OSD: B-52G-110-BW
To MASDC June 11, 1991 and scrapped in January 2001 but the panel with its 'Brute Force' nose-art was removed and it is now displayed at the NMUSAF Wright Patterson AFB, Dayton, Ohio.

BS: 464312   **USAFS:** 58-0244
OSD: B-52G-110-BW
To MASDC October 29, 1992; still present March 2012.

BS: 464313   **USAFS:** 58-0245
OSD: B-52G-110-BW
To MASDC October 20, 1992; still present March 2012.

BS: 464314   **USAFS:** 58-0246
OSD: B-52G-110-BW
The 69th B-52 to be lost and first B-52G to be shot down. 'PEACH 02' was the callsign of this Buff which was hit by an SA-2 over Kinh No railway yards on December 18, 1972 during Linebacker II. The crew managed to nurse the damaged 2nd BW 72nd SW(P) jet back to Thai airspace where the crew of seven ejected safely.

BS: 464315   **USAFS:** 58-0247
OSD: B-52G-115-BW
To MASDC November 5, 1991; still present March 2012.

BS: 464316   **USAFS:** 58-0248
OSD: B-52G-115-BW
To MASDC January 25, 1994. This is the machine that was nearly shot down by an F-4G and was subsequently named 'In HARM's way'. Still present March 2012.

BS: 464317   **USAFS:** 58-0249
OSD: B-52G-115-BW
To MASDC September 10, 1991; The aircraft was still present in March 2012 but the panel with its 'Urban Renewal' nose-art has been removed and it is now displayed at the NMUSAF Wright Patterson AFB, Dayton, Ohio.

BS: 464318   **USAFS:** 58-0250
OSD: B-52G-115-BW
To MASDC October 7, 1993. The aircraft was

still present in March 2012 but the panel with its 'Screamin Eagle' [sic] nose-art has been removed and it is now displayed at the NMUSAF Wright Patterson AFB, Dayton, Ohio.

BS: 464319   **USAFS:** 58-0251
OSD: B-52G-115-BW
To MASDC February 27, 1990 and scrapped in March 1997.

BS: 464320   **USAFS:** 58-0252
OSD: B-52G-115-BW
To MASDC April 18, 1967 ; scrapped.

BS: 464321   **USAFS:** 58-0253
OSD: B-52G-115-BW
To MASDC November 4, 1993; still present March 2012.

BS: 464322   **USAFS:** 58-0254
OSD: B-52G-115-BW
To MASDC December 4, 1990 and scrapped but the panel with its 'Damage Inc' nose-art has been removed and it is now displayed at the NMUSAF Wright Patterson AFB, Dayton, Ohio.

BS: 464323   **USAFS:** 58-0255
OSD: B-52G-115-BW
To MASDC October 28, 1993; still present March 2012.

BS: 464324   **USAFS:** 58-0256
OSD: B-52G-115-BW
The 38th B-52 to be lost. One of the more infamous losses - this 68th BW Buff, callsign 'TEA 16' collided with KC-135A 61-0273 over Palomares, Spain on January 17, 1966. The tanker, engaged on a 'Chrome Dome' mission from Seymour Johnson AFB, North Carolina, exploded killing all four on board but four of the seven crew of the B-52 survived. Of four Mk28R1 hydrogen bombs that were on board the bomber at the time of the crash, three were soon recovered near Palomares. Even though they did not detonate a 2km² (490 acre) area was contaminated with plutonium from the bombs. The fourth weapon fell into the sea and was subject of an enormous effort to recover it. More than twenty US surface vessels and submersibles were used in the search. The bomb was located on April 2 at a depth of 2,900ft (880m); it was eventually recovered intact.

BS: 464325   **USAFS:** 58-0257
OSD: B-52G-115-BW
To MASDC October 14, 1993; still present March 2012.

BS: 464326   **USAFS:** 58-0258
OSD: B-52G-115-BW
To MASDC November 9, 1993; still present March 2012.

BS: 464327   **USAFS:** 59-2564
OSD: B-52G-120-BW
To MASDC August 8, 1991; scrapped April 1, 1997. The forward fuselage and cockpit section have been stored at the ARM scrapyard outside the base; it was first noted

in June 2002 and is believed to still be there.

BS: 464328   **USAFS:** 59-2565
OSD: B-52G-120-BW
To MASDC October 12, 1993; still present March 2012.

BS: 464329   **USAFS:** 59-2566
OSD: B-52G-120-BW
To MASDC September 16, 1992; still present March 2012.

BS: 464330   **USAFS:** 59-2567
OSD: B-52G-120-BW
To MASDC October 22, 1992; still present March 2012.

BS: 464331   **USAFS:** 59-2568
OSD: B-52G-120-BW
To MASDC November 24, 1992; still present March 2012.

BS: 464332   **USAFS:** 59-2569
OSD: B-52G-120-BW
To MASDC February 15, 1994; still present March 2012.

BS: 464333   **USAFS:** 59-2570
OSD: B-52G-120-BW
To MASDC January 24, 1994; still present March 2012.

BS: 464334   **USAFS:** 59-2571
OSD: B-52G-120-BW
To MASDC April 30, 1991 and scrapped April 1997.

BS: 464335   **USAFS:** 59-2572
OSD: B-52G-120-BW
To MASDC January 11, 1994; still present March 2012.

BS: 464336   **USAFS:** 59-2573
OSD: B-52G-120-BW
To MASDC October 26, 1993; still present March 2012.

BS: 464337   **USAFS:** 59-2574
OSD: B-52G-120-BW
The 63rd B-52 to be lost. After an in-flight engine failure, the aircraft aquaplaned during landing at Griffiss AFB, New York on May 8, 1972 and was subsequently written off. The aircraft was taken to Stockbridge Research Facility, Oneida, New York, (Rome Laboratories) in 1973 and used there for radar tests. It was scrapped in July 2008.

BS: 464338   **USAFS:** 59-2575
OSD: B-52G-125-BW
To MASDC August 6, 1991 and scrapped.

BS: 464339   **USAFS:** 59-2576
OSD: B-52G-125-BW
The 26th B-52 to be lost. Six of the eight on board were killed when this 4038 SW 431 BS jet, callsign 'JUDY 24', on a flight from Dow AFB, Maine and taking part in a 'Hot Rocket' intra-Air Force radar-scored bombing competition, crashed 22 nm (40km) southwest of High Point, NC on March 30, 1961 after an accident during refuelling involving 4241st SW KC-135A 'FROSH 60'.

BS: 464340   **USAFS:** 59-2577
OSD: B-52G-125-BW
This B-52G has been preserved as a gate

guard at Grand Forks AFB, North Dakota since January 1992.

BS: 464341   **USAFS:** 59-2578
OSD: B-52G-125-BW > GB-52G
To the 82nd TRW, Sheppard AFB, Texas for use as a GIA; scrapped August 22, 2010.

BS: 464342   **USAFS:** 59-2579
OSD: B-52G-125-BW
To MASDC November 12, 1991. The aircraft was scrapped but the forward fuselage is preserved at the Southern Utah Air Museum, Washington, Utah along with many other US military aircraft cockpits.

BS: 464343   **USAFS:** 59-2580
OSD: B-52G-125-BW
To MASDC June 6, 1992 and scrapped.

BS: 464344   **USAFS:** 59-2581
OSD: B-52G-125-BW
To MASDC October 8, 1992; still present March 2012.

BS: 464345   **USAFS:** 59-2582
OSD: B-52G-125-BW
To MASDC August 7, 1991 and scrapped but the panel with its 'Grim Reaper II' nose-art was removed and it is now displayed at the NMUSAF Wright Patterson AFB, Dayton, Ohio. The accompanying informational plaque incorrectly gives the serial number as 57-2582.

BS: 464346   **USAFS:** 59-2583
OSD: B-52G-125-BW
To MASDC October 1, 1992; still present March 2012.

BS: 464347   **USAFS:** 59-2584
OSD: B-52G-125-BW
This former 93rd BW machine named, 'Midnight Express,' was accepted by the USAF on September 28, 1960 and has been at Paine Field, outside Seattle, Washington, since it was retired on September 23, 1991. It is now on the charge of the excellent Museum of Flight, Snohomish County Airport, Paine Field, Washington. Midnight Express is under threat of being scrapped and B-52 devotee Bob Bogash is involved in administering an 'adopt a B-52' project to help save her. If you'd like to help, Bob can be contacted at Bob2@rbogash.com.

BS: 464348   **USAFS:** 59-2585
OSD: B-52G-125-BW
To MASDC April 15, 1993 - no longer there.

BS: 464349   **USAFS:** 59-2586
OSD: B-52G-125-BW
To MASDC April 22, 1994. Transferred to NASA ownership but still stored with MASDC March 2012.

BS: 464350   **USAFS:** 59-2587
OSD: B-52G-125-BW
To MASDC January 4, 1990 and scrapped in March 1992.

BS: 464351   **USAFS:** 59-2588
OSD: B-52G-130-BW
To MASDC April 5, 1994; still present March 2012.

BS: 464352   **USAFS:** 59-2589
OSD: B-52G-130-BW
To MASDC June 17, 1992 and scrapped in October 1998.

BS: 464353   **USAFS:** 59-2590
OSD: B-52G-130-BW
To MASDC July 13, 1992 and scrapped December 1995.

BS: 464354   **USAFS:** 59-2591
OSD: B-52G-130-BW
To MASDC June 19, 1992 and scrapped.

BS: 464355   **USAFS:** 59-2592
OSD: B-52G-130-BW
To MASDC February 7, 1990 and scrapped in March 1997.

BS: 464356   **USAFS:** 59-2593
OSD: B-52G-130-BW
The 102nd B-52 to be lost and the last B-52G. This 42nd BW machine with a 97th BW crew was assigned to Diego Garcia for operations during Operation Desert Storm with the 4300th BW (P). When returning to base on February 3, 1991 after a mission to Iraq, the bomber crashed into the Indian Ocean near the base after five engines flamed out because of improper fuel management following serious electrical problems. Three crewmembers ejected safely but three others were killed after they ejected outside the ejection seats' parameters.

BS: 464357   **USAFS:** 59-2594
OSD: B-52G-130-BW
To MASDC October 15, 1992 and scrapped but the panel with its 'Memphis Belle III' nose-art was removed and it is now displayed at the NMUSAF Wright Patterson AFB, Dayton, Ohio.

BS: 464358   **USAFS:** 59-2595
OSD: B-52G-130-BW
To MASDC February 24, 1994; still present March 2012.

BS: 464359   **USAFS:** 59-2596
OSD: B-52G-130-BW
One of only two B-52s to be preserved outside the United States, (the other is the B-52D at the Imperial War Museum at Duxford in the UK) 59-2596 left Guam for Australia on March 27, 1989 and, having been given the name 'Darwin's Pride', has been given pride of place at the Australian Aviation Heritage Centre at Darwin, Australia ever since. RAAF Darwin shares its runway with Darwin international airport and because of its location in the extreme north of Australia it has frequently played host to B-52s passing through the region.

BS: 464360   **USAFS:** 59-2597
OSD: B-52G-130-BW
The 94th B-52 to be lost, this 93rd BW example burned out on the ground at Castle AFB, California on November 29, 1982 after a fire in the hydraulic system on landing occurred during a series of touch and goes. The brakes caught fire and blew up into the forward wheel well cutting oxygen lines and battery cables, and puncturing the forward main fuel tank. The crew evacuated the machine safely. Indirectly this led to the loss of B-52G 57-6482 a month later at Mather AFB.

BS: 464361   **USAFS:** 59-2598
OSD: B-52G-130-BW
To MASDC January 13, 1994; still present March 2012.

BS: 464362   **USAFS:** 59-2599
OSD: B-52G-130-BW
To MASDC March 15, 1994; still present March 2012.

The nose art of 57-6498 is preserved at the NMUSAF. USAF

BS: 464363 **USAFS:** 59-2600
OSD: B-52G-130-BW

The 64th B-52 to be lost crashed on take off from Andersen AFB, Guam on July 7, 1972 while operating with the 416th BW attached to the 72 SW(P). The aircraft lost airspeed information on climb-out and stalled. It was reported that the forward BNS radome detached severing the pitot tube system that provides the dynamic air-speed information to the air-speed indicator. Although all six crewmembers ejected, the Radio Navigator's parachute failed and he was killed.

BS: 464364 **USAFS:** 59-2601
OSD: B-52G-130-BW

Preserved as a gate guard at the Langley Air Park, Langley AFB, Virginia since the early 1990s. In July 1983, when serving with the 416th BW this Buff was displayed at RAF Fairford, Gloucestershire in the UK during the International Air Tattoo.

BS: 464365 **USAFS:** 59-2602
OSD: B-52G-130-BW

To MASDC October 27, 1992; still present March 2012 but the panel with its 'Yankee Doodle II' nose-art was removed and it is now displayed at the NMUSAF Wright Patterson AFB, Dayton, Ohio. The accompanying informational plaque incorrectly identifies the aircraft from which it came as 59-2606.

BS: 464366 **USAFS:** 60-0001
OSD: B-52H-135-BW

2nd BW 96th BS 'LA' tail-code; named 'Memphis Belle IV'.

BS: 464367 **USAFS:** 60-0002
OSD: B-52H-135-BW

2nd BW 'LA'.

BS: 464368 **USAFS:** 60-0003
OSD: B-52H-135-BW

307th Wing 93rd BS 'BD'; named 'Master Blaster'.

BS: 464369 **USAFS:** 60-0004
OSD: B-52H-135-BW

5th BW 69th BS 'MT'.

BS: 464370 **USAFS:** 60-0005
OSD: B-52H-135-BW

5th BW 69th BS 'MT'; named 'War Birds'.

BS: 464371 **USAFS:** 60-0006
OSD: B-52H-135-BW

The 86th B-52 to be lost. When serving with the 17th BW, this B-52H crashed at Wright-Patterson AFB on May 30, 1974, after rudder and elevator failure during a GCA approach caused loss of control. In the early 1960s this machine had flown as a JB-52H to test the early EVS.

BS: 464372 **USAFS:** 60-0007
OSD: B-52H-135-BW

5th BW 23rd BS 'MT'.

BS: 464373 **USAFS:** 60-0008
OSD: B-52H-135-BW

2nd BW 20th BS 'LA', code marked '8th AF' on the tail.

BS: 464374 **USAFS:** 60-0009
OSD: B-52H-135-BW

5th BW 69th BS 'MT'.

BS: 464375 **USAFS:** 60-0010
OSD: B-52H-135-BW

To MASDC August 28, 2008, still present March 2012.

BS: 464376 **USAFS:** 60-0011
OSD: B-52H-135-BW

307th Wing 93rd BS 'BD'; 'Mr Jiggs' nose-art and marked '11th BS' on tail.

BS: 464377 **USAFS:** 60-0012
OSD: B-52H-135-BW

5th BW 69th BS 'MT'.

BS: 464378 **USAFS:** 60-0013
OSD: B-52H-135-BW

2nd BW 20th BS 'LA'.

BS: 464379 **USAFS:** 60-0014
OSD: B-52H-140-BW

To MASDC December 11, 2008; still present March 2012.

BS: 464380 **USAFS:** 60-0015
OSD: B-52H-140-BW

307th Wing 93rd BS 'BD'.

BS: 464381 **USAFS:** 60-0016
OSD: B-52H-140-BW

2nd BW 20th BS 'LA'.

BS: 464382 **USAFS:** 60-0017
OSD: B-52H-140-BW

Unmarked but Barksdale-based.

BS: 464383 **USAFS:** 60-0018
OSD: B-52H-140-BW

5th BW 23rd BS 'MT'.

BS: 464384 **USAFS:** 60-0019
OSD: B-52H-140-BW

To MASDC August 7, 2008, still present March 2012.

BS: 464385 **USAFS:** 60-0020
OSD: B-52H-140-BW

To MASDC September 4, 2008, still present March 2012.

BS: 464386 **USAFS:** 60-0021
OSD: B-52H-140-BW

2nd BW 96th BS 'LA'.

BS: 464387 **USAFS:** 60-0022
OSD: B-52H-145-BW

2nd BW 96th BS 'LA'.

BS: 464388 **USAFS:** 60-0023
OSD: B-52H-145-BW

5th BW 23rd BS 'MT'.

BS: 464389 **USAFS:** 60-0024
OSD: B-52H-145-BW

2nd BW 20th BS 'LA'.

BS: 464390 **USAFS:** 60-0025
OSD: B-52H-145-BW

2nd BW 20th BS ' LA'; named 'Ol' Crow Express II'.

BS: 464391 **USAFS:** 60-0026
OSD: B-52H-145-BW

5th BW 23rd BS 'MT'.

BS: 464392 **USAFS:** 60-0027
OSD: B-52H-145-BW

The 48th B-52 to be lost. It was destroyed on April 10, 1968 when serving with the 5th BW. The aircraft was returning to Minot AFB as 'FOG 32' when it flew into the ground with the loss of all six people on board 14 miles (22 km) east south-east of the base. The cause of the crash was attributed to fuel mismanagement during the landing approach causing a multiple engine flameout.

BS: 464393 **USAFS:** 60-0028
OSD: B-52H-145-BW

2nd BW 96th BS 'LA'.

BS: 464394 **USAFS:** 60-0029
OSD: B-52H-145-BW

5th BW 23rd BS 'MT'.

BS: 464395 **USAFS:** 60-0030
OSD: B-52H-145-BW

To MASDC August 21, 2008, still present March 2012.

BS: 464396 **USAFS:** 60-0031
OSD: B-52H-145-BW

307th Wing 93rd BS 'BD'.

BS: 464397 **USAFS:** 60-0032
OSD: B-52H-145-BW

2nd BW 96th BS 'LA'; named 'Iron Eagle'.

BS: 464398 **USAFS:** 60-0033
OSD: B-52H-145-BW

5th BW 69th BS 'MT'; named 'Instrument of Destruction'.

Unthinkable just a few years before, in 2003 B-52s, including 'H' model 61-0027 visited Zhukovsky outside Moscow to take part in that year's Moscow Space and Aviation Show. Former cosmonaut and test pilot Russian Air Force Colonel Magomed Tolboev took the opportunity to inspect the Buff. USAF

BS: 464399 **USAFS:** 60-0034
OSD: B-52H-150-BW

To MASDC August 14, 2008, still present March 2012.

BS: 464400 **USAFS:** 60-0035
OSD: B-52H-150-BW

307th Wing 93rd BS 'BD'.

BS: 464401 **USAFS:** 60-0036
OSD: B-52H-150-BW

412th TW 419th FLTS 'ED'; named 'Tagboard flyer'.

BS: 464402 **USAFS:** 60-0037
OSD: B-52H-150-BW

5th BW 69th BS 'MT'; named 'Wham Bam II'.

BS: 464403 **USAFS:** 60-0038
OSD: B-52H-150-BW

307th Wing 93rd BS 'BD'.

BS: 464404 **USAFS:** 60-0039
OSD: B-52H-150-BW

The 90th B-52 to be lost, it was destroyed on April 1, 1977 when flying with the 410th BW. Flew into the ground whilst approaching to land at K I Sawyer AFB, Michigan during a snow storm. All eight on board were killed.

BS: 464405 **USAFS:** 60-0040
OSD: B-52H-150-BW

The 100th B-52 to be lost. Destroyed on December 6, 1988 when it exploded during a touch-and-go approach to land at K I Sawyer AFB, Michigan. An overheated fuel pump caused an explosion in the aft fuel tank and the jet crashed back onto the runway and split into three pieces. All eight on board survived albeit with injuries.

BS: 464406 **USAFS:** 60-0041
OSD: B-52H-150-BW

307th Wing 93rd BS 'BD'.

BS: 464407 **USAFS:** 60-0042
OSD: B-52H-150-BW

307th Wing 93rd BS 'BD'.

BS: 464408 **USAFS:** 60-0043
OSD: B-52H-150-BW

To MASDC October 2, 2008, still present March 2012.

BS: 464409 **USAFS:** 60-0044
OSD: B-52H-150-BW

5th BW 69th BS 'MT'; named 'Excalibur'.

BS: 464410 **USAFS:** 60-0045
OSD: B-52H-150-BW

307th Wing 93rd BS 'BD'.

BS: 464411 **USAFS:** 60-0046
OSD: B-52H-155-BW

To MASDC October 23, 2008, still present March 2012.

BS: 464412 **USAFS:** 60-0047
OSD: B-52H-155-BW

2nd BW 20th BS 'LA'; named 'Neanderthaul'.

BS: 464413 **USAFS:** 60-0048
OSD: B-52H-155-BW

2nd BW 20th BS 'LA'; named 'Phoenix'.

BS: 464414 **USAFS:** 60-0049
OSD: B-52H-155-BW

53rd Wg 49th TES 'OT'.

BS: 464415 **USAFS:** 60-0050
OSD: B-52H-155-BW

412th TW 419th FLTS 'ED'; named 'Dragon's Inferno'.

BS: 464416 **USAFS:** 60-0051
OSD: B-52H-155-BW

307th Wing 93rd BS 'BD'.

BS: 464417 **USAFS:** 60-0052
OSD: B-52H-155-BW

2nd BW 96th BS 'LA'; named 'Ragin' Red III'.

BS: 464418 **USAFS:** 60-0053
OSD: B-52H-155-BW

The 103rd B-52 to be lost crashed on July 21, 2008 when flying with the 2nd BW 20th BS. The aircraft, 'RAIDER 21', was deployed to Andersen AFB, Guam from its home base at Barksdale AFB. It was about to participate in an airshow to celebrate Guam's Liberation Day when it crashed into the Pacific Ocean with the loss of the crew of six.

BS: 464419 **USAFS:** 60-0054
OSD: B-52H-155-BW

2nd BW 20th BS ' LA'; named 'Mud Buff'.

BS: 464420 **USAFS:** 60-0055
OSD: B-52H-155-BW

5th BW 69th BS 'MT'.

BS: 464421 **USAFS:** 60-0056
OSD: B-52H-155-BW

5th BW 23rd BS 'MT'; named 'Black Widow'.

BS: 464422 **USAFS:** 60-0057
OSD: B-52H-155-BW

307th Wing 93rd BS 'BD'; named 'Nemesis'.

BS: 464423 **USAFS:** 60-0058
OSD: B-52H-160-BW

2nd BW 20th BS 'LA'; named 'War Hog'.

BS: 464424 **USAFS:** 60-0059
OSD: B-52H-160-BW

2nd BW 96th BS 'LA'; named 'The Devil's Own'.

BS: 464425 **USAFS:** 60-0060
OSD: B-52H-160-BW

5th BW 69th BS 'MT'.

BS: 464426 **USAFS:** 60-0061
OSD: B-52H-160-BW

307th Wing 93rd BS 'BD'.

BS: 464427 **USAFS:** 60-0062
OSD: B-52H-160-BW
2nd BW 96th BS 'LA'; named 'Cajun Fear'.

BS: 464428 **USAFS:** 61-0001
OSD: B-52H-165-BW
5th BW 69th BS 'MT'.

BS: 464429 **USAFS:** 61-0002
OSD: B-52H-165-BW
2nd BW 96th BS 'LA'; named 'The Eagle's Wrath II'.

BS: 464428 **USAFS:** 61-0003
OSD: B-52H-165-BW
5th BW 69th BS 'MT'.

BS: 464429 **USAFS:** 61-0004
OSD: B-52H-165-BW
2nd BW 20th BS 'LA'.

BS: 464430 **USAFS:** 61-0005
OSD: B-52H-165-BW
5th BW 69th BS 'MT'.

BS: 464431 **USAFS:** 61-0006
OSD: B-52H-165-BW
2nd BW 96th BS 'LA'.

BS: 464432 **USAFS:** 61-0007
OSD: B-52H-165-BW
To MASDC November 13, 2008, still present March 2012.

BS: 464433 **USAFS:** 61-0008
OSD: B-52H-165-BW
307th Wing 93rd BS 'BD'; named 'We Remember'.

BS: 464434 **USAFS:** 61-0009
OSD: B-52H-165-BW
To MASDC September 25, 2008, still present March 2012.

BS: 464435 **USAFS:** 61-0010
OSD: B-52H-165-BW
2nd BW 20th BS 'LA'.

BS: 464436 **USAFS:** 61-0011
OSD: B-52H-165-BW
Unmarked but Barksdale-based.

BS: 464437 **USAFS:** 61-0012
OSD: B-52H-165-BW
2nd BW 96th BS 'LA'.

BS: 464438 **USAFS:** 61-0013
OSD: B-52H-165-BW
2nd BW 20th BS 'LA'; named 'High Tension III'.

BS: 464439 **USAFS:** 61-0014
OSD: B-52H-170-BW
5th BW 69th BS 'MT'.

BS: 464440 **USAFS:** 61-0015
OSD: B-52H-170-BW
2nd BW 96th BS 'LA'.

BS: 464441 **USAFS:** 61-0016
OSD: B-52H-170-BW
2nd BW 20th BS 'LA'; named 'Free bird'.

BS: 464442 **USAFS:** 61-0017
OSD: B-52H-170-BW
307th Wing 93rd BS 'BD'; named 'Renegade'.

BS: 464443 **USAFS:** 61-0018
OSD: B-52H-170-BW
2nd BW 20th BS 'LA'.

BS: 464444 **USAFS:** 61-0019
OSD: B-52H-170-BW
2nd BW 96th BS 'LA'; named 'Rolling Thunder III'.

BS: 464445 **USAFS:** 61-0020
OSD: B-52H-170-BW
2nd BW 20th BS 'LA'.

BS: 464446 **USAFS:** 61-0021
OSD: B-52H-170-BW
307th Wing 93rd BS 'BD'.

BS: 464447 **USAFS:** 61-0022
OSD: B-52H-170-BW > GB-52H
A crack was found in a wing during maintenance at Tinker AFB, Oklahoma. It was repaired to allow it to make a one-time flight to Sheppard AFB, Texas where it is in use as a GIA with the 82 TRW as a GB-52H.

BS: 464448 **USAFS:** 61-0023
OSD: B-52H-170-BW
Before being delivered to the USAF this jet was bailed back to Boeing to test turbulence effects that had caused the loss of some earlier models when the vertical stabilizer failed. On January 10, 1964 while engaged in a test flight, clear air turbulence caused the entire fin and rudder to be ripped off. However, Boeing's Chief Bomber Test Pilot, Chuck Fisher and Co-pilot Dick Curry were able to safely recover the aircraft to Blytheville AFB. The aircraft could only be controlled by jockeying the throttles; to turn left, reduce power on the engines on that side and increase it on the other. To go up, increase power on all eight. In order to preserve the tapes of data that would be vitally important in solving the problem that had already cost several B-52s and the lives of their crews, the navigator was ordered to eject with the tapes. Fisher did not want the data lost in the crash that looked inevitable. The bomber was subsequently repaired and returned to service, going on to take part in Operation Noble Anvil over the Balkans in 1999. It was the first B-52H to be retired to MASDC on July 24, 2008 and was still present in March 2012.

BS: 464449 **USAFS:** 61-0024
OSD: B-52H-170-BW
To MASDC January 6, 2009; still present March 2012.

BS: 464450 **USAFS:** 61-0025
OSD: B-52H-170-BW > GB-52H
Delivered to NASA Dryden Flight Research Center July 30, 2001 as a replacement for NB-52B mothership 52-0008. Left Edwards AFB May 9, 2008 on a one-time ferry flight to Sheppard AFB, Texas, for use as a GIA with the 82 TRW as a GB-52H.

BS: 464451 **USAFS:** 61-0026
OSD: B-52H-170-BW
The 103rd B-52 to be lost, it crashed on June 24, 1994 when flying with the 92nd BW.

Perhaps the most infamous post-Cold War B-52 crash, 'CZAR 52' crashed with the loss of all on board while rehearsing for an airshow at Fairchild AFB, WA. There has been much controversy since because many of the people on the base had refused to fly with the pilot who was the wing safety officer, but also considered to be a 'hotshot'.

USAFS: 61-0027
OSD: B-52H-175-BW
To MASDC January 23, 2009, still present March 2012.

BS: 464453 **USAFS:** 61-0028
OSD: B-52H-175-BW
2nd BW 20th BS ' LA'.

BS: 464454 **USAFS:** 61-0029
OSD: B-52H-175-BW
307th Wing 93rd BS 'BD'.

BS: 464455 **USAFS:** 61-0030
OSD: B-52H-175-BW
The 44th B-52 to be lost and the first 'H' model, it was destroyed on November 2, 1967 when serving with the 319th BW after it suffered a fire in number six engine, which was shut down only for number five engine warning light to come on. The aircraft returned to Griffiss AFB, New York, but during a go around the aircraft became uncontrollable and the order was given to eject. Four people on board were killed.

BS: 464456 **USAFS:** 61-0031
OSD: B-52H-175-BW
307th Wing 93rd BS 'BD'.

BS: 464457 **USAFS:** 61-0032
OSD: B-52H-175-BW
307th Wing 93rd BS 'BD'. In use as a maintenance trainer at Minot AFB, North Dakota.

BS: 464458 **USAFS:** 61-0033
OSD: B-52H-175-BW
The 89th B-52 to be lost on November 14, 1975 when assigned to the 5th BW. The aircraft burnt out on the ground at its home base, Minot AFB, North Dakota after a booster pump ignited fuel inside a fuel-tank on the aircraft.

BS: 464459 **USAFS:** 61-0034
OSD: B-52H-175-BW
5th BW 23rd BS 'MT'. With the increasing cost of fuel the US has been experimenting with alternative fuels. In September 2006, a B-52 took off from Edwards Air Force Base with a 50/50 blend of Fischer-Tropsch process (FT) synthetic fuel and conventional JP-8 jet fuel powering two of its eight engines.

On December 15, 2006 61-0034 (named 'Checkmate') took off from Edwards AFB using only synthetic fuel for all eight engines. This was the first time an Air Force aircraft was entirely powered by the synthetic fuel. The flight lasted for seven hours and was considered a success.

BS: 464460 **USAFS:** 61-0035
OSD: B-52H-175-BW
5th BW 23rd BS 'MT'.

BS: 464461 **USAFS:** 61-0036
OSD: B-52H-175-BW
2nd BW 96th BS 'LA'.

BS: 464462 **USAFS:** 61-0037
OSD: B-52H-175-BW
The 51st B-52 to be lost, 'MILAN 34' crashed on take off from Minot AFB, North Dakota on January 23, 1969 when flying with the 5th BW following incorrect use of the bopmber's trim controls. As soon as the aircraft left the runway it became uncontrollable and although the crew ejected they were too low for their parachutes to be effective - there were no survivors.

BS: 464463 **USAFS:** 61-0038
OSD: B-52H-175-BW
307th Wing 93rd BS 'BD'; named 'Immortal Soul'.

BS: 464464 **USAFS:** 61-0039
OSD: B-52H-175-BW
5th BW 69th BS 'MT'.

BS: 464465 **USAFS:** 61-0040
OSD: B-52H-175-BW
Last of 744 B-52s built, this jet still flies with the 5th BW 69th BS 'MT from Minot AFB..

B-52H 61-0033 burned out on the ramp at Minot AFB. USAF photo via Greg Spahr